SOLIDARITY WITH THE WORLD

THEOPOLITICAL VISIONS

SERIES EDITORS:

Thomas Heilke
D. Stephen Long
and C. C. Pecknold

Theopolitical Visions seeks to open up new vistas on public life, hosting fresh conversations between theology and political theory. This series assembles writers who wish to revive theopolitical imagination for the sake of our common good.

Theopolitical Visions hopes to re-source modern imaginations with those ancient traditions in which political theorists were often also theologians. Whether it was Jeremiah's prophetic vision of exiles "seeking the peace of the city," Plato's illuminations on piety and the civic virtues in the Republic, St. Paul's call to "a common life worthy of the Gospel," St. Augustine's beatific vision of the City of God, or the gothic heights of medieval political theology, much of Western thought has found it necessary to think theologically about politics, and to think politically about theology. This series is founded in the hope that the renewal of such mutual illumination might make a genuine contribution to the peace of our cities.

FORTHCOMING VOLUMES:

James Reimer
Toward an Anabaptist Political Theology: Law, Order, and Civil Society

David Deane
The Matter of the Spirit: How Soteriology Shapes the Moral Life

Solidarity With the WORLD

*Charles Taylor and Hans Urs von Balthasar
on Faith, Modernity, and Catholic Mission*

CAROLYN A. CHAU

CASCADE *Books* • Eugene, Oregon

SOLIDARITY WITH THE WORLD
Charles Taylor and Hans Urs von Balthasar on Faith, Modernity, and Catholic Mission

Theopolitical Visions 19

Copyright © 2016 Carolyn A. Chau. All rights reserved. Except for brief quotations in critical publications or reviews, no part of this book may be reproduced in any manner without prior written permission from the publisher. Write: Permissions, Wipf and Stock Publishers, 199 W. 8th Ave., Suite 3, Eugene, OR 97401.

Cascade Books
An Imprint of Wipf and Stock Publishers
199 W. 8th Ave., Suite 3
Eugene, OR 97401

www.wipfandstock.com

PAPERBACK ISBN: 978-1-62564-750-4
HARDCOVER ISBN: 978-1-4982-8526-1
EBOOK ISBN: 978-1-4982-3597-7

Cataloguing-in-Publication data:

Names: Chau, Carolyn A.

Title: Solidarity with the world : Charles Taylor and Hans Urs von Balthasar on Faith, Modernity, and Catholic Mission / Carolyn A. Chau.

Description: Eugene, OR : Cascade Books, 2016 | Series: Theopolitical Visions 19 | Includes bibliographical references and index(es).

Identifiers: ISBN 978-1-62564-750-4 (paperback) | ISBN 978-1-4982-8526-1 (hardcover) | ISBN 978-1-4982-3597-7 (ebook)

Subjects: LCSH: Catholic Church—United States. | Taylor, Charles, 1931– —Criticism and interpretation. | Balthasar, Hans Urs von, 1905–1988—Criticism and interpretation. | Christianity and politics—Catholic Church. | Christianity and politics—United States.

Classification: BX1793 .C47 2016 (print) | BX1793 .C47 (ebook)

Manufactured in the U.S.A.   NOVEMBER 14, 2016

*For my parents, Margaret and Peter Chau,
And for all who work to bring the joy and hope of Christ
into the world today*

Contents

Preface ix

Acknowledgments xiii

List of Abbreviations xv

Introduction 1

1. Taylor's Picture of the Modern World 24

2. The Challenge of Secularism for the Church 57

3. Balthasar's Theological Anthropology: Authentic Personhood and the Eschatological Horizon of Freedom 107

4. Balthasar's Vision of a Witnessing Church: The Holy Church, Possibility of a Genuine Christian Inspiration 154

5. Conclusion 189

Bibliography 207

Name Index 223

Subject Index 225

Preface

MORE COMMON TODAY IN twenty-first-century "post-Christian" society than the question, "What kind of Christian should I be?" or "To which church should I belong?" is the question, "Why should I belong to a church?" Alongside this basic question are some other ones: "What kind of person do I want to be?," "How do I make a difference in the world?," and "Where will I find everyday meaning for my life?"

The goal of this work is to examine the cultural context of the contemporary world in the West so as to think anew about the question of Christian mission—and Catholic mission, specifically—in this culture and age. Is it possible for the Catholic Church to evangelize today, to speak of the joy of being in a relationship with Jesus Christ in and through belonging to a community that believes him to be God and the Redeemer of the world, in a way that is not threatening, off-putting, offensive, or simply dismissed? Can Christianity, as an organized religion with a wounding history for many and varied groups and individuals in the West, be a credible source of hope and trust for people once again?

One of the key claims of this work is that "reading the signs of the times"[1] leads one to probe the secularization of Western cultures. Amid debates about whether updating the Church to meet the modern world is continuous with or is a rupture with tradition, secularity, a notable feature of the modern Western world, and mission, a key trope within the Christian tradition, have receded significantly in Catholic theological discourse. Mission has even been considered by some to be anathema to authentic Christianity in the modern world. This work contends that exploring secularity and mission together will yield a fresh energy for

---

1. Like "*aggiornamento*" this was an exhortation famously associated with Vatican II.

renewing Catholicism in the spirit of Vatican II. It will offer a possible approach to mission in a secular age through a reading and mining of the corpus of two significant Catholic thinkers of the twentieth century on modernity and the Church: Charles Taylor and Hans Urs von Balthasar. My proposal here works out the claim that Charles Taylor helps the Church appreciate the cultural context of secularity with a complexified historical lens, and this perspective helps the Church approach the world in all of its secularity with, above all, charity.

I use Taylor primarily as a diagnostician of the ills and desires of modern selves, in light of his opus, *Sources of the Self: An Ontology of Modern Selfhood*, and *A Secular Age*, his work on secularity that has received a remarkable reception. I interpret and appropriate Hans Urs von Balthasar's accounts of ecclesiology and personhood to indicate what aspects of the Church's identity may need to be recovered to reach a world that is seemingly indifferent or hostile to religion. The book proposes, ultimately, that taking *aggiornamento* or updating the Church seriously today leads to the discovery of the need to shift our understanding of Church from one that is focused primarily on its official hierarchical profile to how the Church can play a central role in helping people realize and embody their true and best selves. It is my hope that by the end of the book readers will be persuaded or will begin to consider seriously the claim that Christianity is an important source, if only a pedagogical one, for fulfilled personhood.

There exist real challenges, however, for retrieving the significance of mission as an intrinsic aspect of Catholic identity. Mission seems to have become a casualty in contemporary theology due to its past associations with colonialism, coercion, and political oppression. The increased awareness of plurality in religion and cultures also implies to some a need to cease evangelizing altogether. Despite frequent mention of the mission of the Church and, particularly, the social mission of the Church in the seminal documents of the Second Vatican Council, postconciliar appropriation has tended to emphasize learning from the world, almost at the expense of meeting the call to share the transforming message of God's love, revealed in Jesus Christ, with the world also.[2] The Church

---

2. "It is for God's people as a whole, with the help of the Holy Spirit, and especially for pastors and theologians, to listen to the various voices of our day, discerning them and interpreting them, and to evaluate them in the light of the divine word, so that the revealed truth can be increasingly appropriated, better understood and more suitably expressed" (*Gaudium et Spes*, 44). Often, the first part of this exhortation is

faces challenges, moreover, around how to conceive of mission today due to false assumptions that mission must involve gaining power over vulnerable cultures through indoctrination, violence[3] (the Crusades are the notorious example here), or that mission denies the truth and goodness inherent in other faiths and other cultures.

This book was born out of a desire to think with the spirit of the Council Fathers of Vatican II about the ongoing engagement of the Church with modernity, as well as a perceived diminishment in the evangelical dimension of Roman Catholic ecclesial existence. Secularism is, indisputably, a key form of "new cultural reality" that the Church in the West faces. In thinking anew about how to be the Church in the world, and in North America in particular, this work thus seeks to gain greater understanding of the secularity of the modern Western world. It aims to discern, moreover, a possible shape of effective Catholic witness and mission in a contemporary post-Christian culture.

Engaging key aspects of the thought of Taylor and Balthasar for discerning contemporary Catholic mission in a secular age is an implicit argument for moving beyond the politicization of Catholic witness (that is, the often lamented but entrenched divisions between "right" and "left") within the contemporary Church, and the necessity of ecclesial unity for effective mission in and to secular cultures in the West.

---

emphasized, and the aspect of listening so as to increasingly appropriate, understand, and express *divine* truth minimized.

3. For an important work that challenges the identification of religion with violence, see Cavanaugh, *The Myth of Religious Violence*.

Acknowledgments

MANY PEOPLE HAVE BEEN a part of this work as inspiration, support, guides, and mentors. Thank you to Gill Goulding CJ, and to John Berkman for supervising the dissertation that formed the basis for this book, and to Ronald Kuipers and Joseph Mangina for their helpful comments and encouragement as readers of the dissertation. Heartfelt thanks to D. Stephen Long for his tremendous support, which made the publication of this work possible.

Thanks to Regis College, the Jesuit Faculty of Theology at the University of Toronto, the Social Sciences and Humanities Research Council of Canada, and the Edmonton-Toronto Province of the Congregation of the Most Holy Redeemer for helping to fund my doctoral research. My formation and exposure to the Redemptorists' charism, "to evangelize and to be evangelized by the most poor and abandoned," largely informed my choice to explore mission and secularity in my dissertation. I am deeply grateful to King's University College at Western University for research grants that allowed for the completion of this book. Thank you to Monica Marcelli for her assistance with chasing footnotes and to my excellent copy-editor at Cascade Books, Jacob Martin. I would like to express my gratitude to Charlie Collier and Heather Carraher of Cascade Books as well for their editorial work and assistance with typesetting.

Thank you to Ron Mercier, Travis Kroeker, John Robertson, Margaret Farley, the late Margaret O'Gara, Janine Langan, and Scott Lewis—your encouragement, your mentorship, and above all your example inform this work. What I have learned from you I have tried to put into the heart of this book.

I am grateful to Peter Casarella, Adriaan Peperzak, Bill Cavanaugh, Bishop Bill McGrattan, and David Schindler, whose support and encouragement were an enormous impetus to write fearlessly.

All works of theology must have a spiritual foundation. Balthasar reminds us of this. Ignatian spirituality has been a great gift to my theological formation. Deepest thanks to my Jesuit friends Sylvester Tan, SJ, Javier Gomez Sanchez, SJ, John Meehan, SJ, Teo Ugaban, SJ, and Edmund Lo, SJ for your friendship, wisdom, and virtue. The spirituality of the Redemptorists, of l'Arche, and the friendship of Communion and Liberation have also been a part of the spiritual bedrock of this book.

Fr. Mike Traher, SM; Fr. Bill Clarke, SJ; Fr. Mark Miller, CSsR; Fr. David Louch, CSsR; Leo English, CSsR; and Fr. Francis O'Connor, thank you for your support and guidance along the way, and especially at key junctures of my spiritual and theological formation..

To my friends Laura Colantoni, Brandon Vaidyanathan, Jing Qin, Sydney Choi, Lawrence Yu, Howard Jung, Erik Ranstrom, Mark Scott, Andrea Chan, and Boyon Koh, I couldn't have done it without you.

To my wonderful colleagues in the Department of Philosophy and Religious Studies at King's University College, especially Antonio Calcagno and Mark Yenson, for inspiring me with their own dedication to scholarship, the life of the mind, and for their personal kindness.

To my dear husband, Greg Gehl, thank you so much for your love, friendship, and amazing support.

Finally, I thank my wonderful parents, Margaret and Peter Chau, for their incredible love, endless support, and encouragement.

For the daily work of serving Him with heart, mind, and strength: *gratias Deo*.

Glory to the Father, to the Son, and to the Holy Spirit, as it was in the beginning, is now, and will be forever.

Abbreviations

Works by Charles Taylor

CM	*A Catholic Modernity?*
CP	*The Concept of a Person*
MM	*The Malaise of Modernity*
MSI	*Modern Social Imaginaries*
SA	*A Secular Age*
SS	*Sources of the Self*

Works by Hans Urs von Balthasar

B	*Bernanos*
CSL	*The Christian State of Life*
EG	*Engagement with God*
ET	*Explorations in Theology*
GL (I–VII)	*Glory of the Lord*
HW	*Heart of the World*
IFF	*In the Fullness of Faith*
LC	*Love Alone Is Credible*
LLC	*Laity and the Life of the Councils*
MT	*Mary for Today*

MCW		Moment of Christian Witness
MP		Mysterium Paschale
OP		Office of Peter and the Structure of the Church
P		Prayer
RB		Razing the Bastions
TE		Test Everything: Hold Fast to What Is Good
TA		A Theological Anthropology
TD (I–V)		Theo-Drama
TH		A Theology of History
TL (I–III)		Theo-Logic
TS		Truth Is Symphonic
UC		Unless You Become Like This Child
WC		Who Is a Christian?

Introduction

Retrieving Mission for Contemporary Catholic Ecclesial Identity

VATICAN II WAS A moment of unparalleled significance in the contemporary history of the Roman Catholic Church. It signaled to many a spirit of hope and new life breathing through the Church, especially in the area of the Church's encounter with the world. *Gaudium et Spes*, the document that most explicitly names the call of Christians to transform their cultures, stands as one of the most important legacies of the Council. The Second Vatican Council was also marked by a deeper sense of communion within the Church herself: laity and ecclesial and religious others were engaged in a manner hitherto unseen through liturgical reforms, episcopal collegiality, ecumenical dialogue, and interreligious relations. All of these developments, in the name of *aggiornamento*,[1] seemed to indicate signs of a Church moving forward.

However, the receptive history of Vatican II has become a point of divergent and increasingly divisive response within the Church. Debate has raged over the hermeneutics of what happened at the Council: was it an event of continuity or rupture?[2] Does the Church need to take a step back or do we need to go further? Despite the genuine riches that flowed

---

1. This term, translated literally, means "updating" and, in the Catholic ecclesial context, has been understood as meaning the quest of the Council to update the Church to engage the modern world.

2. See O'Malley, "Vatican II: Did Anything Happen?"; Alberigo and Komonchak, *History of Vatican II* (5 vols.); Schloesser, "Against Forgetting: Memory, History, Vatican II"; Alberigo, *A Brief History of Vatican II*; Lamb and Levering, *Vatican II: Renewal Within Tradition*.

from the Spirit present at the Council, battle lines have been drawn within the Roman Catholic Church regarding the precise way in which the Church is called to open herself to the modern world. Even with the intention of increasing a sense of unity and belonging, there have developed, arguably, a greater disunity and forms of exclusion within the Roman Catholic Church. Division is evident on issues ranging from liturgy and authority to Christian morality. Additionally, the world seems to have become ever more indifferent to the transforming power of the gospel on human lives.[3] This receptive history of Vatican II and the current state of ecclesial tensions within the Roman Church indicate the ongoing challenge that the Church faces in her engagement with modernity.

How can a new appropriation of Vatican II enable the Church to meet the deepest needs of the present age? Instead of remaining mired in a debate about continuity and discontinuity that has seen both sides level charges of fear and misunderstanding at one another, this work proposes that examining the Church in the modern world anew, at the beginning of the twenty-first century, may bring about a rediscovery of ecclesial mission that can lead to a more effective transformation of the world through love. The debate about continuity or discontinuity has often been reduced to reactions to *aggiornamento* and *ressourcement* as too forward-thinking, on the one hand, or inclined to retrenchment, on the other. In this work, however, I proceed on the assumption that an interpretation that reconciles the two is possible. I propose that thinking

---

3. As Ghislain Lafont has so eloquently put it, "If we rejoice humbly in the gifts of the Spirit which the Church has received and capitalized on, as rarely before in its history, the believer is still obliged to admit that very little of this vast wealth shines brightly on the world of our contemporaries. . . . Even if one were to point to an occasional sign of rejuvenation, passing or lasting, or if one or another person catches the attention of the media and is listened to, still the Church itself can hardly be considered as a herald of the gospel or of humanity. The Church today is aware that it is not the kingdom of God and that its mission is not to enlist all people in its fold. It also has the task of entering into dialogue with others. But how does it measure the effectiveness of its dialogue? How can it come to an understanding of the extent of the 'de-Christianizing' process (with all the nuances that this complex term entails), which has appeared precisely at the moment that the Church seems to have received impulses fostering the spread of the gospel? . . . To the extent that the Church is still committed to its mission of evangelization and of dialogue, we still need to ask what appearance the Church will put on in order to surmount such indifference and even such hostility. Next to the fundamental values of holiness and intelligence we have just considered, is there something else necessary which is not happening in the Church and thus obfuscates the true visage of the Church for those who genuinely yearn for wisdom and salvation?" Lafont, *Imagining the Catholic Church*, 5–6.

today about the relation between the Church and the modern world in the vein of both "updating the Church" and "returning to the sources" leads to a need for greater understanding of the *secularity* of the modern Western world and the retrieval of *mission* as a key, ongoing aspect of Christian ecclesial identity. Such a perspective, arising from fifty years of receiving the Council, would lead to a new appreciation for the meaning and shape of a lived spirituality of the Council, half a century later.

Some have recognized, however, that mission is not a negotiable element of Christianity and that new thinking about how to do mission is necessary. David Bosch, for instance, expounded the importance of the normative context of postmodernity for mission. Though written more than twenty years ago, Bosch's challenge to renegotiate the breadth and scope of what we mean by "rationality"; his objection to the objectifying stance to nature; his encouragement to think in terms of vision, revision, repentance, conversion rather than cause and effect; and his emphasis on collaboration remain salient injunctions for how to renew mission for today.[4] Mission conceived as "the Church with others," as "inculturation," and as "common witness" are among those terms that resonate with this writer's sense of how mission may best be refigured for a secular age.

Purpose, Methodology, and Vatican II as Context

A key interest of this work is to try to facilitate the process of *communio* in contemporary Catholic theology between warring parties in the Roman Catholic Church whose antagonism is rooted in divergent perspectives on the meaning and implications of the event of Vatican II for the Church's engagement of the modern world and contemporary culture. An appreciation for the work of Taylor and Balthasar individually and a sense of their subtle compatibility on the question of contemporary Catholic witness leads me to take the two of them as forming a path to such reconciliation. Both Taylor and Balthasar have shown attention to the reception of the Council in their respective works. Yet neither of them takes hermeneutics of the Council as their subject matter. This work, like both Taylor and Balthasar, will try to think *in the spirit* of the Council about how to live Catholic mission to the world in contemporary Western cultures such as Canada but will not be a work that proceeds to

---

4. Bosch, *Transforming Mission*, 349–62.

elucidate the Council based on detailed textual analysis of the documents themselves.

> The danger is that people will not *seek* any more, but will simply explore the inexhaustible warehouse of Vatican II. This will simply open a post-Vatican era, as once there was a post-Tridentine era. It would be a betrayal of *aggiornamento* to think it has been fixed once and for all in the texts of Vatican II.[5]

Yves Congar's statement illustrates the perspective that, rather than a culmination of Roman Catholic theological reflection or the only starting point for theological reflection, the texts of the Council are significant doctrinal records of a moment of an incredible burst of life in the Roman Catholic Church.[6] *Aggiornamento* is, however, a choice and a task to update the Church continually by reflecting on her life in the modern world afresh, with the same spiritual ethos of loving service toward all people, but open to the possibility that such love and faithfulness to mission may take a different form as the world shifts and changes.

How then to arrive at a better understanding of the secularity of the modern Western world and the missionary dimension of the Church that would take into account this secular context? The guiding contention of this work is that a synthetic and comparative analysis of Charles Taylor's and Hans Urs von Balthasar's respective work concerning faith, personhood, and modernity reveals a potential way out of the darkness of ideological division over how to be the Church in the modern world. Taylor's acclaimed work on secularity, *A Secular Age*,[7] offers an approach to secularism that seeks to speak with a charitable and discerning voice on the phenomenon. In this work, Taylor engages the question of how to consider the implications of the most recent five hundred years of history for the present and future of Latin Christianity.[8] Balthasar lends

---

5. Yves Congar, cited in Duffy et al., *Vatican II*, 6.

6. Thank you also to Dr. Ronald Mercier for first encouraging a hermeneutic approach to the documents of the Second Vatican Council as works of ecclesial imagination that seek to create an alternative social imaginary.

7. Taylor, *A Secular Age*. Hereafter cited as *SA*.

8. To clarify, Taylor's Catholic faith is evident in much of his scholarship, as James Heft has noted: "His [Taylor's] Catholicism has been a central, if mostly implicit, element in his philosophical writings." Heft, "Introduction," 3. *A Secular Age* is, however, generally observed to be the work in which Taylor has been most explicit about his Catholic perspective on the world. E.g., "In fact, *A Secular Age* is Taylor's most explicitly theological work." Long, "How to Read Charles Taylor," 94. Yet it should also be said that Taylor shares his vision of life as a committed Catholic in *A Secular Age* not to

an unabashedly Catholic theological approach to questions of identity that arise in the midst of the cultural shift to a "secular" world. A critical and synthetic engagement of Taylor and Balthasar may therefore help clarify the path of contemporary Catholic witness in a North American context and redraw the lines of intra-ecclesial controversy surrounding the question of evangelization. This work may be seen as an attempt to bring the social, cultural, and philosophical thought of Taylor and the ecclesiology and theological anthropology of Balthasar into engagement so as to achieve greater clarity on how the Church may retrieve a sense of her personal being and mission.[9]

Ultimately, my argument is that some of the challenges and ecclesial division arising from disagreement about how the Church ought to engage the modern world may be ameliorated by recognition of the importance of personhood as a locus of evangelization and that rapprochement between the Church and modernity rests particularly on the question of fulfilled personhood or, in the language of the Church, holiness. The work of Taylor and that of Balthasar will be brought to bear on the question of contemporary Catholic witness in two ways. On the one hand, Taylor's oeuvre will be used to deepen and complexify the Church's understanding of modernity. In particular, Taylor's approach to modernity through a mining of Western modernity's "social imaginary," his attempt to read out the longings and malaises of modern persons through various historical shifts, and his delimitation of the Western experience of modernity, modernization, and secularization as a contingent and historically particular experience will be used to clarify the implications of

---

be seen as presenting a view of secularity from "the Catholic perspective," but because he believes that the narrative of secularity that he is trying to tell—a story that is full of a variety of religious positions, all of them more fragile than in the past—warrants "full disclosure" of his own position in the current scene, which happens to be Catholic. See Kuipers, "The New Atheism and the Spiritual Landscape of the West."

What I want to do in this work is to acknowledge the Catholic theological *a priori* operative in Taylor's work as a philosopher, particularly as a moral philosopher, and to trace how his philosophical works may then take a disaffected person living in this age from interest in questions about the good life to openness to faith, to see how mapping this journey may be a clue to the Church as to how far she can go with a dialogical approach to mission. I say this to be clear that I am interested in mobilizing Taylor's form of Catholicism and philosophical work (as that of a Catholic thinker) for the purpose of understanding one possible way to do mission in this age.

9. Incidental hopes of the work are that it may perhaps contribute to new readings of Taylor's project (particularly his social, political, moral, and religious writings from 1989 to the present) and a new lens of appreciation for that of Balthasar.

Vatican II for the present Church. Taylor's deepened understanding of the modern world will be synthesized with Balthasar's understandings of the Church. This first form of engagement looks at the basic terms of Vatican II's seminal ecclesiological document, *Gaudium et Spes*, namely, "church" and "world," and attempts to view them again with greater texture and complexity.

On the other hand, Taylor's insight into the relationship between horizons and selfhood will be used to draw out the implications of his narrative on secularity and the need for a more open and relational community of faith to keep religious faith and experiences of fullness alive in the world. Aspects of Taylor's philosophical anthropology and theories of identity will be brought into conversation with Balthasar's theological account of personal identity and will lead, ultimately, to new reflections on the relationship between ecclesial existence, spirituality, and authentic personhood. Indeed, Balthasar's ecclesiology will in some sense turn Taylor's understanding of the Church on its head. The insights of Taylor on the malaises that attend modern selfhood, and those of Balthasar on the relationship between the person of Christ and personal identity, will be culled so as to underscore the Church's role in forming persons. The goal is to meet the challenges to retrieving mission previously mentioned, such as attentiveness to history, pluralism, issues of power, the importance of tradition, and ecclesial authority, through a combination of their thought. Taylor's work contributes to the retrieval of mission through attention to the formation of modern selfhood that involves a deep awareness of history, appreciation for pluralism, and of both religious and secular power in the making of modern selves and their social imaginary. Balthasar's approach to personhood mines the Catholic tradition widely, includes a spiritual Christology,[10] attention to post-Christian reality, and a revisionary account of ecclesial authority.

The challenge of secularization and how to rediscover the evangelical impulse of the Roman Catholic Church are not new, unconsidered issues for the ecclesial hierarchy. Pope John Paul II and Pope Benedict XVI showed with their papal addresses regarding "the new evangelization" that secularization and evangelization are key concerns of their papacies. Pope Francis has discussed from the beginning of his papacy the

---

10. Cf. McIntosh, *Christology from Within*. McIntosh's demonstration of the profoundly spiritual and incarnational Christology of Balthasar helps show the relevance of Balthasar's Christology for the situation of the contemporary Church in a secular age.

need to become a vibrant missionary Church once more, full of zeal and love for those who suffer and those on the margins. Despite this awareness and some growing literature on the new evangelization, this work chooses to approach these topics through applying a combination of methods—philosophical theology, literary analysis, and hermeneutics—to the works of Charles Taylor and Hans Urs von Balthasar on modernity, personhood, and the Church. The reasons for this alternative approach are threefold: first, certain hermeneutical and political complexities attend the exegesis of theological works of persons who speak with official authority in the Church. Approaching questions of the nature of "the secular" and "mission" through a Catholic philosopher and a Catholic theologian who have not held positions of distinguished ecclesial authority, in contrast, may allow for a greater reception of their work among the theologians, philosophers, religion scholars, and interested laypersons to whom this book is primarily addressed. This approach aims, thereby, to avoid some of the politicized tensions around "the new evangelization" within contemporary Catholicism and to enlarge the Catholic audience for whom mission signifies a constitutive part of ecclesial identity.

In addition, the choice of Taylor and Balthasar is premised on an understanding of both writers as eminently alive to the dynamism evoked by the event of the Second Vatican Council. Taylor has stated on numerous occasions that it was the spirit of the Council and the authors associated with *nouvelle theologie* that first awoke in him a genuine resonance with his Catholic heritage.[11] Balthasar, though not directly involved in the Council, was deeply attuned to its spirit,[12] and this consonance is famously evident in his early programmatic work, *Razing the Bastions*,[13] which advocated change in the Church and a radical surrender of postures of defensiveness and stasis. It is important for pursuing the chief question of this work, namely, how to understand what it means to be the Church "open to the world" in an increasingly secular culture such

---

11. Cf. Taylor, *A Catholic Modernity?*; Taylor, *Sources of the Self*; and public lectures, including "The Future of Religion in a Secular Age: Charles Taylor and Jonathan Sacks in Conversation" (Hillel Center, Toronto, November 2011).

12. "I did not attend the Council and therefore did not share in experiencing the enthusiasm of its participants. The Council produced a great number of papers, more perhaps than the average Catholic (or bishop) can master.... I tried to listen carefully to that spirit which rushes through the great forest of papers, although you will not detect many literal quotations in my work." Balthasar, *Test Everything*, 22–23. See also Balthasar, "The Council of the Holy Spirit," in *ET* III, 245–67.

13. Balthasar, *Razing the Bastions*.

as that which characterizes North America, and Canada in particular, that the inquiry take place within the context of Vatican II. The Council is indisputable among many as an essential horizon for doing Catholic theology in the twenty-first century. Yet, as Congar notes, the documents are not the totality of Catholic wisdom on Catholic identity and witness today. Rather than interpreting the letter of the constitutions, decrees, and declarations, this work aims to work in the spirit of the Council, affirming the Church as a mystery who is called to extend the drama of the Incarnation in history until God is all in all.[14]

Interestingly, Taylor and Balthasar hold varying degrees of commitment to Vatican II in its thinking about the Church in the world, although in both cases, their reception of Vatican II seems rooted in a fundamental understanding of and affinity for its original aims and goals. In particular, most would see Taylor as fitting well in the aggiornamento 'camp' of Vatican II, and Balthasar in the camp of ressourcement thinkers. While there is validity to this characterization, my work also seeks to disrupt the clean lines of these categorizations. Nonetheless, it should be noted that there are points of real divergence between the interpretation of modernity by Taylor and by Balthasar. Taylor's account of "the Nova effect" indicates an openness to religious pluralism that contrasts with Balthasar's view on the same topic, while Balthasar's sense of the permanence of certain shifts in modernity is more complicated than that of Taylor.[15] This theological difference forms part of the fecundity that this pairing hopefully yields for the question of Catholic witness and mission in a secular age. One may see, for example, how an aggiornamento approach can be more effective in dealing with religious pluralism but a ressourcement approach can handle more adeptly questions of identity. We will show how the ways in which Taylor and Balthasar respectively agree and disagree with the Council leads to a renewed attentiveness to how the wisdom of the Council may be lived in the present time.

Finally, Taylor and Balthasar have been chosen to understand the situation of the Church in the modern world anew because each has produced works that show not only sympathy for but also divergence from and development of some of the key concepts of the Council. As a first glance in that direction, Taylor's work offers a greater exegesis of

---

14. This is not to minimize the great importance of understanding the letter of the documents and their genesis, but simply to note the different approach to Vatican II that this work will take.

15. Many thanks to Stephen Long for suggesting this nuance.

the central importance of authenticity for contemporary persons. He also provides an analysis of "secularity" in terms of a cultural shift in the conditions of belief that has taken place since the Second Vatican Council. Of note in Taylor's historical narrative on the development of secularity is the sustained effort to remain in the mode of descriptive analysis rather than normative claims about an ideology, "secularism." Taylor does raise questions about human existence that arise from within a "flattened" horizon or "immanent frame." What is interesting, however, is the manner in which Taylor allows for self-examination and critique of secularism in his interlocutors. Indeed, Taylor's analysis of the ontology of modern selfhood includes intimations of the ways in which modern selves experience the multiplication of moral sources in modernity in a rather tragic fashion. This rhetorical shift is, I believe, part of Taylor's contribution to a new approach to secularism that may be appropriated by the Church in its ongoing mission to peoples in the West. An exploration of the nuanced thought of Taylor and Balthasar on the world and the Church respectively may, therefore, add to the conversation on the hermeneutics of Vatican II without the issues attending thinkers with official status in the Church, such as the popes mentioned, thereby to receive more deeply what happened at Vatican II, what has happened in the Church since, and in which direction theologically and practically the Church may be called to go at this time.

Given the unconventional and previously untried pairing of these two figures (and there are indeed tensions between their thought), the remainder of the chapter will offer an initial sketch of each thinker's contributions to understanding the Church in the modern Western world at the beginning of the twenty-first century. Taylor's work will be mined for its understanding of modernity and the implications of his work on modern selfhood and modern malaise for discerning Catholic mission today. Balthasar's emphasis on ecclesial personhood and holiness will be elucidated, at a general level, to highlight the significance of his ecclesiology and anthropology for the project of discerning the same.

Before doing this, however, I offer a note about the literary styles used by these authors. Significantly, both Taylor and Balthasar employ styles of argumentation that are uncharacteristic, at best, of contemporary conventional academic discourse. Taylor insists that he has to "tell a story" in *A Secular Age*; Balthasar turns to the resources of the theatre and the leitmotif of *drama* to present his account of Christian theology for modern persons. Taylor chooses narrative rather than an apologetic argument expressed in the traditional Anglo-American analytic style of philosophy of religion to underscore a point, seemingly, on the need for a different form of communication about faith in the present secular culture. Balthasar's depiction of orthodox Christian claims in terms of a glorious and ongoing drama between God and humanity also seems aimed at a culture no longer interested in "doctrine," as such.

The fact that these thinkers compel through their appeal to a more artistic and persuasive mode of expression underscores the importance, too, of beauty in sharing the good news of Christ in a secular age.[16] Taylor's elucidation of the nature of a social imaginary, which is carried in "images, stories and legends" rather than in theoretical terms,[17] may help the Church to attend, for example, to the power of story, song, film, and dance to speak to a secular culture.

CHARLES TAYLOR, LEADING INTERROGATOR OF WESTERN MODERNITY

Charles Taylor is best known as a philosopher of modernity, a phenomenologist working within the tradition of modern philosophical hermeneutics, a Hegel scholar, and a social, moral, and political thinker who has written some classic texts on the issues of multicultural and political belonging in a pluralistic context.[18] His more recent works on Catholic modernity and secularity have led to increasing interest in his thought on religion and, in particular, on how his Catholicism informs his other writings.[19] More than ever, theologians are beginning to engage the work of Taylor and the meaning of his narrative of secularity for their understandings of culture, modernization, and the future of religion.[20] This

---

16. Balthasar, *Theo-Drama*, vol. 1, *Prolegomena*, 89–135.

17. Taylor, *Modern Social Imaginaries*, 23. Hereafter *MSI*.

18. Cf. Taylor, *The Explanation of Behaviour*; *Hegel and Modern Society*; "What's Wrong with Negative Liberty"; *Human Agency and Language*, including "What Is Human Agency?," "Self-Interpreting Animals," and "The Concept of a Person"; *Philosophy and the Human Sciences*; "The Politics of Recognition"; *Philosophical Arguments*; *Sources of the Self*; *The Malaise of Modernity*; *A Catholic Modernity?*; *Modern Social Imaginaries*; and *A Secular Age*.

19. See, for example, Fraser, *The Dialectics of the Self*, and Colorado, "Transcendence, Kenosis and Enfleshment: Charles Taylor's Religious Thought."

20. See, for example, Baum, "The Response of a Theologian to Charles Taylor's *A Secular Age*"; DeVries, "The Deep Conditions of Secularity"; Flanagan, "*A Secular Age*: An Exercise in Breach-Mending"; Hauerwas and Coles, "Long Live the Weeds and the

work seeks to broaden Taylor's disciplinary significance further still, by investigating his significance for the theological question of mission.

Few have attempted to explore Taylor's contribution to theological reflection on mission and evangelization, and there is reason for this. To some extent, Taylor would likely disagree with the project.[21] Despite his commitment to retrieving the spiritual sources of Judeo-Christianity in the history of modern selves, Taylor seems to be, above all, a social and political thinker interested in addressing the problems of contemporary conflict that emerge from historically unprecedented experiences of pluralism and human diversity. His interest in Christian spirituality seems, at times, to be out of a concern that important sources of human ideals and wisdom for life are not left behind in the wake of the modern project.[22] Taylor has argued for the riches of *many* spiritual traditions, though he will admit to being personally formed and transformed by his Catholic faith.[23] Taylor's Catholicism informs his many writings on social, moral, and political life as the impetus to affirm and embrace plurality for the sake of an ultimate reconciliation. Indeed, Taylor in recent years has become very frank and open about his "form of Catholicism":

> It's possible to build friendship across these boundaries based on a real mutual sense, a powerful sense, of what moves the other person. . . .We're in the business of friendship, which

---

Wilderness Yet: Reflections on *A Secular Age*"; Kerr, "How Much Can a Philosopher Do?"; Kerr, "Comment: Christians in a Secular Age"; Long, "How to Read Charles Taylor: The Theological Significance of Charles Taylor's *A Secular Age*"; Milbank, "Review Article: A Closer Walk on the Wild Side; Some Comments on Charles Taylor's *A Secular Age*"; Ormerod, "Charles Taylor and Bernard Lonergan on Natural Theology"; Rossi, "Review of *A Secular Age*"; and Ward, "History, Belief and Imagination in Charles Taylor's *A Secular Age*".

21. Taylor has expressed antipathy toward the biblical injunction that is most frequently associated with mission and evangelization, "Go ye and teach all the nations." Taylor asserts that the injunction is at the heart of a misunderstanding of Catholicism as meaning "to take the global worldview of us who are Christians and strive to make over other nations and cultures to fit it. But this violates one of the basic demands of Catholicism. I want to take the original word, *katholou*, in two related senses, comprising both universality and wholeness; one might say universality through wholeness. . . . Unity-across difference as against unity-through identity." Taylor, *Catholic Modernity?*, 14. Hereafter *CM*.

22. This theme was made prominent in *Sources of the Self* but continues and is augmented in *A Secular Age*.

23. Cf. Warner et. al, *Varieties of Secularism*, 320.

incorporates the kind of understanding where each can come to be moved by what moves the other.

Now what has this got to do with Christianity? Everything, to me: that is what it's all about. It's all about reconciliation. It's all about reconciliation between human beings, and it doesn't simply mean within the Church, and it doesn't mean that it's conditioned on being within the Church. . . .

I resonate with Herder's idea of humanity as the orchestra, in which all the differences between human beings could ultimately sound together in harmony.[24]

Taylor seems to indicate that reconciliation between human beings finally happens through mutual openness to the differences between human beings, which can potentially lead to a fusion of horizons. A shared vision, a shared mission, does not seem to be essential, to Taylor, for reconciliation to happen, unless that shared mission is a willingness to understand the space from which another person or community is coming. The premise of evangelization, which is a sharing of the good news, seems on the face of it to be in tension with Taylor's view of reconciliation in so far as it is premised on (if the Church is understood as one social group among others) a unidirectional self-mediation.

Yet Taylor has penned significant essays on topics related to mission that suggest some interest and insights on the question. *A Catholic Modernity?*, the Marian Award Lectures in which Taylor reflects most explicitly on what it means to be Catholic in this age, considers the Jesuit missionary to China of the sixteenth century, Matteo Ricci. In the lecture Taylor gestures approvingly to the model of inculturation that he sees expressed in the life of Ricci, who knew how to express his Catholic faith persuasively within a culture radically distinct from his own.

From the example of Ricci, Taylor indicates that an approach of "learning a culture," even one's own, is an important criterion for moving toward an effective incarnation of true *catholica* in the world, including the culture of modernity. Taylor advocates a similar kind of discernment of Western culture "from a distance," a kind of being with the other and learning from the other so as to begin a dialogue that may lead to greater understanding of both the culture and one's tradition. This becomes, in Taylor's view, an inculturation of the gospel or, at the least, "an instantiation of the Catholic principle."[25] Some—Ian Fraser, for example—have

---

24. Ibid.
25. *CM*, 15.

criticized Taylor for having an overly positive depiction of Ricci and have countered that Ricci's intention was much less openly dialogical for the goal of mutual understanding and self-understanding than Taylor suggests. Fraser claims that Ricci's intention as a Jesuit missionary in China was to propagate the Christian faith, contrary to Taylor's intention in referring to Ricci as a way to think through deepening catholicity through affirmation of diversity. Ricci's attempts to assimilate the practices and transform aspects of his identity to conform to Chinese culture were entirely for a missionary end and not for the end of unity in diversity. Taylor's approach, Fraser avers, "fails to recognize that Ricci worked within a 'unity-through-identity' framework and 'winning' a culture for the one, true Faith through a tactical approach of convincing the ruler of the nation, the Emperor, who would then disseminate it to the masses in a uniform way."[26]

This critique, while valid from an historical perspective, does not necessarily imply that Taylor's proposal is without merit or ought not to be considered, however. Taylor's appropriation of Ricci is for the sake of presenting his view that living up to the demand of being Catholic means "taking our modern civilization for another of those great cultural forms that have come and gone in human history, to see what it means to be Christian here, to find our authentic voice in the eventual Catholic chorus."[27] His interpretation of a Riccian approach to being Catholic means a willingness to engage seriously with the culture of modernity so as to sift out what is a deepening of the gospel in the culture, and what is not.

James Heft and others have remarked on Taylor's style of engagement with modern culture as one of discernment and charity. Something of both seems necessary in considering an approach to mission today in the North American secularized context. Taylor acknowledges that the distance natural to learning a truly foreign culture is not easy to model in the case of Western persons when it is one's own culture, but Taylor nonetheless concludes that a Catholic modernity, a sense of how best to express the universal truthfulness of the Catholic claim in this age, ought

---

26. There was also no sense of self-conversion in Ricci's case, Fraser states, following the research of Jean Lacouture on the history of the Jesuits. Thus, Taylor's use of Ricci as an example seriously weakens the sense in which he seems to advocate for modernizing Catholicism through an inculturation in diverse ways, and through an openness to difference. Cf. Fraser, "Charles Taylor's Catholicism," 231–52.

27. *CM*, 15.

to involve such a detached "first look" at a local culture so as to engage the same culture with true charity.

In order to communicate with the modern world, it is necessary to understand the world. This is particularly true of evangelizing communication. Robert Schreiter has observed the importance of understanding the different interests of listeners and speakers when engaging in dialogue and evangelization.[28] One of my basic premises is that, while not working in a strictly sociological or anthropological vein, Taylor's "philosophy of modernity" may be treated as a body of work that clarifies the cultural or "world" aspect of mission for Catholics in the West.[29] Taylor presents a picture of Catholic mission as a deepening of true universality through examining a local culture—his own, in this case—with an openness and readiness to learn about it and to see the good in it.

While many thinkers have considered the phenomenon of modernity, Taylor's work is particularly insightful for its attention to the features of the modern world such as its secularity, and how the modern world has formed or impinges on the human person. Taylor has written persuasively on certain features of modern selves, such as authenticity, universal beneficence, and expressivism, which are positive developments and even aspirations of contemporary persons living in the West. Taylor has also named certain malaises—atomism, subjectivism, and instrumentalism—as losses that attend the passage of Western culture into modernity.

Even more interesting is that it is possible to see in Taylor the development of a work over the past twenty years about the spiritual nature of human persons. The end of his most recent magnum opus, *A Secular Age*, discusses "conversions" and hints at the significance of Christ and Catholicism for the experience of true human fulfillment (Taylor's term in this text is a sense of "fullness"). However, Taylor stops short of naming the Church as a necessary vehicle for "contact with transcendence." In this work I will present a reading of Taylor that shows that Taylor's investigation of secularity, which he takes to mean the conditions of belief in our age, is in fact the culmination of a long line of persevering efforts to recuperate something of a true vision of personhood and meaning that resonates with modern, secular selves. Moreover, his line of thinking

28. See Schreiter, *The New Catholicity: Theology Between the Global and the Local*.

29. Implicit in my methodology is a Lonerganian approach to mission, i.e., theology as mediating between a culture and a religion, and theology of mission as being a particular instance of such an understanding of theology. I look later to Balthasar to clarify the ecclesial aspect of the same question.

actually may lead modern selves to consider the importance of religion as constitutive of authentic, fulfilled human existence. Taylor's insights into the modern world, modern selves, and the relationship of authentic self-transcendence to faith are thus the resources this work will mine to show that Taylor's work may help the Church in developing a better sense of her missionary task.

This work proposes, however, that Taylor's work alone does not suffice to create a template or path for Catholic mission in a secular age. Taylor's understanding of the modern world from within, though undergirded by a Catholic theological *a priori*, does not, understandably,[30] take the reality of Christ for granted. Balthasar, a theologian who is more known for his work on the objectivity of God ("divine glory") than human subjectivity, provides further indications, then, of a potentially fruitful path for mission with his work on personhood and the Church. Balthasar notes that the defining aspect of theological personhood, true personhood, is receptivity to the call of Christ.[31]

Balthasar's work on personhood and holiness may thereby be appropriated as a step in contemporary Christian understanding that builds on Taylor's claims about what faith offers. Balthasar's work expounds what Taylor's narrative on belief and unbelief today only hints at, namely, the need of persons for the person of Christ in their quest for authenticity and a genuinely creative, original, and benevolent life. The possibility of a true faith, moreover, one that surpasses an aspiration of self-improvement toward genuine reverence and love, is rendered coherent by Balthasar's fundamental claim regarding the reality of God as self-donation.

Additionally, Balthasar's ecclesiology, though often mistaken for an apology for the Church's hierarchical structure, in fact identifies the primary responsibility of the Church to be generating *subjective* holiness

---

30. Taylor, *Catholic Modernity?*, 13. Speaking of the constraints of philosophy, Taylor has stated that his view of the nature of philosophical discourse is that it "has to try to persuade honest thinkers of any and all metaphysical or theological commitments."

31. There have, of course, been notable feminist critiques of Balthasar's understanding of receptivity as singularly unhelpful to women, as women already suffer from systemic oppression and a socially pervasive expectation of submission. However, these critiques seem to me to misunderstand the active and paradoxically subversive quality of receptivity in the face of worldly "power" at the heart of Balthasar's endorsement of receptivity. I have written on this subject elsewhere (cf. Chau, " 'What Could Possibly Be Given?': Towards an Exploration of Kenosis as Forgiveness — Continuing the Conversation between Coakley, Hampson, and Papanikolaou.") but note particularly the work of Sarah Coakley on this issue. Cf. Coakley, "*Kenosis* and Subversion: On the Repression of 'Vulnerability.'"

or fulfilled personhood. Particularly in *Bernanos*, Balthasar's work on ecclesial existence, Balthasar describes the role of the Church in knowing Christ. His theological anthropology and ecclesiology will thus form the focus of this work's consideration of Balthasar's contribution to clarifying a possible shape for contemporary ecclesial mission in the West.

Just as Taylor's work will be mined for its portrait of modern selves and modernity to integrate a nuanced understanding of "the modern world" into a conception of Catholic mission for today's "secular age," so Balthasar's work will be explored for understandings of the Church that may assist in the task of reconceiving Catholic mission. It will be argued that Balthasar offers an *ecclesial hermeneutic* that holds great possibility for the post-Vatican II Church at the beginning of the third millennium. It may be said that Balthasar does for "ecclesial" hermeneutics what Rowan Williams has done for scriptural hermeneutics: that is, just as, according to Williams, a believing community is the necessary context for reading and hearing Scripture, so *the Church's relationship with Christ as Christ's handmaid is the context for understanding and receiving the moral teachings of the hierarchy*. In addition to mining Balthasar's understanding and refiguration of the Church in terms of her love for Christ (as spouse and as a community of friends), this work will also look to Balthasar's christological approach to mission ('embodied revealing,' one may say) as a necessary supplement to the more anthropological/incarnational ("bottom-up") approach of Taylor to ecclesial mission and witness in a secular age.[32]

Key Terms

Before we begin I would like to clarify a few terms.

"Mission"

"Mission" is notoriously difficult to capture. According to Georgia Masters Keightley, Vatican II shifted ecclesial understanding of mission to

---

32. It should be noted that while the emphasis in this work is on how Balthasar's ecclesiology may enhance understanding of the present situation of mission in the West, Taylor's profound recognition of cultural and religious diversity (cf. Taylor's discussion of the "nova effect," the rapid diversification of ways to be spiritual as secularization unfolds) may supplement Balthasar's ecclesiology also and provide a needful contribution to contemporary Catholic ecclesiology from a different direction.

mean a constitutive aspect of the identity of the Church: "The Council's key assertion is that mission is simply not something the Church does. Rather, mission is what the Church is and it is thus because ecclesial reality originates and participates in the very missions of the Son and the Spirit."[33] The Council signaled such a close identification of the Church with its mission that the question "What is the mission of the Church?" was effectively another way of asking, "What is the nature of the Church?" In light of the centrality of communion ecclesiology in the aftermath of Vatican II, Keightley asks about the relationship between mission and communion, for mission must be, she then argues, a task for the entire communion of God's people. The author of this work takes mission to mean the call and task of the Church to go beyond itself and to share its message of good news with the world both in word and in deed. Similar to Keightley and, indeed, the Council, she takes mission and communion to be inextricably bound with one another. In this she also follows the insights of Lesslie Newbigin, the Protestant missiologist who understands mission and unity to be the two core realities that constitute the nature of the Church.[34]

The author understands the division over how to be the Church in the modern world as a challenge, then, of both communion and mission. The need for a renewal of the Church involves, then, both communion and mission and deepening of communion must be a part of deepening mission. Mission is the Church's response to God's call to give herself in love and truth to the service of the world. I will argue that the Church needs to discern the shape of her service in and through her relationship of adoring love of the triune God and that the diminishment of the vertical dimension of ecclesial self-understanding has led to a compromised experience of communion and mission over the past fifty years. Service of the world does not mean that the Church is called to help the world become more secular insofar as secular implies a nonreligious, solely temporal reality. Service of the world involves, simply, a sharing of the reality of God who is Love that enables all to participate in the mutual, dynamic, self-giving love that Christians know as the Trinity.

---

33. Georgia Masters Keightley, "Vatican II: The Church's Self-Understanding," in Cernera, *Vatican II: The Continuing Agenda*, 9.

34. Newbigin, *The Household of God*.

"Witness"

"Witness" denotes the more general category of Christian existence that expresses belief in and fidelity to the reality of the triune God made known through Jesus Christ and his Church. It will be used in this work to include evangelization, the act of proclaiming the good news, but will not be considered reducible to evangelization, which implies an intentionality toward the other through verbal communication that is less central to the term "witness" as here used. This work follows Balthasar in understanding witness as the manifestation in human existence of the recognition that "the Church has her origins in the crucifixion"[35] and to live from this basis. While not "merely inward,"[36] there is a hiddenness to witness. "Existence in the openness of this realm of [the mystery of God's glory] is what we call belief—the acceptance and affirmation in being taken possession of by God in Christ. Hidden within itself, it contains the hope of partially sharing in the eternal life of love, of which the opening-up of this realm is already an offer."[37]

"Secular"

At the time of the council in the early 1960s, secularism signified a new ideology that was distinctly nonreligious and antireligious. "Secular" was understood as an -ism that represented all stances rooted in a commitment to nonreligious meaning or the absence of religion. Although the roots of the term "secular" lie within a Christian context to signify "the age" as opposed to the realm of the eternal, it gradually came to mean a kind of commitment to the absence of religion in public life and in personal beliefs.

With classic works such as *The Secular City* by Harvey Cox, secularism received some significant attention in the 1960s. Interest in secularism and secularization theory waned over the past forty years, however, as the resurgence of religion has proven such theories wrong. In very recent years, secularism has again enjoyed renewed interest, in large part due to Taylor's work *A Secular Age*,[38] which constructs a historical

---

35. Balthasar, *Moment of Christian Witness*, 38.
36. Ibid., 56.
37. Ibid., 57.
38. As Craig Calhoun, Mark Juergensmeyer, and Jonathan Van Antwerpen have stated in the introduction to their recent book on secularism, "The book opens with

narrative of the development of secularity in the West. This work takes up Taylor's definition of secularism, redefined more neutrally as *secularity*, which defines secularity as the contemporary *conditions* of belief. Secularity, in other words, is the tacitly held foundation that undergirds most contemporary reflection and questioning about faith. The importance of Taylor's new conception of secularism is that it understands secularism more charitably and more deeply than as mere ideology. To think about secularity as underlying and circumscribing *conditions* for religious belief today is, I think, to begin to move toward a more accurate vision of what is entailed in evangelizing the age. While Taylor also acknowledges more conventional notions of secularization as the decline in religious practices and the diminishment of religious presence in public institutions, he considers these to be instantiations and concretions of his more fundamental sense of secularity, which is as a shift in the very conditions of belief.

"Church"

For the purposes of this work, "Church" will refer to the Roman Catholic Church, and true Church will signify (following de Lubac, Augustine, and others) the Church in heaven and that which is only partially realized in the community of faith on earth. It will be in great sympathy with the Church as a communion, symbolized in language as "the people of God" but even more so by the life she receives through being the spouse of the Word and his body. By that locution, it will identify the Church neither with her hierarchy nor with her laity, *tout court*. Church will be taken to mean communion in the broadest and deepest sense of the term. Two chief constitutive markers of the nature of the Church are unity and mission.

"Modern"

"Modern" will mean, to some degree, Taylor's understanding of modernity as being a deeply historical process and one that may look different in different times, places, and cultures in the world. This is otherwise

---

a chapter by philosopher and political theorist Charles Taylor, whose massive and complex *A Secular Age* has singularly shaped current discussions of secularism and secularity." Calhoun et al., *Rethinking Secularity*, 20.

known as the concept of "multiple modernities" that Taylor and some of his collaborators have begun to explore.[39] It will also refer, therefore, to *Western* modernity, in particular. The "modern world" refers to the reality of industrialization, and various shifts that have led to the experience of the world as smaller and more connected, with increasing challenges brought about by rapid technological development.

"Person"

This term will be used throughout the work to mean "person" according to philosophical and theological treatments of the term, rather than sociological, political, or legal meanings of the term (though in many cases the latter derive from the former). Person will include the concept of agency but, following Taylor and Balthasar, will go beyond that to suggest horizons of significance that help constitute agency. "Person" will designate something more than a locus of human consciousness, sentience, or cognition, and an individual instantiation of human being. It is also to be distinguished from personality. While "person" will be understood as the substance underlying and manifest in intention and action, it will also signify the sustained finite being capable of love, gift, and relationality apart from explicit intention and action. A helpful definition of the person in terms of gift and generosity—drawn from and informed by the history of the word *person*, including, in particular, the development of the term through the early fathers of the Church from Cappadocia—is the following:

> "Person" will be reserved for the most authentic aspect of the temperament-inheriting self: its loving, generous, and "freest" opening. . . . The human "person" is mainly led out of the limits of the primitive "self" by the gifts of other persons who

---

39. This concept observes that modernity has developed in a particular way in the West, in tandem with a growing secularity, but that the Western experience is only one historically contingent experience of a culture modernizing, and modernization may not occur with secularization in other cultures. Political scientist Rajeev Bhargava, one of Taylor's interlocutors, looks at the experience of modernity and secularization in India, for example. The last pages of *Modern Social Imaginaries* begin to hint at the concept. See also Taylor, "On Social Imaginary" in *Contemporary Sociological Theory* 2001, blog.lib.umn.edu. Taylor's attunement to the particularity of individual cultures through his embrace of the concept of multiple modernities and his reflections on catholicity as unity-through-diversity are some of the foundations for deriving a hermeneutics for intercultural theology from his thought.

work lovingly and methodically, striving to educate a person authentically.[40]

According to this definition, a person is fundamentally a relational identity made in the image of the one who is most authentically relational, the triune God. Taylor's philosophical anthropology and Balthasar's theological treatment of personhood will be mined substantively in subsequent chapters of the book.

"Self"

In contrast to "person," "self" will designate that individual locus of experience that is understood to be the center of experience, thought, and agency in the modern world. To some degree, "self" is a term that may be viewed as a modern development of the term "person," originating from a Cartesian notion of identity as intrinsically related to the mind. I will understand the self to be a conflicted reality that emerges out of the moral confusion of modern identity and multiple and competing moral sources, after the fashion of Taylor's narrative of modern selfhood.[41]

STRUCTURE OF THE WORK

This work will proceed in five steps. Chapter 1 will consider Taylor's account of modernity, treating his philosophical, historical work on modern identity as a source of cultural "data" for the question of mission to modern Western cultures. I will focus on Taylor's account of modern selves, their aspirations and their challenges. I will also begin to examine Taylor's phenomenology of personhood and his philosophical arguments for the relationship between horizons and identity formation. The chapter will conclude with a first look at Taylor's description of the social imaginary that pervades general consciousness and undergirds the daily functioning of persons living in contemporary Western cultures.

Chapter 2 will mine Taylor's insight into the secularity of the modern social imaginary and the genesis of secularity as a pervasive feature

---

40. Langan, *Human Being*, 11.

41. One way to articulate what this work proposes as the Church's mission to a secular culture is to enable the process whereby individual and individualistic selves become persons. Thank you to Sr. Gill Goulding for underscoring the centrality of the latter for Balthasar.

of contemporary societal understanding and practice in the West. It will derive five claims from Taylor's account of secularity that the Church ought to consider in its reflection on how to evangelize in this age. The second half of chapter 2 will offer an interpretation of how Taylor's work on modernity, the phenomenology of the human person, and secularity comprise a subtle proposal regarding the role of faith and spirituality in achieving authentic personhood. His work *A Catholic Modernity?* will, on my interpretation, function as a hinge work opening up the religious and even missiological import of his work for theologians. It will also consider the degree to which a philosophical approach to questions of religion may help the Church's discernment of mission today. I will suggest that Taylor's approach can be appropriated by the Church to move from a "first reception" of Vatican II toward a "second reception" of Vatican II,[42] as Taylor traces a missionary path for the Church communicating itself in a secular culture (that is, begin with persons in culture, understand the power of social imaginaries in cultural and personal formation, and move to an articulation of holiness as that which most meets certain culturally held values, and is the Church's own deepest commitment).

Chapter 3 will explore Balthasar's theological anthropology and argue that Balthasar retrieves the dimension of transcendence to which Taylor alludes, at the metaphysical level of the foundations of freedom. Balthasar's *theodrama* describes the intrinsic relationship between becoming a person and God's self-giving freedom. It proposes a consideration of Balthasar's anthropology as a radical retrieval of the notion that the *action of God* and *human-divine interaction* lie at the foundation of any genuinely creative, loving, good, transformative human action.

Chapter 4 will develop an interpretation of Balthasar's ecclesiology as progressive and fresh in its account of the Church's missionary task. It will examine in particular Balthasar's account of the role of ecclesial authority in the formation of persons. It will show that Balthasar's account of the Church's many "profiles" reorients every aspect of the Church around holy intimacy[43] with Christ, a genuinely ecclesial spirituality, and the communion of saints.

These five steps of 1. appropriating Taylor's account of modern selves—the phenomenology of identity formation, 2. Taylor's account of

---

42. This language of a second reception of Vatican II is in many ways consonant with and in sympathy with Lamb and Levering's work on Vatican II (2012).

43. Thank you to Sr. Gill Goulding for shining a light on this felicitous turn of phrase and concept in Balthasar.

secularity, 3. synthesizing Taylor's claims about identity formation and secularization to develop a proposal about the path of Catholic mission in a secular age, 4. appropriating Balthasar's theodramatic account of personhood in Christ, and 5. Balthasar's refiguration of ecclesial essence —will, I argue, bring the Church to a greater awareness of a potential path forward for Catholic mission in a secular age—one that, importantly, unites the Church in her desire to open herself to the modern world.

The goal of this work is, finally, to argue that essential to Christian mission today is a committed and sustained formation of transformed Christian persons. While mission is generally understood to comprise the activity of the Church *ad extra*, "to the nations," the following chapters will demonstrate that the priority of Christian mission in the light of secularity is to retrieve her relationship to Christ, and from that 'space' to form persons in Christ whose radiance will invite others into relationship with the triune God. Missionary emphasis must be then, paradoxically, on rediscovering the Church *ad intra* and her ability to form saints for a new age.[44] The new cultural context of the modern western world, namely, its decidedly secular character, must be recognized so as to distinguish the call to deepen interior faithfulness as a united, holy, catholic, and apostolic Church from mere "retrenchment." Thus, I turn to the first hermeneutical task of the work, that of appropriating Taylor's account of modernity and the making of modern selfhood, for understanding the Western culture and selves that the Church is called to transform through loving and compassionate service.

---

44. A stronger way of framing the enormity of the propaedeutic work involved in proclaiming Christ to secular Western cultures today might even be to say that before we can get to mission proper as a Church, we need to look within and work on the deep problems of division within our body that are symptoms of a great separation from the person of Christ.

CHAPTER 1

Taylor's Picture of the Modern World

INTRODUCTION

IN THIS CHAPTER, I mine the resources for a vision of contemporary Catholic witness according to Taylor. Guided by Taylor's proposal of a catholic modernity as outlined in his work by the same name, I consider Taylor's works *Sources of the Self*, *The Malaise of Modernity*, and *Modern Social Imaginaries* as steps in which Taylor, and we with Taylor, discern how to meet modern, Western, secular culture "where it is." I use and read *A Catholic Modernity?* as the hinge piece for my interpretation of Taylor. From this consideration, I retrieve the following elements of Taylor's narrative of modernity. Taylor identifies in modern culture positive desires for justice, authenticity, and fulfillment in ordinary life that are attended by forms of modern malaise—subjectivism, relativism, atomism, instrumentalism, loss of fullness, flattened horizons, excarnation, and potential spiritual lobotomy. Based on Taylor's approach of understanding (and Augustine's also: understanding precedes love just as love precedes understanding[1]), this cultural and moral "data" enables the Church to discern how she might serve the contemporary cultures of Western modernity, such as that of Canada. Taylor also outlines the

1. See Augustine, *The Trinity*.

social imaginary and the new fundamental pre-reflective understanding of identity in Western modernity: namely, in economic, public, and self-legislating terms. He underscores that this imaginary is decidedly secular in character, "unmoored from higher times and Great Chains of Being."[2]

Taylor's "genealogy" of modern morals reveals that the challenge for modern individuals fifty years after the Council is much greater than the Church may have anticipated. In contrast with the much "cleaner" picture of "Church" called to serve "the world" in *Gaudium et Spes*, Taylor's historical accounts highlight the manner in which "Church" and "world" are mutually implicated and complicated in the history of modern Western identity. Sources *other than* theism have contributed significantly to modern identity and ethos. The decision for many modern selves in Western culture today lies in whether to retrieve theistic sources or to undergo "spiritual lobotomy." There exists a temptation toward immanentization in modernity in light of other proposals of how best to live, namely, neo-Nietzschean endeavors of self-realization without transcendence and morality, and exclusive humanism, that is, human morality without transcendence. Describing it as a three-cornered battle, he notes the seriousness of this root conflict over how best to live.

Taylor himself is opposed to the position that spiritual mutilation is necessary and seeks to retrieve some of the deep ontological commitments ("hypergoods") that, he believes, all persons have, and which involve theistic sources. Taylor's insight into the loss of certain languages and the conception held by most modern selves as self-legislating agents leads him to go beyond a straightforward account of the good of a Christian vision of the world. Indeed, Taylor "updates" the Church in helping it see that the theological horizon of human life can be taken much less for granted as the social imaginary of modern Western cultures evolves. There exists in place of the theological horizon of faith the unnamed,

---

2. Taylor, *Modern Social Imaginaries*, 157. "The public sphere is an association constituted by nothing outside of the common action we carry out in it: coming to a common mind, where possible, through the exchange of ideas. Its existence as an association is just our acting together in this way. This common action is not made possible by a framework that needs to be established in some action-transcendent dimension, either by an act of God or in a Great Chain or by a law that comes down to us since time out of mind. This is what makes it radically secular" (ibid., 94). See also, "A purely secular time-understanding allows us to imagine society horizontally, unrelated to any 'high points,' where the ordinary sequence of events touches higher time, and therefore without recognizing any privileged persons or agencies, such as kings or priests, who stand and mediate at such alleged points" (ibid., 157).

"unthought" (or pre-reflective) secular social imaginary. Rather than gifted recipients of salvation, sons and daughters of God, and *imago Dei*, people now see themselves primarily in terms of the economy, the public sphere, and as members of self-legislating polities.

Recognizing the reality of "the modern moral order,"[3] Taylor seems to try to find the "narrow" path in his dialogue with modern culture between the charge that Christianity is mere moralism (the Nietzschean critique that Christianity prevents genuine—self-originating—creativity) and the claim that nothing is lost with reliance on human morality alone ("exclusive humanism"). As Taylor tries to "save transcendence" in modernity, he notes the need of Christianity for secular society—that the latter in fact helped the gospel ethos to be more fully realized—and seeks a viable manner in which to present the gospel message. These are all ways in which Taylor proves to be an immensely discerning and formidable contributor to contemporary understanding of Christian existence in the wake of modernity.

Perhaps the most insightful of all is Taylor's implicit acknowledgment of the challenge of discussing transcendence in contemporary Western culture without recourse to morality, for that seems, indeed, to be the cultural condition that constrains all religious discourse. Morality is (even for neo-Nietzscheans, Taylor would say) the common ground. Thus, of all of Taylor's insights into the historical nature of modern selves, I wish to lift up the moral ideal of authenticity in contemporary culture as one of the key loci for missiological efforts. That and the challenge of a loss of ends are the key features of modern identity in the West that I believe can be further harnessed in developing a vision of Catholic mission in a secular age.

Interpreting Taylor

In *A Catholic Modernity?*, Taylor expresses a certain unhappiness with the traditional formulation of Catholicism in terms of mission and evangelization, claiming that the biblical injunction "Go ye and make

---

3. In *SA*, Taylor notes that while it is perfectly reasonable to lament the conflict between exclusive humanism and transcendent religion (and other options of varying degrees of similarity to one or the other), Taylor states that it is simply a fact: "The multi-cornered debate is shaped by the two extremes, transcendent religion, on one hand, and its frontal denial, on the other. It is perfectly legitimate to think that this is a misfortune about modern culture; but I would argue that it is a fact" (*SA*, 20).

disciples of all nations" has too often been used to support the project of Christendom and colonial forms of Christianity.[4] He makes an appeal, instead, to consider the call of faith in the contemporary world to be a deepening of catholicity through embracing the diversity of spiritual paths to faith that are possible today.[5] Taylor emphasizes that universality through wholeness and unity through difference are the ways we need to think about the question of catholicity today, rather than unity through identity.[6] Just as Matteo Ricci sought to make Christianity available to people in China, so, too, it is worth reflecting on the culture of Western modernity and how to enable the possibility of faith in this culture. *A Catholic Modernity?* is as close to an explicit perspective on Christian witness as exists in Taylor's corpus. Thus, for the purpose of answering the question at the heart of this work, *A Catholic Modernity?* will be treated as the "hinge piece" for understanding Taylor's works on modernity and secularity from 1989 to the present.

This chapter will thus begin with a discernment of modern selfhood through Taylor's works *Sources and the Self* and *The Malaise of Modernity* to show how one may apply Taylor's proposal of deepening *catholica* through first understanding a particular culture to his own work on the

---

4. "'Go ye and teach all nations.' How to understand this injunction? The easy way, the one in which it has all too often been taken, has been to take the global worldview of us who are Christians and strive to make over other nations and cultures to fit it. But this violates one of the basic demands of Catholicism. I want to take the original word *katholou* in two related senses, comprising both universality and wholeness. . . . Redemption happens through Incarnation, the weaving of God's life into human lives, but these human lives are different, plural, irreducible to each other. Redemption-Incarnation brings reconciliation, a kind of oneness. This is the oneness of diverse beings who come to see that they cannot attain wholeness alone, that their complementarity is essential, rather than of beings who come to accept that they are ultimately identical. . . . . Our great historical temptation has been to forget the complementarity, to go straight for the sameness, making as many people as possible into 'good Catholics'—and in the process failing of catholicity: failing of catholicity, because failing wholeness; unity bought at the price of suppressing something of the diversity in the humanity that God created; unity of the part masquerading as the whole. It is universality without wholeness, and so not true Catholicism" (*CM*, 14).

5. "So a Catholic principle, if I can put it in this perhaps overrigid way, is no widening of the faith without an increase in the variety of devotions and spiritualities and liturgical forms and responses to Incarnation" (*CM*, 15).

6. "This unity-across-difference, as against unity-through-identity, seems the only possibility for us, not just because of the diversity among humans, starting with the difference between men and women and ramifying outward. . . . But it seems that the life of God itself, understood as Trinitarian, is already a oneness of this kind. Human diversity is part of the way in which we are made in the image of God" (*CM*, 14–15).

culture of Western modernity. I will consider Taylor's account of the various aspirations and challenges from within an historicized moral ontology that reveals the complexity of modern identity—namely, that there exist myriad sources and some of them, theistic sources, are suppressed. I will then turn to Taylor's earlier work on horizons and his later work on social imaginaries, which names the deeply secular character of the cultural imaginary of modern Western polities. Expositing these facets of Taylor's account of modernity sets us up to understand where Taylor's approach to secularity may lead us on the question of viable Christian witness in a secular age (the latter forms the content of chapter 2).

A key way in which Taylor frames his approach is to ask, How can we be Catholic in this age so as to help those of us who live in modernity to be part of the eventual Catholic chorus?[7] Importantly, Taylor's signature approach, which seeks to appreciate perspectives from every side and apply evaluation with even-handedness, leads him to clarify that he does not mean by his question an inquiry into how to restore Christendom, nor a quest for becoming the most superior form of Catholic that history has yet seen, simply through existing at this latter point in time.[8]

As stated in the introduction, Taylor alludes to Jesuit missionary Matteo Ricci as a model of discernment and indicates that the possibility of a Catholic modernity might proceed in a similar fashion to first "learn the culture of modernity" with a certain critical distance and openness. It is true that there are some limitations to the application of a Riccian approach to inculturation or interculturation, as North American and Canadian society in particular is post-Christian and even anti-Christian in many ways; that is, there is a decided even though at times implicit antipathy to Christianity that was not necessarily present in pre-Christian societies such as the one Ricci was trying to evangelize. Nonetheless, it remains salient to bring this hermeneutic of openness and charity to one's approach of evangelization. Notwithstanding the debate about whether Taylor was accurate in his depiction of Ricci (as Ian Fraser has raised; see

---

7. *CM*, 15.

8. "The point is not to be a 'modern Catholic,' if by this we (perhaps semiconsciously and surreptitiously) begin to see ourselves as the ultimate 'compleat Catholics,' summing up and going beyond our less advantaged ancestors (a powerful connotation that hangs over the word *modern* in much contemporary use). Rather, the point is, taking our modern civilization for another of those great cultural forms that have come and gone in human history, to see what it means to be a Christian here, to find our authentic voice in the eventual Catholic chorus, to try to do for our time and place what Matteo Ricci was striving to do four centuries ago in China" (*CM*, 15).

Introduction, note 25), it seems reasonable that the challenge of being authentically Catholic today involves "making new discriminations: what in the culture represents a valid human difference, and what is incompatible with Christian faith."[9] Taylor's view is that there are authentic developments of the gospel, of an incarnational mode of life, mingled with a closing off to God that negates the gospel. Taylor points out, further, that a discerning look at modern life will reveal "facets of Christian life were carried further than they ever were taken or could have been taken within Christendom."[10] Understanding the culture is an important first step to learning how best to serve it. While much of what Taylor outlines is acknowledged in *Gaudium et Spes*, Taylor's narrative from within the modern world shows how modern identity in the West is inscribed far less by theistic sources (even less by ecclesial sources) and more by the intellectual inheritance of the Enlightenment and Romanticism. Taylor thus helps the Church understand more deeply one of the key dimensions that form the task of mission, namely, *the world*. Taking the Second Vatican Council's principle of dialogue seriously, and Lonergan's understanding of theology as mediating between a cultural matrix and the significance and role of religion in that matrix, I will appropriate Taylor's conception of the making of modern identity for understanding the task of mission.

For the purpose of this work, Taylor's account of modern identity includes four crucial aspects. First, Taylor highlights an integral development in Western culture: an increasing commitment to the ideal of universal beneficence. Taylor claims that the degree to which individuals are now inclined to give charitably and to bond together in common cause around the granting of equal rights is unprecedented in history. A second key dimension of modern selfhood and ever more prominent in culture today is the belief that ordinary life, the life of production and reproduction, is the locus of true human fulfillment. Taylor describes this development as "the affirmation of ordinary life." Third and most importantly, a strong ethos of authenticity is a key modern ideal; that is, the deep desire arising from a culture of expressiveness has become linked to a sense of one's life as a work of art. To be "true to oneself" becomes a principal ideal of modern selfhood. Attending these modern ideals is, however, a fourth marker of modern identity: the sense of fragmentation and incompleteness that marks modern experience, losses that Taylor names

9. *CM*, 16.
10. Ibid.

specifically as the problems of atomism (in politics), instrumentalism (in thinking), subjectivism,[11] and lack of a sense of fullness.[12] Presenting Taylor's account of these facets of modern Western experience shall form the first main task of this chapter.[13] Subsequent to laying out the main features that emerge from Taylor's developmental inquiry into the making of modern selves, Taylor's earlier theoretical work on agency and horizons will be discussed, which is important for framing the larger hermeneutical argument this work proposes concerning Taylor's accounts of personhood and secularity, and their implications for mission.

Modernity's Achievements and Laudable Ideals

Morally and epistemically, Taylor judges that we have made great gains. The ideals of modernity are great achievements. They include, for Taylor, several positive developments: (1) the development of universal rights, (2) the ethos of universal benevolence, (3) the affirmation of ordinary life, and, above all, (4) the aspiration to authenticity. Taylor affirms the fullness of a rights culture that has been attended by a sense of universal justice and benevolence, and praises the enlarged emphasis on equality as a moral norm. He also sees beauty in the affirmation of ordinary life that arose with the Protestant Reformation, and the Puritans in particular, as well as the development of an ethic of authenticity and freedom. Although the discussion of modernity's positive aspects will be distinguished here from modernity's darker aspects, it should be clear from the outset that Taylor's treatment of modernity understands modernity's *grandeur* and *misère* as arising from the same sources.[14]

---

11. Taylor, *The Malaise of Modernity*. Hereafter *MM*.

12. Taylor, *A Secular Age*.

13. While it might be more succinct to simply list the key ideals and malaises that have been abstracted from Taylor's expansive inquiry into modern identity, they will be expounded in Taylor's terms of historical and intellectual context to underscore the degree to which Western modernity is a culture, with its own developmental history and shifting ethoi.

14. Another way of stating the matter is that modernity's achievements are all in some sense double-faced goods.

A Culture of Rights

According to Taylor, the primacy of the modern rights culture has led to "something quite remarkable: the attempt to call political power to book against a yardstick of fundamental human requirements, universally applied."[15] The rights to life and liberty, crafted after the fashion of the right to property, were developments of the seventeenth century that saw the growing significance of self-responsible independence and recognized particularity.[16] For Taylor, the latter originates from Montaigne, whose development of modern individualism aims to "identify the individual in his or her unrepeatable difference."[17] Descartes is also a chief figure in the development of the modern self, articulating the general essence of the self as disengaged, scientific, instrumental rationality.[18] Taylor traces all of these, in turn, to Augustine's shift of attention from the cosmos outside the subject to one's self (there to find God), which Taylor designates the evolution of "inwardness." Thus, for Taylor, a line of development stretches from Augustinian inwardness to the radical reflexivity that characterizes the modern subject that then, through further layers of influence, develops into an understanding of individual rights with respect to political order.

In Taylor's narrative, seventeenth-century theories of social contract added to the traditional understanding of social contract a prior *contract of association*.[19] The roots of rights culture lie, in particular, with John Locke, Grotius, and Pufendorf. Through their work, individuals came to be seen as political atoms with an existence prior to the founding of political community. "Membership of a community with common power of decision is now something which needs to be explained by the individual's prior consent."[20] Taylor observes that this was a key development from the previous view of the individual as existing within a larger meaningful order, whether cosmic or social. The individual now stood outside of a cosmic order as well as outside of political society, as a sovereign individual who is by nature not bound to any authority.

15. *CM*, 18.
16. Taylor, *Sources of the Self,* 185. Hereafter *SS*.
17. Ibid., 182.
18. Note that not all interpreters of Descartes would understand his legacy in this way. Cf. Jean-Luc Marion and David Tracy.
19. Ibid., 193.
20. Ibid.

The value of equality, which arose through the development of modern subjective consciousness and especially the Protestant Reformation, had a leveling effect on social understanding, in general. It is involved in the fullness of rights-culture that Taylor affirms. The developments of a constructive, productive interest in securing the common good, through Calvinism, combined to bring into effect the moral norm that affirms that basic goods are owed to every individual and, thereby, the universalization of rights. It becomes clear, then, that another value, that of universal benevolence, is also closely related to the virtuous character that Taylor attaches to modern rights-consciousness.

Universal Benevolence

Universal benevolence is a second great ideal of modernity. Taylor writes, "We live in an extraordinary moral culture, measured against the norm of human history, in which suffering and death, through famine, flood, earthquake, pestilence, or war, can awaken worldwide movements of sympathy and practical solidarity."[21] The road to universal benevolence is a long one. Taylor traces the development of universal benevolence to three key figures and movements: the rise of *sentiment* as a central moral source for moral agents (Shaftesbury and Hutcheson are associated with this); the Calvinist penchant to remake the moral structure of society; and, ultimately, the deistic views of Locke that led to a move away from God's grace as part of moral action and resituated God as the great designer, whose universe individuals were called to care for according to its natural order.

For Taylor, Shaftesbury is a cross between the modern philosophy of Locke and that of the neo-Platonist philosophers of his time. Like Locke, Shaftesbury affirms deism and the general importance of resonance with human rationality as a criterion of the good. Like the Greek philosophers, Shaftesbury affirms an ethic of order and harmony. According to Shaftesbury, our nature is to love, and "our highest good is to love and take joy in the course of the whole world."[22] This love exists spontaneously in us. While the Platonic note sounds loudly in the aspect of love of the good, Shaftesbury's modernization is that the cosmic good is loved because of

---

21. *CM*, 25.
22. *SS*, 251.

our "natural affection," rather than the loveable character of the good.[23] The good is found in our loving; in this lies the "order."

Taylor states that Hutcheson, following Shaftesbury, was part of the modern process of internalizing the sources of the good in human persons. In particular, Hutcheson understood sentiment as a source within us that was naturally oriented to the good; as such, we could trust that our feelings and engagement of them would move us toward the good. Hutcheson, who takes the tradition from Shaftesbury, begins to see beyond the Lockean vision of the self as disengaged, toward the importance of reengagement of the world through a sense of the movement of the good within us.[24] The emphasis begins to turn to the way in which the feelings in us call us to the good. Indeed, Hutcheson believes so deeply in the correspondence of the movement of the good in us and the benevolence of God that he deems "our bent toward the good to be our sentiments of universal benevolence," which rests, of course, on the benevolence of God, who makes our nature.[25] Hutcheson reframes the picture of the relationship between the good and the self by claiming that we are in the moral order through engagement of our sentiments of benevolence. The heightened sense of sentiment as a moral source is one key element of the rise of the modern hypergood[26] of universal benevolence.

For Taylor, Hutcheson also provides the groundwork for the utilitarians, who make the end of happiness the chief criterion upon which to base a rational procedure to determine right action. Underlying the utilitarian norm of universal happiness is also a Calvinist sensibility, which understood the task of life to be to remake and restructure the world according to the natural order, established by the creator. Because Lockean deism as well as Locke's understanding of the human subject stood behind Calvinism, an ethic of rational control informed the Calvinist drive to make the world more orderly according to the laws of God. Calvinist societies placed a high emphasis on self-control and the mutual admonishment of one another so as to realize God's vision in the world.

A final moral source of universal benevolence was Lockean deism. Locke's vision of God is that of the maker of order, the great designer. While human moral striving still depends on God, the nature of moral

23. Ibid., 256.
24. Ibid., 265.
25. Ibid., 264.
26. Hypergoods are the goods against which other goods are evaluated and measured. They form the standard of moral measure, so to speak.

action is reconfigured to lie not in the will, as in Augustine, and openness to God's gracious action, but in the mind's capacity to know the will of God. Rationality, and particularly disengaged rationality, enables us to see clearly. Following Descartes, the discovery of reality in one's reasoning process is such that we come most clearly to the will of God in understanding the way his universe works. Rather than personal relationship with God, we come to know his will through understanding the workings of his creation. This procedural, instrumental outlook of the Enlightenment also greatly informs the dominance of the ethical imperative of universal benevolence in our day. Notably, a Christian ethos is tied to many of these new "sources."

The Affirmation of Ordinary Life

A third and widely discussed aspect of Taylor's view of modernity is the ideal that he describes as the affirmation of ordinary life. Taylor's view of this ideal is almost unequivocal appreciation: "[I] think that the practical primacy of life has been a great gain for humankind."[27] Taylor's narrative emphasizes the sweeping influence of this constitutive norm. He traces to it the development of one main family of moral sources, *nature*. Affirming everyday life involves the shift wherein the ordinary life of production and reproduction came to be seen not merely as infrastructural to more ultimate ends of society, nor as inferior, but as important in itself. Within this shift, the ideal of companionate marriage came to the fore, along with a more explicit sanctification of family life. Business and economic life, a view of science as serving the ends of practical life (*techné*) rather than knowledge in itself, the development of the contemporary novel with its shedding of a certain formalism in style, and a new appreciation for the relaxed aesthetic of the English garden over the more styled and elaborate French garden were all part of the culture that developed from within and through the affirmation of ordinary life.

All of it was rooted, Taylor claims, in a fundamental and strong rejection by the Reformers of certain aspects of the Catholic vision. In particular, the resistance was directed at the Catholic understanding of the sacred, which saw God's action as "in a sense imprisoned, tied to an action which it was in men's power to perform: the Mass." Taylor connects this with a rejection of Catholic practices of elevating certain times

---

27. *CM*, 29.

and places as special, and therefore "Protestant (particularly Calvinist) churches swept away pilgrimages, veneration of relics, visits to holy places."[28] All of these practices were jettisoned along with the basic sense that the Church was the locus of divine meaning. Rather, meaning was to be found in life itself, and "calling" was the privilege of all and not merely those with a monastic vocation. The priority of universal calling came with the Puritans and followed the general dismissal of God's way in the world as particularly exemplified in monasticism rather than in every form of life. Related to this was the spirit/flesh distinction originating with Plato, which privileged the spirit. Hierarchies and mediation were rejected in favor of a sense that each believer was authorized to "row his own boat" to salvation.[29] A great leveling took place socially.

The affirmation of ordinary life was rooted in a theology. Taylor notes that it was rooted in the basic sense of Judeo-Christian spirituality that life is good in itself, as expressed in Genesis. During the Enlightenment and in light of Enlightenment values of equality and democracy, the superiority of vocations to the religious life or monastic life over vocations to the lay life was denied. Despite this transformation of existing theology, the point of all things according to the theology of ordinary life was still to serve the glory of God. The Puritans, Taylor writes, aimed at a balance between the errors of monasticism[30] and attachment to life. One's work and the love of one's spouse were for the greater glory of God, not for these realities in themselves. Regarding work, Taylor describes the shift with Puritanism from *what* one does to *how* one does it.[31] All individuals, through Calvinism, were driven by a desire to reorder the world to the purposes of God. In light of deism, this was how order was now conceived, as "reciprocal effects toward a set of interlocking purposes."

Authenticity

Authenticity is perhaps the ideal upon which Taylor has shed the most light. Taylor praises the ethic of authenticity as a powerful and valid moral ideal, despite the degraded expressions of this ideal that modern

---

28. SS, 216–17.
29. Ibid., 217.
30. We are not dealing with Taylor's view of Catholicism in this chapter so much as exegeting his view of modernity, which is to say that Taylor's understanding of monasticism is not necessarily affirmed.
31. SS, 222.

culture has developed.[32] "Authenticity points us towards a more self-responsible form of life. . . . At its best authenticity allows a richer mode of existence."[33] The richness lies in the fullness and differentiation that life acquires when individuals actively appropriate their lives.

The ideal of authenticity is perhaps the paradigmatic ideal of modern and contemporary persons in the West. According to Taylor, the roots of the ethic of authenticity lie originally in the subjectivist visions of Descartes and Locke, elaborated respectively as disengaged rationality and political individualism. Authenticity is also grounded in the Romantic rejection of "disengagement." Expressivism developed through Rousseau's articulation, in particular, of heeding the voice of nature within us,[34] and Herder's idea that "each of us has an original way of being human."[35] Herder helps give strength to the idea that to be true to oneself is to be true to one's own originality, and this is the fruit of a process of self-discovery that only one can undertake.[36] A close link is forged through the ideals of Romanticism between an authentic life that involves defining one's life and life as artistic creation.

Taylor notes that while it might be easy to decry the culture of authenticity *tout court*, he thinks it is preferable to make distinctions about when the idea of authenticity can lead to the "slide to subjectivism." Taylor concludes that the ideal of authenticity cannot be met through a thoroughgoing freedom of self-determination, or be reduced to an ethic of self-fulfillment in which others figure only as instruments to one's self-actualization. The logic of authentic self-determination requires the understanding that significance only arises through a horizon *beyond* one's own choosing; that significance arises from something being acknowledged more generally. Taylor designates the latter "horizons of significance." Without recognition that one's choosing acquires significance from a larger and external horizon of meaning, be it society, nature, or the will of God, one risks reducing authenticity to mere choosing, such that one achieves only a trivialization of the meaning of choice. Taylor's example, involving Nietzsche, distinguishes the achievement of choosing to create a new understanding of values from choosing what to order

---

32. *MM*, 13–23.
33. Ibid., 74.
34. Ibid., 27.
35. Ibid., 28.
36. Ibid., 30.

at a fast food restaurant. A key problem that Taylor has with certain postmodern varieties of authenticity is their destruction of the greater horizons of significance, which Taylor notes are the condition for the possibility of genuine authenticity.[37]

Moreover, evidence of the need for horizons of meaning is given in experience itself, particularly in the experience of its absence. Treating relationships as instrumental to self-fulfillment and the right to determine oneself in whatever way, without "horizons of significance," leads to inauthenticity, as we are fundamentally dialogical and need relationships to fulfill us.[38] At a social level, the absence of agreed-upon senses of meaning leads to merely procedural justice, which Taylor decries as a "sham." Taylor concludes that authenticity "perhaps can only be achieved through connection to a wider whole."[39] Taylor arrives at this judgment through a consideration of authenticity as it exists for most people who live in this culture of authenticity, who privilege self-fulfillment and the sphere of intimate relationships. Taylor shows that while authenticity is inherently self-referential in method, for the ideal to be actualized it must not be self-referential in content.

Thus, to summarize, *Sources of the Self* yields a portrait of modern selves as moved and motivated by certain moral ideals. The first part of this chapter elaborates Taylor's description of three of these ideals in particular: (1) benevolence as a key modern ideal, which includes developments of the value of equality and a culture of rights; (2) ordinary life as the locus of genuine fulfillment; and (3) authenticity as perhaps the highest human ideal of modern selves. The next section discusses some of the challenges that modern selves face as well, which Taylor has famously described as "the malaise of modernity" in his book by the same name (also released under the title *The Ethics of Authenticity*). These include an ongoing and underlying struggle to ward off atomism, instrumentalism, and a loss of meaning and sense of ends.

The Malaise of Modern Selfhood

One of the key aspects of Taylor's approach to modernity that aids the Church today concerning mission is his reminder that, despite

---

37. Ibid., 66.
38. Ibid., 33.
39. Ibid., 91.

modernity's great achievements, *losses* attend the passage to modernity. While such recognition exists within the documents of the Council, reception of Vatican II has also been summarily construed by many as an unequivocal affirmation of the modern world and its realities. The shift in the Church's ethos in the name of *aggiornamento* to "what we might learn from the world" occludes in some cases the sense of the world this side of the eschaton as always in need of transformation and conversion. Taylor's account of some of Western modernity's fundamental challenges helps clarify that the call to mission and evangelization remains in the Church's engagement of the modern world.

As previously stated, modernity's ideals are implicated with certain modern malaises. Each of the positive facets of modernity is attended by problematic tendencies: the tendency to political atomism and "soft despotism," to loss of meaning, to loss of heroism, and to loss of ends. Taylor enumerates these losses as the malaise of subjectivism, instrumentalism in reasoning, and political atomism.

Subjectivism, Instrumentalism, and Atomism

Taylor names three modern malaises in various ways throughout his corpus. Subjectivism is also known as individualism, and loss of meaning is one of its associated effects. Instrumentalism is alternately described as a loss of ends. The third dimension of modernity's malaise, which is related closely with the first, is a political loss or "soft despotism"—that is, a loss of freedom and a sense of "impending social dissolution."[40] Taylor also cites confusion with respect to moral sources and morality itself as a further intellectual loss. This loss is more pervasive because it is suppressed.[41]

Let us consider the first aspect of modern malaise, subjectivism. It is often the case that the ideal of authenticity is lived as subjectivism, with the subject referring only to himself or herself in his or her quest for self-fulfillment. Taylor acknowledges that part of the malaise of subjectivism is due to social change, which includes the processes of industrialization, increasing mobility, technologization, and bureaucratization of modern

---

40. *MSI*, 1.

41. In an important way, the confusion we experience in understanding our moral sources, moral agency, and experience drives Taylor's genealogical work in moral philosophy.

societies.[42] In addition, subjectivism is due to the stream of moral sources that combine to identify fulfillment and individuality, such that fulfillment is now centered on the individual and modes of self-fulfillment become self-centered.

From another direction, there is the challenge of loss of meaning and radical subjectivism that comes from a Nietzschean sense of self-fulfillment and expression, where art is pitted over against morality. Into this form of expression is the imperative to struggle against some internally imposed rules, as conformity is the enemy.[43] According to Taylor, this trend of malaise attends deconstructionist theories of human existence. The problem with deconstruction is that it delegitimates horizons of significance so that creativity comes without due respect to the dialogical setting. Where value itself becomes created, Taylor acknowledges that there is a tremendous sense of freedom and power, but this radical freedom is also the source of many contemporary enactments of violence. In short, such self-determining freedom in its most thoroughgoing sense undercuts itself. Value ends up being choice itself, which "undoes the underlying [necessary] value of recognizing difference."[44] While Taylor does not tend to elaborate on the problem of relativism, it is certainly a version of this aspect of modern malaise.

The three forms of modern malaise are inextricably related. An attendant effect of subjectivism is, for example, atomism and alienation. The cost of a radical "subjectivization" is experienced as malaise in our political life. The more we identify ourselves as atoms with desires prior to political community, the less likely we are to engage in the life of the polity. While Taylor on the whole affirms the fullness of rights as a substantial and positive development of moral selfhood, he also notes that understanding society as a mere instrument for individual good has significant problems. For Taylor, our theories of rights, "the modern tendency to frame the immunities accorded people by law in terms of subjective rights," is the legacy of the seventeenth century, but so, too, is its corollary, political atomism. Both give pride of place in our legal system to the individual.[45] The less we engage in common projects with fellow citizens and the more we leave to the efficiency of the market and

42. *MM*, 59.
43. Ibid, 63.
44. Ibid., 31–41.
45. *SS*, 195.

state planning, the more likely it is that we will live in a state of "soft despotism."[46] Taylor believes that the dual power of state and market, taken together, can weaken democratic initiative.[47]

Atomism leads also to social fragmentation and, reciprocally, fragmentation leads to atomism since individuals "fail to identify with political society as a community" and so are more likely to see society in purely instrumental terms.[48] The lack of identification with political life leads to a sense of political powerlessness and the cycle devolves. Taylor alludes to theories by modern thinkers who are trying to "recapture a more holistic view of society, to understand it as a matrix for individuals rather than as an instrument."[49] For this he is sometimes described as a communitarian.

Instrumentalism, Taylor shows, is bound up with the ideal of authenticity and its aberrant form, subjectivism or individualism. Instrumentalism arose in part out of a response to a universe that was no longer enchanted. Disenchantment and an eroded belief that meaning was to be found in the cosmos led to increasing identification of freedom with self-expression and self-legislation. Persons unmoored from a cosmos with inscribed meanings found themselves moving into a deistic conception of God that ultimately led to a sense that freedom comes only in choosing and, further, in a sense that reality is partially constituted by our ability to give creative expression to it.[50]

Without traditional horizons of meaning in place—for example, the social hierarchies of an honor society—it is possible for the ethical ideal of authenticity and individualism to slide into subjectivism, a degraded form of itself that culminates in a lack of meaning. The lack of meaning arises from a denial of horizons of significance and a dialogical context for all self-creating; freedom in creation comes at the expense of freedom as dialogical.[51] Together they undercut self-determining freedom: there are "no meaningful choices because there are no meaningful issues."[52] The world becomes "flattened." Instrumentalism is bound up with subjectivism or the loss of meaning since, where the subject and subjective choice

---

46. *MM*, 111.

47. To some extent, the situation has changed since Taylor presented these ideas in 1991, as cultural phenomena such as the Occupy movement show.

48. *MM*, 118.

49. *SS*, 196.

50. This causal connection is developed more explicitly in *A Secular Age*.

51. *MM*, 66–67.

52. Ibid., 69.

settle things, it becomes easy to see ourselves as inhabiting a universe that we can consider "raw material" for our purposes.[53] Instrumentalism is the upshot of disengagement: we become disengaged from our bodies, our dialogical situation, our emotions, and traditional life forms, "to be pure, self-verifying rationality."[54]

Thus, Taylor's affirmation of the modern self also includes a caution that this identity often seems to demand a choice of modern persons, to accept some sort of spiritual loss, some "sacrifice" of meaning or sense of fullness and wholeness, or else, seemingly, rejection of ourselves as modern. Some destruction of some part of ourselves, moved as we are by moral sources that exist in tension, seems inevitable.

Loss of Relationality

The disembedding of the modern individual is experienced in the relationship of the self to society. Previously, persons received their value from the divinely instituted order that was inscribed in both the cosmic and social order. Persons experienced their value and sense of purpose in virtue of where they found themselves in the social hierarchy. According to Taylor's account, with the developments of modern social contract and economic theories, the modern individual became the bearer of rights prior to political belonging and social ordering. A shared narrative of participation in a Great Chain of Being or other transcendent order no longer bonded the cultural "we" in the West, but rather, common "action." Relationships in the modern age are characterized by mutual benefit and disinterested benevolence. What drops out, Taylor observes, are understandings of sacrifice that attended relationships founded on Christian *agape* and heroism.

Heroism is another articulated loss that persists in Taylor's writings that show the point of convergence between Taylor and Nietzsche. At the beginning of SS, Taylor cites heroism as comprising part of the key problematic that he worries about.[55] On the one hand, we have become convinced of the majesty and beauty of "ordinary life." Part of this

---

53. Ibid., 89.
54. Ibid., 102.
55. "We sympathize with both the hero and the anti-hero; and we dream of a world in which one could be in the same act both. This is the confusion in which naturalism takes root." SS, 24.

appreciation derived from the efforts of the Reformation to challenge and refigure the belief that certain forms of higher existence, essentially the special religious existence of Christians, are more superior than that of honest work ("production") and family ("reproduction"). Taylor reveals that this attitude coexists in tension with the experience we have had and still remember: traces of the experience of living within an "honor" society, where only great deeds of selfless bravery count as significant action. There is something in Taylor's question concerning the loss of heroism that connects up with the dismissal of theistic sources. We can begin to see how Taylor's cultural project is motivated by a certain underlying interest in the question of faith and secularization in modernity.

The Search for Meaning, the Loss of Ends

Finally, in *A Secular Age*, where Taylor provides his most direct argument against one form of modern morality, exclusive humanism, Taylor weaves throughout his narrative on the development of secularity a nagging question about whether persons living within a frame closed to transcendence are truly fulfilled. *A Secular Age* suggests that our experience of "fullness" and "emptiness" has something to do with the presence of the spiritual dimension in our lives, particularly as it impacts our moral vision. Moreover, Taylor claims that how we understand our lives in time has also to do with their sense of fullness. He argues that modernity has brought about a certain diminishment in our sense of fullness.[56]

Taylor suggests that he is personally compelled by some sources more than others and believes that the primary predicament of modern moral existence is to preserve a sense of the spirit as one faces the incredibly high demands that modern morality has generated in us for benevolence, universal justice and beneficence, equality, and freedom.[57] Taylor does not, however, take a moralistic stance or make an absolute pronouncement on the goodness of modern moral identity. Taylor acknowledges the voices in our age that express concern over the instrumentalism that leads to marginalizing purposes that are of more intrinsic value, and that a threatening sense of the loss of meaning pervades modern experience

---

56. Because Taylor ties spirituality into modern moral identity, we may later ask whether faith as a moral horizon suffices as a way to envision being Catholic in a contemporary secular culture and age.

57. This is a theme that surfaces repeatedly through Taylor's works on modernity.

in terms of a concern for disenchantment and personal fragmentation.[58] Nevertheless, Taylor does not consider modernity in itself the problem. Rather, the problem, he finds, is the tendencies that are latent in modernity, that have at times actualized themselves as inauthentic forms of the ethic of authenticity, such that our sense of meaning and freedom are in fact compromised. Thus, Taylor believes that the best approach to modernity is to see it in such a manner as to aid modern culture and modern individuals in actualizing modernity's greatest potentialities, and minimize its tendencies toward its most base and shallow forms.

Phenomenology of Personhood

> I want to talk of how wonder and puzzlement intruded into my life, and pushed me where I have gone. At first, I studied history. This seemed to be the best way. Then I became involved in politics, in the ways that politics could transform human life. But underlying all these was an interest in philosophical anthropology: what were human beings, these beings who can speak and therefore articulate, and in this way transform themselves?[59]

At this point, I move retrospectively from Taylor's constructive work on the moral sources and malaises of modern individuals to Taylor's earlier analytic work in philosophical hermeneutics. The second half of this chapter will consider Taylor's description of persons as essentially agents, that is, autonomous and "self-interpreting." I will focus in particular on Taylor's contention that human agency is fundamentally constituted by shared horizons of understanding. This claim concerning the role of horizons in forming identity is, I argue, a thread that unites and clarifies much of what Taylor is ultimately proposing in his later works on modern social imaginaries and his much-lauded interpretation of the development of secularity in the West. It will enable us to see the upshot of Taylor's discernment of modern Western culture. The chapter will conclude with an account of Taylor's depiction of the modern social imaginary and the implications of considering imaginaries as a platform for the Church's engagement with the world. This last prepares us for receiving Taylor's narrative of secularity in chapter 2.

---

58. *SS*, 501.
59. Taylor, "What Drove Me to Philosophy."

Agency

In 1985, Taylor considered a generally held concept of person: by person, we mean "an agent, with purposes, desires, aversions, and so forth. But obviously more than this because many animals can be considered agents in this sense, but we don't consider them persons. So generally philosophers consider that to be a person in the full sense you have to be an agent with a sense of yourself as an agent, a being which can thus make plans for your life, one who also holds values in virtue of which different such plans seem better or worse, and who is capable of choosing between them."[60] Taylor then clarified that the general understanding of person in terms of consciousness and representational powers is a distinctly modern one that equates personhood with being an individual. While noting that it is an historically located understanding of the human person, Taylor did not disagree with such a definition of the human person but simply sought to show that the concept of person needed to involve more than the agency associated with consciousness and the ability to think representationally; it had to include the question of significance. Taylor's understanding of humans as self-interpreting animals and as creatures who are constantly involved in strong evaluation is well known: our self-understandings are not arbitrary construals, though we can be wrong in our construals of ourselves; as self-interpreting animals we constantly engage in strong evaluation, or the practice of recognizing goods that are seen as intrinsically worthy, and not only worthy in their relation to us; and we find ourselves and our sense of significance through language and conversations with others. Shared horizons are essential for constituting meaning. These aspects of personhood, Taylor claims, are given to us in our experience of ourselves as perceiving, acting, moral agents.

The Importance of Horizons to Identity

The importance of horizons derives from the phenomenological fact of human sociality. Taylor articulates the dialogical nature of identity formation in *Malaise of Modernity* thus:

> The genesis of the human mind is in this sense not "monological," not something each accomplishes on his or her own, but dialogical. . . . [Yet] we are expected to develop our own

---

60. Taylor, "Person," 257.

opinions, outlook, stances to things, to a considerable degree through solitary reflection. But this is not how things work with important issues, such as the definition of our identity. We define this always in dialogue with, sometimes in struggle against, the identities our significant others want to recognize in us. And even when we outgrow some of the latter—our parents, for instance—and they disappear from our lives, the conversation with them continues within us as long as we live.[61]

Taylor outlines the place of horizons in determining the significance of things and thus authenticity:

> Things take on importance against a background of intelligibility. Let us call this a horizon. It follows that one of the things we can't do, if we are to define ourselves significantly, is suppress or deny the horizons against which things take on significance for us. [Yet] this is the kind of self-defeating move frequently being carried out in our subjectivist civilization.[62]

Taylor notes that one pervasive form of modern malaise is the slide into a subjectivistic mode of being. Contrary to being a mode of authentic existence, subjectivism emphasizes the aspect of creativity in self-becoming, without due attention to the dialogical character of becoming human: the need, that is, for dialogue with others and a shared framework of significance. Due to this neglect of the dialogical character of identity formation, Taylor argues, subjectivism fundamentally undercuts itself as a method or results in the trivialization of personal choice. For Taylor, this is the problem with Nietzschean and related postmodern understandings of selfhood.

The Secularity of the Modern Social Imaginary

In *Modern Social Imaginaries* Taylor begins to explicitly underscore the manner in which the social imaginary in modern Western cultures is decidedly secular. Our current social imaginary in the West, Taylor claims, is comprised of "realities" such as the economy, the public sphere, and self-determining peoples, and hinges on the conception of social/political, temporal realities as unmoored from all forms of transcendence, including founding narratives. Taylor maps the process in historical

61. *MM*, 35.
62. Ibid., 37.

consciousness whereby we have received and cultivated our current Western, secular experience of social relationships, showing how we have moved from a social order that reflected a cosmic order where God was at the helm to an ordering of the social according to the sovereignty of the autonomous individual, in which the shared goal of life together is mutual benefit.

Taylor's investigation of modern Western culture through an examination of its social imaginary takes place not primarily in laying out an historical tour but in articulating the background that shapes the lived space of where we are now. A particular modern moral order has become legitimized, which powers our current social imaginary. Taylor thus explores the roots of this order. He finds that the roots of the modern moral order lie at a fundamental level in a desire to get beyond the destruction caused by the wars of religion, and that Grotius and Locke are among key theorists who "aimed to find a stable basis of legitimacy beyond confessional differences."[63]

An ethic of rights, freedom, and mutual benefit drives the development of the modern social imaginary. Taylor traces this form of individual and social self-understanding to Locke and Grotius. They along with others refigured natural law theories of contract such that mutual respect and service of individuals came to the fore along with the primary task of society as serving two ends, security and prosperity. Economic activity, through Locke, was considered the primary mode for human behavior and key to its harmonious existence.[64] In short, the modern moral order is premised on the hypergoods of the individual, security, economic flourishing, rights, freedom, and equality.

A social imaginary develops in light of this moral order. The economy, the public sphere, and the practices and outlooks of a self-determining people become the horizon that defines modern sociality. All take place in "profane time," namely, a time that counters any notion of higher times and is a place to stand outside of political order.[65] With the development of the public sphere, in particular, action becomes the ground of commonality, rather than any founding moment tied to a higher time.[66] Taylor writes, "Secularity is the condition where the constituting

---

63. *MSI*, 31.
64. Ibid., 15.
65. Ibid., 98–99.
66. Ibid., 97.

factor is nothing outside of the common action," rather than any "action-transcendent dimension; [there is] no God or Great Chain of Being."[67] There is no shared goal beyond the common action of an exchange of ideas and the development of a common mind among individuals who are understood as constituted by rights pre-politically and who have a kind of metatopical agency that is legitimized by rationality rather than power or traditional authority.[68]

Along the way, there is greater distance from founding moments and, with Calvinism, the possibility of founding and refounding at any point in time. This emphasis on founding at any time contributes, too, to the reality of the sovereign people. The legitimized form of the self-determining people reshapes social relations from personal and hierarchical to impersonal and equal.[69] A "direct access" society emerges that is characterized by horizontality rather than verticality. Narrating this transformation as "progress" or "maturation" helps entrench the social imaginary.

Taylor finds, significantly, that the modern social imaginary in all of its characteristic forms is profoundly secular. By this Taylor means a certain kind of time—a time unattached to any kind of eternal order or other form of "higher time." Taylor notes that at the heart of the moral order itself, and so understandably in the social imaginary, is an orientation to and for the "here and now." He contrasts this with a moral political order that is ultimate, such as the communion of saints, the medieval Christian ideal.[70] Moreover, the new idea of moral order, as it develops, "begins to inflect and reformulate the descriptions of God's providence and the order he has established among humans and in the cosmos."[71]

Taylor's method of narrating secularization recognizes the shifting character of ethics "on the ground" and reads history with an eye to seeing within it the pursuit of the good, if not the fulfillment of it. He might be said to reveal in a new key—that of social imaginaries and the historical narrative of Western culture—the insight articulated by Augustine on the nature of human souls: the line between good and evil runs through each one. Otherwise stated, Taylor disrupts the clean lines between sacred and

67. Ibid., 94.
68. Ibid., 90.
69. Ibid., 152.
70. Ibid., 7.
71. Ibid., 5.

secular history. In writing about the development of secularization in the West over the past five hundred years as he has, Taylor's implicit claim is that all of us who live today in a secularized Western culture share a common history in which the sacred and secular are intermingled.

The upshot of all of this for the question of Catholic mission seems to be, on the one hand, that the secular social imaginary forms the background understanding of many Catholics today. Moreover, Taylor seems to question whether modernity's goods must come with the adoption of a secular conception of time, society, and hence life. In *CM*, Taylor becomes more explicit with regard to the competitive dimension and points of exclusiveness between theism, now crystallized as "transcendence," exclusive humanism, and the Nietzschean version of freedom. It seems to Taylor that modernity can demand something akin to a "spiritual lobotomy."[72]

The point of tracing the imaginary seems to be to get clearer on how we live together, how we have gotten to where we are, and how we relate to others who are different from us on matters of ultimate value and fidelity. Taylor acknowledges that there seem to be conflicts and confusions over personhood that have arisen with the modern social imaginary of our time. While modern society is more homogenous than the premodern and different classes are much closer together,[73] modern individualism's notion of belonging is to "ever wider and more impersonal entities."[74] Society is, then, "a field of common agency," and also a terrain to be "mapped, synoptically presented, analyzed."[75] There is the phenomenon of the lonely crowd that sometimes, nevertheless, may break into a new identity as a genuinely collective agent. Taylor cites the example of the shared experience of Princess Diana's death: people from around the world came together to mourn a celebrity who was in many cases a complete stranger to them and yet, somehow, a dearly beloved individual as well.

Taylor notes that the sense of lack and malaise is derivable, to some degree, from a loss of frameworks of meaning and significance. The challenging implications of modernity for persons and identity where persons are disembedded from cosmic and social orders of the good include

---

72. See *Sources of the Self* and *The Malaise of Modernity*.
73. *MSI*, 161.
74. Ibid., 160.
75. Ibid., 164.

the experience of a sense of truncated freedom, loss of meaning or sense of fullness, fragmentation/atomism, and the felt pressure in the face of a naturalistic conception of moral norms to choose what Taylor terms "a spiritual lobotomy."

As Ron Mercier has noted, relationality and responsibility shift in modernity: the question left without clear contours is, to whom do modern selves answer?[76] A profound vulnerability and uncertainty exists in the light of the modern world's "sweeping away" of ultimate horizons. Taylor notes, in spite of the cultural narrative, an ongoing striving for communion. Simply put, modern selves' experience of agency, relationality, and moral core are greatly transformed by their transition into a disenchanted cosmos where they become "buffered selves" facing an endless series of choices toward a series of uncertain ends.

In a secular age the spiritual search and the spiritual seeker therefore rise to prominence. Taylor observes the phenomenon of world tourism and exploration by young persons of different cultures, peoples, and religions. The phenomenon of spiritual quest or search marks the modern age with unavoidable force. This, too, Taylor asserts, indicates something of the desire for ends that remains unsatisfied in a culture of punctual selves[77] living in horizontal time.[78]

Taylor's Alignment with Vatican II on the Question of Modernity

Taylor's appreciative yet critical approach to modernity shows, then, a clear alignment with the Church's desired approach to the modern world at Vatican II. In addition to speaking to the best aspirations and achievements of a culture, Taylor speaks to the experience of the modern person and to the way in which the spiritual dimension of the modern self can be accessed through a discussion of moral sources and moral imagination.[79] The Second Vatican Council was notable for emphasizing and enlarging the sense of moral responsibility of individual Catholics. While the

76. Mercier, "Holy Spirit and Ethics," 43–65.
77. Taylor, *Sources of the Self*.
78. Taylor, *Modern Social Imaginaries*.
79. William Greenway's version of stating the person-centered character of Taylor's approach is that Taylor speaks from within moral experience to God rather than from God as a primary source to a constitutive good according to experience. See Greenway, "Charles Taylor on Affirmation, Mutilation, and Theism."

Church certainly recognizes the central importance of the human person, Taylor's account adds a dimension of complexity to understanding the nature of the human person through providing a fuller account of the mixed development of the modern moral self through time. Taylor seldom directs normative claims at the human person *tout court* however, but points to human culture and to where modern culture's truest strivings fall short of arriving at a truth that adequately sustains the human desire to be whole.[80]

Taylor's take on modernity is also unique in being a recuperative and hopeful project that traces the roots of spiritual malaise through an historical narrative of cultural shifts. Taylor explicitly engages the spiritual question in terms of culture, trying to give an account of the *Zeitgeist*.[81] Importantly, Taylor both affirms and challenges certain aspects of modernity, arguing that development in the understanding of human rights, for example, only occurred with the unfolding of the modern age and its social imaginary.

Taylor's Alignment with Modernity

Yet Taylor's view of modernity is more complicated: on the one hand, Taylor seeks to affirm much more of modernity's moral landscape as it has developed in the West than many in the official Church might, including the ethic of authenticity in its most principled form. On the other hand, Taylor is critical of the Nietzschean hyper-claim of self-authenticating

---

80. "Is the naturalist affirmation conditional on a vision of human nature in the fullness of its health and strength? Does it move us to extend help to the irremediably broken, such as the mentally handicapped, those dying without dignity, fetuses with genetic defects? Perhaps one might judge that it doesn't and that this is a point in favor of naturalism; perhaps effort shouldn't be wasted on these unpromising cases. But the careers of Mother Teresa or Jean Vanier seem to point to a different pattern, emerging from a Christian spirituality.... My aim has been to ... identify this range of questions around the moral sources which might sustain our rather massive professed commitments in benevolence and justice. This entire range is occluded by the dominance of proceduralist meta-ethics, which makes us see these commitments through the prism of moral obligation, thereby making their negative face all the more dominant and obtrusive and pushing the moral sources further out of sight. But the picture I have been drawing of the modern identity brings this range back into the foreground.... The intention of this work was one of retrieval, an attempt to uncover buried goods through rearticulation—and thereby to make these sources again empower, to bring the air back into the half-collapsed lungs of the spirit" (SS, 517–20).

81. Smith, *Charles Taylor: Meaning, Morals and Modernity*, 199.

will to power over and against *agape*. Taylor also recognizes, however, the value of Nietzsche's critique of a false Christianity parsed as moral code.[82] Taylor clearly feels resonance with the Romanticists' protest against Enlightenment reason. Taylor holds, thereby, an important and unusual stance, uncommon in so far as it belongs to one who advocates the presence of strong evaluation based on transcendent realities. Taylor believes that Nietzsche is correct with respect to Christian morality: "As Taylor notes, Nietzsche took this thought further to challenge the worth of morality itself. If the pursuit of morality inhibited or compromised authentic self-creation and the intensification of experience through art, so much the worse for it: better to drop the moral (Christian) hypergood altogether. Taylor takes seriously Nietzsche's diagnosis of the impoverishment of modern life due to the slavish and ultimately self-destructive obedience to the moral hypergood."[83] In *A Catholic Modernity?* Taylor describes the situation as a three-cornered battle, where two are always joined in resistance to the third.

How, then, may Taylor's appreciation of the fuller reality of modern culture and its ideals serve Catholic mission in a positive way? One example is the way in which effective witness and evangelizing would be enriched by acknowledging the power of *expressivism* in the moral consciousness of modern persons. Although Taylor himself might hold to a Christian metaphysics, Taylor would claim that any discussion of angels today could not occur on such a plane but would require refiguration so as to resonate with a sense of individual feelings, sentiment, and self-expression.[84]

Taylor also helps show that, in modernity, morality functions as the entry point into discussions of the spiritual. Though only an inference from Taylor's method, it seems that Taylor recognizes that morality may open up into the dimension of ultimate sources through articulating the reality of backgrounds in "universal" modern moral experience, regardless of one's consciously appropriated sources. Taylor's work attends critically to the continuities and transformations between a Christian spirituality and a secular modern humanism. This careful tracking allows for the possible retrieval of those less-favored sources, those related to theism. Taylor even makes an appeal to modernity's high ideals of benevolence

---

82. Redhead, *Charles Taylor: Thinking and Living Deep Diversity*.
83. Smith, *Charles Taylor: Meaning, Morals and Modernity*, 222.
84. *MM*, 86–87.

and justice to suggest that belief in transcendence may be necessary to sustain these goals. Indeed, Taylor seems to find that utilitarian moral theorizing and attunement to the expressive self are, paradoxically, ways to open up receptivity to more traditional spiritual sources.

There is an additional way in which Taylor's complex investigation of the sources of modern selves may be insightful for Christian evangelization. Taylor wants to argue that, in addition to theistic sources spawning or giving rise to other kinds of moral sources, these other sources and variations—Taylor calls them "possible substitutes for grace"—have also cooperated with one another in various combinations to give people the moral energy modernity's ideals call for. This is true both of ideas of the good and moral motivation: the conceptions are mingled in the actual life of the times. And there is another form of causality at play. Taylor observes,

> It is not just that the secular replacements issue historically from the Christian notion of grace; they in turn have influenced it. Modern notions of agape have been affected by the ideal of austere and impartial beneficence, which emerges from disengaged reason. This is already evident in Hutcheson and becomes salient in Christian utilitarianism. But they have also been transformed by Romantic conceptions of spontaneous feeling, of a goodness which flows from inner nature.... The belief in a unilinear process called "secularization" is the belief that the crisis only affects religious beliefs, and the beneficiaries are the secular ones. But this is not an adequate view of our situation.[85]

As early as 1989, Taylor sought to acknowledge the relationship between religious beliefs and the secularizing process of modernity to be mutually implicating and enhancing.

Fundamentally, Taylor shows an appreciation for the evolution of life and identity in contemporary Western societies even as he observes the moral and spiritual challenges that attend modernity. Taylor's method of analyzing contemporary Western culture at a distance[86] involves a tone of nonjudgmental charity that resonates with the ethos of Vatican II toward the modern world as well as the pluralist and humanist temper of our age. His nuanced understanding of modern Western culture through its intellectual and cultural history appeals to both the historicist and rationalist ethos of the contemporary Western consciousness, and Vatican II's affir-

---

85. *SS*, 413.
86. *CM*, 36.

mation of the same. Moreover, Taylor's examination of modern selfhood underscores that both gains and losses, moral and spiritual, are an aspect of the enhanced, "progressive" life of modern Western existence.

Implications of Discernment as a Propaedeutic for Presenting the Gospel Message

We can glean from Taylor's approach to modernity and modern persons some preliminary regulative ideals for an incarnational approach to communication in a secular culture. First, the genesis of the modern self includes many gains such as the aspirations to authenticity, creativity, freedom, responsibility, self-appropriated understanding, empowered participation in institutional decision-making, and benevolence. These must be acknowledged, as well as the fact that some of these ideals depended on a break from Christendom. In addition, a Catholic witness of truthful love must attend to the fact that deep challenges characterize much of the experience of modern selves in the West, such as atomism, instrumental rationality (where a contemplative appreciation is needed), and disinterest and disengagement in political and civic life. Finally, the malaise of modernity, while traceable to spiritual uncertainty and crisis, will not be most effectively addressed by direct theological or metaphysical discourse, as the imagination of modern societies in the West has become distinctly secular and operates out of a shared self-understanding as an economy, public sphere, and self-determining peoples. To each of these three implications for communications from Taylor's general analysis of the modern self and culture we now turn.

From Taylor's account of key aspects that have gone into the making of modern identity, the significance of beauty emerges as a key value for modern subjects. Taylor highlights the transformation in Romantic and modern art that linked experiences of the beauty of nature with transcendence and became a chief way in which modern persons came to experience something like fullness. Moreover, the aspect of beauty in modernity that rendered it meaningful, increasingly, was that it was created, "indexed to a personal vision." Taylor highlights the discovery of the symbol, and what Romantic poets may keep alive through their attention to the thing "beyond."

> Virtually nothing in the domain of mythology, metaphysics, or theology stands in this fashion as publicly available background

today. But that doesn't mean that there is nothing in any of those domains that poets may not want to reach out to in order to say what they want to say, no moral sources they descry there that they want open for us. What it does mean is that their opening these domains, in default of being a move against a firm background, is an articulation of personal vision. It is one that we might come to partake in as well, as a personal vision. . . . We know that the poet, if he is serious, is pointing to something—God, the tradition—which he believes to be there for all of us. But we also know that he can only give it to us refracted through his own sensibility. We cannot just detach the nugget of transcendent truth; it is inseparably imbedded in the work—this is the continuing relevance of the Romantic doctrine of the symbol.[87]

This insight helps the Church in understanding the ideals of modern persons to which she must speak in order to be heard. The truth of Christian existence must involve, I submit, a response to this desire for creative self-expression. Authenticity attends this desire to express oneself as a sign of robust identity, and language, poetic language in particular, is key to such expression. Brian Braman[88] notes Taylor's allusion to the importance of the "epiphanic" as a mode of retrieving a source of meaning and value external to oneself, as an awareness of how the objective must resonate now and must be discovered within. Taylor notes the discovery of nature as a moral source, as well as affirmation of creativity and plurality as ideals for modern persons.

Sources also emphasizes the understanding of the self as residing in one's ability to choose a way of ordering the world rather than accepting one's identity as originating from a predetermined cosmic source or order. Identity involves a way of detaching from one's surroundings to understand situations and oneself in relation to them as a rational agent. One's choices are not predetermined, but prepolitical; that is, one's rights inhere prior to one's belonging to a polity; social existence ratifies rather than confers rights. Taylor traces the genesis of the importance of autonomy in modern selfhood to developments in the Enlightenment such as those of Descartes, Locke, and Grotius. Despite what other changes arose in response to Cartesian rationalism, this ideal of autonomy and a certain disengagement as the proper mode of being a self is rather firmly

---

87. SS, 491–92.
88. Braman, *Meaning and Authenticity*.

entrenched in the modern subject. We all, to some degree, understand much of who we are in terms of what kinds of realities we can control through our rational capacities to understand and to know. The Church must also speak to the sense of self as critically aware and rational.

Finally, in addition to autonomous rationality and authenticity through creative and original self-expression, there is also the search for wholeness that marks modern persons, and the location of this in ordinary life—and particularly in the relationships of ordinary life, those pertaining to reproduction and work. That goodness is to be found in the immanence of ordinary life is a key aspect of a modern self's creed and expectation. This ideal entails affirmation of the flattening of hierarchies, understanding rights as universal, accepting the moral duty to universal benevolence (though since certain versions of utilitarianism have come to be dominant, this duty could be said to be reduced to a "no harm" principle),[89] and a positive valuation of a plurality of goods and the natural diversity of life. Resistance to code is also central, a culmination of the Romantic resistance to the Enlightenment and the drive to reform that raised up the goods of ordinary life as opposed to norms propounded in a top-down manner by religious authority.

Taylor's project will thus have strong resonance with those who reject codified ethics—Christian or otherwise. A fundamental goal of *Sources* was to broaden the moral space of modernity beyond the pervasive schemas of naturalism and proceduralism. Taylor's insight into the modern moral predicament—of which, one may say, naturalism and proceduralism are manifestations or symptoms—is that there are *four* related terms that circumscribe moral space, namely, "our notions of the good," "our understandings of self," "the kinds of narrative in which we make sense of our lives," and "conceptions of society."[90] Taylor's attentiveness to the quality or the predominant shape of the modern narrative (namely, flattened and decidedly secular) and the economic, instrumental conceptions and experience of human social relationship receive more developed treatment and focus in Taylor's *Modern Social Imaginaries*.

---

89. Cf. *A Secular Age* on authenticity and how the meaning of "harm principle" has changed since Mill's articulation.

90. SS, 105.

The Ethic of Authenticity—a Potential Site of Conversion?

Is it possible for the ethic of authenticity to be transformed from within? I propose that the ideal of authenticity in contemporary culture may be one of the key resources for mission in a secular age. Part of the problem of inauthenticity is the lack of shared horizons of significance. For Taylor, it can seem that the presence of shared horizons is sufficient for the possibility of significance and the project of being authentic.[91] If, however, we follow Taylor's original desire in 1989 to retrieve theistic sources for the sustenance of modernity's greatest ideals, and we understand Taylor's presentation of the possibility of religious faith in a secular age as another proposal of hope in what faith offers, then we can infer that Catholic mission in a secular age will involve opening persons up to the transcendent horizon of identity. Christians, that is, the Church, can thereby make it their aim to accompany persons on their spiritual search, revealing to the latter the possibility of authenticity through the unity, fullness, joy, and purpose of their lives. To understand how that may be the case, however, we first require a consideration of the challenge that secularity poses to such an endeavor, what Balthasar's theological anthropology will reveal about the nature of personhood and mission, and what becoming a person in Christ, through the Church, allows.

---

91. Cf. Laitinen, *Strong Evaluation without Moral Sources: On Charles Taylor's Philosophical Anthropology and Ethics*. Also insightful on this point is Cécile Laborde's "Protecting Freedom of Religion in the Secular Age".

CHAPTER 2

The Challenge of Secularism for the Church

NOW THAT TAYLOR'S APPROACH might be understood as making a charitable discernment of the presence of the gospel in the culture of modernity, and an interpretation proffered of how his corpus instantiates stages of such discernment, we turn to *A Secular Age*, which we read as Taylor's consummate response to his own question of how "to find our authentic voice in the eventual Catholic chorus, to try to do for our time and place what Matteo Ricci was striving to do four centuries ago in China."[1]

This chapter considers Taylor's narrative of the development of secularization in the West and the possibility he proposes for faith in an age with a penchant for nonreligious ways of framing the world. Taylor's account of five hundred years of development of the contemporary context for religious belief and unbelief indicates the significant challenge of contemporary evangelization of Western cultures. Taylor's story of how the secular age came to be signals some important conceptual shifts from a Vatican II context for how to configure the Church in relation to the world. *A Secular Age* highlights that the developments of theism and atheism share a history of events and ideas; it leads one to consider more concretely the complexity of history in the life of the Church, which is, also, the complex history that shapes the life of modern persons. Together with Taylor's work on modern identity, Taylor's work on the pervasive secularity of social and cultural existence in the contemporary West

1. *CM*, 15.

comprises Taylor's contribution to developing a contemporary Catholic understanding of witness and mission, or, as Taylor would say, *a catholic modernity*.

Recap

In the previous chapter we noted that Taylor's approach toward mission may be understood as that of making a charitable discernment of the presence of the gospel in the culture of modernity. Taking *A Catholic Modernity?* as a hinge work, we looked "back" in Taylor's corpus to see how *Sources of the Self* and *Malaises of Modernity* constitute an initial stage in such discernment, sifting out the ideals and struggles of modern selves in the West. We then considered *A Catholic Modernity?* and *Modern Social Imaginaries* as a continuation of Taylor's early work on horizons and identity, and read them as exemplifying a further stage in Taylor's discernment of modern social existence and the real challenge of self-transcendence within it.

The present chapter considers Taylor's account of secularity. Grounded in the theoretical work of his previous text, *Modern Social Imaginaries*, Taylor presents in *A Secular Age* a story of the development of the secular social imaginary of modern culture and its implications for faith today. Taylor asserts in this work that secularity is a feature of modern societies; however, rather than describe secularity in normative terms, and merely critically, Taylor shows by way of a complicated historical narrative that secularity is better understood as the condition of belief in our age and one that Christianity had no small part in producing.

In the present chapter, I consider five key points from Taylor's narrative of secularity and their implications for discerning the shape or path of contemporary Catholic mission. Taylor's analysis of secularity in Western cultures (his study is limited to the North Atlantic West) yields the following insights: (1) secularity concerns not only a decrease in religious practices or the diminished involvement of religion in public life and public institutions, but also a profound transformation in the social imaginary which, at the beginning of the twenty-first century, is more defined by secular humanism than theistic faith; (2) we cannot "go back" from this point of development, which is the result of five hundred years of historical shifts and morally motivated transitions; (3) Latin Christendom and the failures of various institutional and cultural expressions of

Christianity have contributed to the development of Western secularity; (4) faith will be "fragilized" in a secular age, as it is a choice made in the face of cross-pressures from Nietzschean and immanent humanist critiques; and (5) religious faith remains a live option and a good option in a secular age, as there are important losses associated with living closed to transcendence within the "immanent frame" (that is, faith offers a kind of fullness that cannot be found without belief in transcendence). Taylor ends with a note of warning that there is also need for much more critical self-reflection among all Christians, and especially the Church. A key implication of these observations about Western secularity and faith, I wish to argue, is that secular humanism with its horizon of immanence so greatly frames the option for religious faith that apologetics is rendered nearly impossible today. By this I mean that the condition of a common understanding of what we mean when we say "God," "life," and "eternal life" is so fractured that a different mode of witnessing is required.[2]

SECULARITY AS A SHIFT IN THE CONDITIONS OF BELIEF

In *A Secular Age*, Taylor considers the various movements—social, intellectual, and political—that led to belief in God being only one option among many, and "frequently not the easiest to embrace."[3] While there exist a number of ways to understand the term "secularity," Taylor chooses to explore secularity taken as "the whole context of understanding in which our moral, spiritual, or religious experience and search takes place." By "context of understanding," Taylor means "matters that will probably have been explicitly formulated by almost everyone, such as the plurality of options, and some of which form the implicit largely unfocussed background of this experience and search, its 'pre-ontology,' to use a Heideggerian term."[4] Taylor makes it clear, from the outset, that his interest in probing the condition of secularity is one with his interest in probing the implicit and explicit limits and possibilities of spiritual quest in the present age.[5]

  2. Let me qualify this claim with a caveat that insofar as the example of human holiness may be considered "apologetic" in character and in effect, as philosopher of religion Victoria Harrison has suggested, apologetics is still possible today.
  3. SA, 3.
  4. Ibid.
  5. Ibid. "So what I want to do is examine our society as secular in this third sense, which I could perhaps encapsulate in this way: the change I want to define and trace is

Taylor identifies more conventional understandings of secularity as other possibilities for what he means to describe with the term "secularity," namely, as (1) a decline in religious practice or (2) the diminished presence of religion in public institutions and public life. However, he pursues the meaning of the term that signifies *conditions of belief* to indicate, in part,[6] his conviction regarding the depth and comprehensiveness with which secularity is entrenched in our age. Throughout the text, Taylor alludes to the metaphor of a three-storey house to explain the various levels at which the phenomenon of modern secularity may be discussed, and that the level that his historical narrative aims to "excavate" is the "basement," which gives an explanatory account of how the current situation of decline in religious practices and a diminishment of religion in the public sphere came to be.[7] According to Taylor, secularity, or thinking immanently, has become a habit of being for many modern persons liv-

---

one which takes us from a society in which it was virtually impossible not to believe in God, to one in which faith, even for the staunchest believer, is one human possibility among others. I may find it inconceivable that I would abandon my faith, but there are others, including possibly some very close to me, whose way of living I cannot in all honesty just dismiss as depraved, or blind, or unworthy, who have no faith (at least not in God, or the transcendent). Belief in God is no longer axiomatic. There are alternatives. And this will also likely mean that at least in certain milieux, it may be hard to sustain one's faith. There will be people who feel bound to give it up, even though they mourn its loss. This has been a recognizable experience in our societies, at least since the mid-nineteenth century. There will be many others to whom faith never even seems an eligible possibility. There are certainly millions today of whom this is true. . . . An age or society would then be secular or not, in virtue of the conditions of experience of and search for the spiritual."

6. This is one possible interpretation of why Taylor chooses this definition of secularity.

7. That is, one of Taylor's primary aims in *A Secular Age* is to challenge the theory of secularization prominent among some sociologists of religion that modernity and secularization necessarily go in hand; that, as civilizations mature in reason and capability, they will gradually slough off the "irrational" elements of human experience such as are exemplified in religious modes of being. Taylor seeks to argue against the dominant "subtraction theory" in sociology of religion and to show that while "the scope and influence of religious institutions is less than before" (sociologist Steve Bruce's claim), the story about religion in modernity is not simply one of decline (ground level claim) "but also of a new placement of the sacred or spiritual in relation to individual and social life. This new placement is now the occasion of recompositions of spiritual life in new forms, and for new ways of existing both in and out of relation to God" (SA, 437). Taylor contends that his claim about the possibilities of religious existence in a secular age is substantiated through his historical account of how the situation of contemporary secularity came to be (basement level of discourse) (ibid., 427–37).

ing in the West; it forms a background understanding, which means that it is a root picture of the world, often unconscious or "unthought," that circumscribes most other thinking in people's lives.

No Single Factor behind the Development of Secularism

Having established secularity as a horizon of understanding, Taylor gives an immensely detailed and wide-ranging historical account of the genesis of the secular imaginary of our time, which Taylor designates "the immanent frame." The immanent frame is the culmination of five hundred years of the past's sedimentation in the present. With patience and at length, Taylor portrays the process of the disenchantment of the cosmos for humans; the development of a sense of identity as buffered from the world rather than porous; and the shift in understanding of the ends of society in terms of Lockean contract and security. He elaborates the transition from "cosmos" to "impersonal universe," with providential deism as a step along the way, and the turn to nature as a source of meaning. The latter, Taylor shows, concurred with an ever dimming sense of a Christian God through a new understanding of the beginning of things in terms of materialism; also through time understood as apart from eternity and as, rather, a dark abyss, through the aesthetics of the sublime or the American valorization of the wilderness through poetry and literature. The drive to reform, Taylor argues, led to the rise of civility as a key feature of social order—the same drive that led to rapid and revolutionary transfer of faith to science and, subsequently, various Nietzsche-inspired developments as a reaction against "code morality." Expressivism, the age of authenticity, further mobilizations by the religiously resolute in the United States, and many more subsidiary moral motivations and configurations of fullness and meaning combined and recombined in different and unexpected ways to lead to the situation of the present.

Taylor's narrative reveals that secularity is not merely an ideological, structural, personal, or idiosyncratic matter but is, to some extent, utterly historical. *SA*, like its predecessor, *SS*, is a narrative that encompasses the history of ideas. In a more conscious way than *SS*, however, *SA* also includes accounts of life "on the ground" to show that historical effects are not merely generated "from above," in the realm of ideas, but also from the "bottom up." The vast, panoramic, yet detailed account of secularity yields the deduction, at the very least, that there is no simple, causal, linear relationship between a single facet of modernity and the rise of secularism. Indeed, perhaps one of Taylor's most emphatic though tacit points is that *one cannot be reductive in one's approach to secularity.*

Secularity Is the "New Normal"

"What happened five hundred years ago such that where it was once normal to throw a stone in the street and in every case hit a believer, faith is only one option today and not the most often taken?" Taylor's genealogy of secularity proposes that it is the gradual development of "the immanent frame," a worldview informed by myriad historical developments and vectors, which implicitly understands God as inert after the generation of the universe, or utterly irrelevant to the same, denies transcendence, and arguably qualifies our freedom to be religious in the twenty-first century rather significantly. The immanent frame that we collectively inhabit is, in some manner of speaking, a non-neutral matrix with regard to religious identity, a conceptual filter through which some constitutive elements of a religious imaginary are strained off and we are left with:

- buffered identities rather than porous selves;
- living in a disenchanted cosmos;
- disciplined individuals whose ends society serves;
- the realm of the social as ordered toward mutual benefit;
- God as an irrelevant concept for both social and cosmic order; and
- the end of life together as the promotion of human flourishing.

Taylor sees the immanent frame as the functional context for our beliefs: the frame usually goes unquestioned; we seldom stray beyond the borders of our "picture."[8] The emphatic degree to which the frame is a "moral order" is clear from Taylor's description of life within it:

> Four strong benchmarks of the new order are: liberty: the move is meant to liberate; power: it is meant to empower; mutual benefit: this is the basic point of the society; and reason: whether freedom, power, mutual benefit has been achieved, or how to achieve them, is meant to be arbitrable by rational discussion.

---

8. Ibid., 549.

Their achievement is meant to be something demonstrable. These, as well as the basic premises of equality, and the foregrounding of rights, are the crucial constitutive concepts of the new understanding.[9]

According to Taylor, the immanent frame of modernity can seem to those who live in it to incline one to a sense of closure to transcendence:[10] it is a frame in which the human good, scientific reason,[11] and the greatest possible flourishing of human beings dominate the discursive space, and within which a religious sense of "fullness" has little place.[12]

A Secular Age thus shows that although the waters of belief are historically muddy, the resulting secular social imaginary has some very well-defined features. Awareness of pre-existing transformations in which secularity, and not the horizon of a simple faith, is the "new normal" must now foreground the conversation of what religion is and how we are to engage one another where belief or unbelief is concerned. As mentioned earlier, an important corollary of Taylor's insight into the immanent frame as the default baseline for discussions about belief in our current culture is that mission cannot take place at the level of reasoned apologetics in the traditional manner because that shared context of understanding between believers and unbelievers no longer exists. The "shared" context is in fact decidedly secular, non-metaphysical, and frequently subjectivistic.

WE CANNOT "GO BACK"

The understanding of secularity as a background understanding that emerges from centuries of social and cultural negotiation underscores the challenge of contemporary witness: a new horizon of understanding

9. Ibid., 578–79.

10. Taylor is actually somewhat ambivalent on this point. At some points in *SA*, Taylor states that the immanent frame allows for both readings—openness to transcendence and closure to transcendence—"without compelling us to either" (544, 550). At other points Taylor notes that "the immanent frame may incline toward closure" (556). But in interviews subsequent to the publication of *SA*, Taylor tends to maintain that life in the immanent frame allows for both possibilities.

11. Ibid., 566: "The buffered identity, with its disciplines, modern individualism, with its reliance on instrumental reason and action in secular time—make up the immanent frame. Science, modern individualism, instrumental reason, secular time, all seem further proofs of the truth of immanence."

12. Ibid., 548.

exists as a backdrop to our culture and we cannot go back. There has been a loss of a certain ontic horizon. The horizon of metaphysical realism, of either Platonic or theistic varieties, wherein order is objective and external, is no longer believable for many in modern culture. The modality of metaphysics is not even comprehensible for most modern persons living in the West today—or, if comprehensible, is not considered to be a viable "background story" for their lives. Taylor claims that a turn inward for moral sources came with the thought of Augustine,[13] since which point the notion of order came increasingly to be constituted by the subject. Subjectivism hardened over time and became a prevalent form of naturalism, which denies the existence of metaphysical horizons of meaning that contextualize all understandings of moral action. The relativism of today has its roots in the unique, historical amalgamation that saw the turn to subjectivity overlaid and mixed with the scientistic turn of the Enlightenment, Romantic Expressivism, the rediscovery of nature as a moral source, and modernism. Myriad and varied layers of shift have, according to Taylor, contributed to the development of the secular social imaginary. Thus, these horizons are to some extent irreversible.

Seeing the "goods" of modernity as hard-fought and painfully won achievements, Taylor is not interested in "undoing history" either.[14] In-

13. It should be noted that Hauerwas (Hauerwas and Matzko, "The Sources of Charles Taylor") and, more recently, Thomas Harmon ("Reconsidering Charles Taylor's Augustine") have written critically of Taylor's ascription of the beginning of the turn to subjectivism to Augustine.

14. Traditionalists in the Church, for example, are sometimes charged with trying to "undo history" with their resistance to the liturgical reforms of Vatican II. Taylor makes it quite clear that he is opposed to those who think that we need to be anti-modern to be truly Catholic today. In the second segment of a three-part interview with philosopher Ron Kuipers, Taylor elaborates his position on the needful orientation of Catholic Christianity at this time:

TAYLOR: The place where many people make a mistake, or I should say, where they have a totally different framework in which to see this than I am proposing, is that they see it (the culture of authenticity) as just a kind of contemporary fad, a fad about fads, which we could call people back from and get back into the old days when people were recruited into massive battalions, either Marxist revolutionary in Adorno's case, or orthodox Protestant or Catholic in other cases. I think this is really a massive mistake. It's analogous to the Catholic Church prior to Vatican II, which failed to see that something happened in the French Revolution that made it impossible to go back to tightly knit Catholic societies ruled from on top, yet they were always trying to reestablish these kinds of societies. . . .

KUIPERS: So what I hear you saying is that, first, we should accept the fact that this is simply the way the world is, and second, that there really have been gains.

TAYLOR: Yes, and further, that the proper stance toward it is not saying something

deed, he believes, perhaps following Hegel, that such undoing is actually impossible. There is not only an immense sedimentation of historical development that burdens our moral imagination, but also it has become our imaginary; it is embedded in our practices and outlooks. Taylor is, in this regard, quite unapologetically modern (and realistic, one might say) in his assessment of the death of certain horizons:[15]

> The [qualitative] change [in artistic languages] is more far-reaching than that. What could never be recovered is the public understanding that angels are part of a human-independent ontic order, having their angelic natures quite independently of human articulation, and hence accessible through languages of description (theology, philosophy) that are not at all those of articulated sensibility. . . . In these circumstances, the very idea that one such order should be embraced to the exclusion of all

---

like, "let's roll it back." See Kuipers, "Religious Belonging in an 'Age of Authenticity.'"

It is also noteworthy, however, that Taylor would not identify wholly with the "progressives" in the debate about "getting Christianity right." Rather, as we will see later, Taylor is critical of any approach that discerns the Christian faith to be epitomized by one historical instantiation or cultural expression over another. For Taylor, there is no "golden age" of Christianity—not five hundred years ago, not through Trent, and not through Vatican II. Taylor explicitly states that to think the debate is between Trent and Vatican II is misguided (SA, 753). He recommends, instead, that in the ages or societies in which Christian faith has existed, "They differ because each mode of Christian life has to climb out of, achieve a certain distance from its own embedding in its time (in the 'saeculum'), one might say. But far from allowing these modes to be neatly ranked, this is the difference which enables them to give something to each other" (ibid., 745).

15. One ongoing point of contention among commentators is whether Taylor is committed to metaphysics or not. On the one hand, Taylor seems to go quite far in the direction of certain commitments typical of twentieth-century phenomenology that to some extent bracket the question of the reality of "things in themselves." On the other hand, Taylor asserts that he is mapping a moral ontology and confesses adherence to traditions that are clearly metaphysical in their presuppositions. Taylor's appreciation of Nietzsche is interesting as a case in point. Alexandra Klaushofer astutely notes the manner in which Taylor's approach to religion follows from an acknowledgment that "Nietzsche's legacy presents a legitimate challenge that must be answered [and so] is marked by a turn away from metaphysical foundationalism and absolutism, issuing in a creative search for other forms of grounding and authority." Klaushofer, "Faith Beyond Nihilism," 135-49. Taylor's phenomenological approach falls within such a category following, according to Klaushofer, the Ricouerian ideal of rescuing the significance of religion from the fall of ontotheology. Taylor's affirmation of the value of theistic sources for the modern moral self can be seen as a cultural argument for religion that affirms pluralism at its core and thus affirms theistic sources as one important source of value for modernity but not the only one.

the others—a demand that is virtually inescapable in the traditional context—ceases to have any force. It is only too clear how another sensibility, another context of images, might give us a quite different take, even on what we might nevertheless see as a similar vision of reality. So contemporary "angels" have to be human-related, one might say language-related, in a way their forebears were not. They cannot be separated from a certain language of articulation, which is, as it were, their home element. And this language in turn is rooted in the personal sensibility of the poet, and understood only by those whose sensibility resonates like the poet's.[16]

However, currently we also live within certain moral horizons, namely, those of an individualist, subjectivist nature. Taylor's sense of the inauthenticity at the root of such orientations leads him to seek those theistic sources and religious ways of being that may be expressed in a new way for this age, a way that has "resonance."

A Transformation of "Time"

The challenge of unearthing these sources is great, as the subjectivism of the disengaged, buffered self, has a wide reach. Change in time consciousness was key to the shift into secularity as the condition for belief in the West. In parallel with the shift from a sense of the world as cosmos to world as universe, the basic shift from the medieval understanding of time was the move from understanding and experiencing life in two kinds of times, secular ordinary time and higher times or times of "*kairos*"—eternity breaking in—to time as basically homogeneous and "empty."[17] Time in the Middle Ages was understood to be fundamentally kairotic, meaning that even ordinary time involved participation in what Taylor terms "higher times," which, in the Christian conception of eternity, is participation in God's time. "Rising to eternity is rising to participate in God's instant."[18] Other notions of higher time include eternity as eternal regress or "time out of mind"[19] and the time of origins spoken of by Mircea Eliade.[20] While Taylor notes that there are still "kairotic knots" in "the

16. *MM*, 86–87.
17. *SA*, 58, 209.
18. Ibid., 57.
19. Ibid., 208.
20. Ibid., 57.

stories we tell ourselves in our time, related to revolutions and founding histories of nation-building, for example, our outlook "enshrines homogeneity and indifference to content." Our contemporary sense and experience of time is not ordered by or organized by higher times; our experience of time is pervasively linear or horizontal.

In the Middle Ages, participation in higher time, which lent a kind of texture to time, involved a dialectic between order and disorder, through oscillation between ordinary time and carnivals and "feasts of misrule." Societies were ordered to and reflected an eternal order; with the move to providential deism, such feasts diminished in prominence. The development of the impersonal order of deism also saw a rise in a sense of the world as standing reserve to be ordered by humans rather than exhibiting an order to be discovered and observed. The horizon of society became flattened, God was not seen as the originator and sustainer of social order (for example, in the doctrine of the divine rights of kings), and the horizontality of social order was also reflected in a flattened sense of time.

The "direct-access society," as Taylor terms it, does not take order to be mediated in any way; all individuals have access to time in the same way, as such, time becomes something of an empty "container" for events happening everywhere in simultaneity.[21] Simply put, "The imbrication of secular time in higher times is no longer for many today a matter of common naïve experience."[22] A sense of being at home in the world in light of an experience of it as God's creation involved a sense of time as "depths of the past already given shape by the divine-human drama played out in it."[23] On the way to our experience of time as horizontal and linear, a space for simultaneity, Taylor notes the growing sense of time as unfathomable, and later, in the nineteenth century, discovery of the sublime and the wilderness leads to entrenchment of the concept of time as opaque to us.[24] We find ourselves in "immeasurable time." The narrative of greater control over our environment, however, has also come with a development of the need "to measure and organize time as never before."[25]

---

21. Taylor draws on Benedict Anderson for part of his account of simultaneity in modern nations.
22. *SA*, 59.
23. Ibid., 324.
24. Ibid., 326–27, 336–43.
25. Ibid., 59.

CHRISTIANITY'S CONTRIBUTION TO WESTERN SECULARIZATION

In narrating the development of secularity in the West, Taylor prescinds from distinguishing sacred history from secular history, or from taking the side of religion, simplistically, against the secularists or the converse. Taylor claims that secularity is a process in which Western cultures affirmed ideals over five hundred years that in some instances were in tension with and replaced ideals grounded in a theistic picture of the world. In other words, ironically, some of the ideals associated with the secular social imaginary arose from theistic ideals and trumped them, often in an unintended manner. He shows, for example, that Christianity's historical expression as Latin Christendom and its reactionary development, the drive to reform, epitomized by Calvin's Geneva and the Puritan movement, were key steps that led to the establishment of the new, secular, moral order. The religious context of axial religions such as Confucianism and the Reformation, with their accent on and valorization of the disembedded individual and entrenchment of a codified Christianity, respectively (though the latter was potentially a corruption of Christianity), also contributed, perhaps inadvertently, to the modern social imaginary that currently exists in the West.[26] God was in the picture with Calvinism and Lockean deism, so there was at some point a God-justification attending these modifications in the idea of moral order. Nonetheless, they were also drivers of the modern moral order's basic goals: peaceable existence among individuals who lived together for mutual benefit, particularly the ends of security and prosperity, the individual rather than hierarchy and the rights of the individual, strengthened by the emphasis on consent.

Taylor minces no words in claiming that Christendom contributed to secularity. For example,

> One can even imagine another chain of events, in which at least some important elements of the Reformation didn't have to be driven out of the Catholic Church, and to a denial of the sacraments (which Luther for his part never agreed to) and of the value of tradition (which Luther was not as such against). But it would have required a rather different Rome, less absorbed with its power trip than it has tended to be these last centuries.[27]

---

26. Ibid., 141.
27. Ibid., 75.

A Secular Age shows, in large part neutrally, the great range of positions with regard to faith and unbelief one may take up today. Yet it also reveals the myriad ways in which present-day misconceptions of Christianity, though wrong, are based, in part, on corruption and errors in history—of power, magic, moralism, and excarnation—by the religious establishment through the Middle Ages and the Reformation. As adamantly as Taylor maintains that great development of Christian life came through the passage to modernity, Taylor also tries to show that Christianity played a large role in the emergence of contemporary secularity. As we have already seen from Taylor's account of the making of modern identity, modernity's gains and losses come through intricate weavings and cross-pollinations of moral sources, theistic and nontheistic. To take the example of the challenge of undoing instrumentalism: "The tremendous importance of the instrumental stance is overdetermined. It represents the convergence of more than one stream. It is supported not just by the dignity attaching to disengaged rational control; it has also been central to the ethic of ordinary life."[28] In *SA*, Taylor says something similar about secularity: it is a story of the weavings and cross-pollinations of "sacred" and "secular" history.

Taylor's account of secularity underscores, then, with new intensity the degree to which Church and world are enmeshed; secular culture is the result of choices made by multiple and various Western cultures, which together have ensconced naturalism and exclusive humanism as the unthought thought that forms the background understanding of our sense of what is true and worthy of human pursuit. The upshot of this for the question of Catholic mission seems to be, on the one hand, that there is no space apart from that of the secular social imaginary from which many can claim to stand, and that includes those living in the earthly Church at this time in history.

The recognition of the minglings between Church and modern culture means also that to some degree, the mere idea of evangelization will be challenging and unattractive to many Catholics—the degree of repulsiveness corresponding to the degree to which the modern social imaginary that affirms that selves live and ought to live in a buffered state among other buffered selves has been received and appropriated as the "unthought." We experience the power of this unthought social imaginary, for example, when we encounter resistance to moral difference in

---

28. *SS*, 232.

70 Solidarity With the World

the form of the attitude, "who are you to tell me anything about me?" In this context, friendship, too, has certain valences, valences of solidarity and identification. Whether transformation is part of modern friendship is a question, and this then also has implications for the degree to which Taylor's understanding of how best to engage one another in the modern world, Christian and secular humanist alike, will be instructive.[29]

The Problem of Excarnation

A key theme that pervades the latter part of SA is the shift from an incarnate background picture of personhood and deity to an excarnate vision of self and God. Taylor shows how the development of deism was an important step in this process of excarnation which continues to bear significantly on the modern sense of personal identity and contemporary understandings of religion. It is interesting to consider the way in which Taylor's narrative of excarnation in fact challenges us to reflect on whether our sense of alienation from our bodies and a healthy sensuality lies in the ethos of a puritanistic culture or whether it is the secularizing materialism and despiritualization of the cosmos, en route to modernity, that is responsible. In either case, Taylor is explicit about seeing excarnation as a *devolution*.

If we consider that Taylor is interested in what forms of spirituality Catholicism may take in the twenty-first century, we should note that for Taylor there is a common and indispensable feature they must share: they must recognize and embrace embodiment once again. Indeed, Taylor's apt phrase in SS "the punctual self" is deepened here by an historical analysis of how culture from the ground up has led to the increasingly

---

29. As MacIntyre notes in *After Virtue*, the pursuit of certain goods consists in participation in some shared understandings, which are lacking in modernity. MacIntyre's retrieval of the virtue tradition poses the strongest challenge, in my opinion, to what seems to be a lacuna in Taylor's account of conversions, namely, the role of tradition in facilitating transformation. This is not to reduce the experience of conversion to social conditions of change, nor is this the understanding of tradition with which I am working. My understanding of tradition involves crucially the sense that tradition is a condition for the possibility of means of grace, such as the sacraments, such as the Church, to be a part of one's life. MacIntyre's persistent question about Taylor's moral realism can also be seen in his review of *Philosophy in an Age of Pluralism: The Philosophy of Charles Taylor in Question*, edited by James Tully, wherein he praises the questions that Rorty poses for Taylor's realism as "just the ones to which an answer is most needed" (MacIntyre, review of *Philosophy in an Age of Pluralism*, 523). We will return to these issues in the critical section of this chapter.

common necessity of experiencing personhood as "buffered." Perhaps this also informs Taylor's affirmation of Jean Vanier, who through his work with persons with profound physical and developmental disabilities creates a new itinerary of faith that retrieves from within a Christian view of the world a profound affirmation of the body.

The Fragilization of Faith

Taylor argues that although we live in a society with an imaginary that inclines toward a closed perspective to transcendence, both a posture of closedness and one of openness to transcendence remain options for us in our age. Taylor inquires extensively into the possibility of the open "option" on the ground even as the closed option enjoys a certain naturalization and hegemony in our current cultural discourse.[30] According to Taylor, considering either the closed or the open option to transcendence obvious and certain is to fall prey to "spin,"[31] for neither option can be clear and obvious in light of the history of choices that have been made for and against religion in its many forms in the Latin West. Fragility is the condition of faith today and, if anything, living networks of love are needed to sustain belief in a largely secularized social context. Even then, Taylor thinks that belief will never be as robust and free from doubt as it was previously, nor skepticism or atheism as resolved and closed as it might have been in another age. Both belief and unbelief are now "fragilized." Notably, Taylor follows the question of secularity beyond the story of the conditions for the growth of "unbelief" alone in modern Western cultures. By casting light on the immanent frame, one could say that Taylor holds open the conditions for *belief*.

The Possibility of Faith and Lives of Conversion

Taylor does show that openness to transcendence remains a viable possibility in a secular age. While there is no simple, causal, linear relationship between a single facet of modernity and the rise of secularism, and although certain values of modernity are prominently involved in the secularization of the lives of all who live in the modern West, there is still

---

30. *SA*, 550–51.
31. Ibid., 551.

the possibility of belief and openness to transcendence in a secular age.[32] Belief, Taylor asserts, is always surfacing in new and unintended forms.

The possibility of religious faith in a secular age is most evident in the lives of those who reveal genuine conversion or re-conversion. These lives show that being alive to transcendence, and to the infinite, is possible even through all the transmutations of understanding that have unfolded in the passage to modernity. Taylor believes that living networks of *agape* are what will testify most profoundly to the possibility and desirability of faith in our time, and open up life in the immanent frame. Taylor alludes to various figures, from Bede Griffiths and Ivan Illich to Mother Teresa and Jean Vanier to Gerard Manley Hopkins and Charles Peguy, to illustrate what he means by lives that reveal a true "conversion."

Interestingly, Taylor's narrative introduces the believing path, and in fact a Catholic path, as an *option* in this secular age. If we take this to be intentional on Taylor's part, then with *A Secular Age* Taylor has crafted a narrative that embraces the common modality of radical choice and presents a subtle argument, within a story, of why that choice is a desirable option. On this reading, Taylor has upended the logic of modernity quite brilliantly and, more importantly, offers a clue to mission in a secular age: the Church must speak in the idiom of *choice*; she must respect that most beloved concept of modernity, "freedom." Taylor's work on secularity importantly takes Western culture's own ideals, namely, the ideal of choice, at face value. It speaks from within the "immanent frame" of the modern social imaginary in the West and to modern persons' own self-understanding as rational, economic agents to open up the possibility of belief in God again.

Taylor states, "The scope and influence of religious institutions is now less than in the past."[33] This is part of what it means to live in a secular age. Taylor believes nonetheless that despite the absence of a social and cultural context that alludes to the sacred, individual lives can "break out" of the immanent frame, and "conversion" is possible.[34] "This sense that others have been closer is an essential part of the ordinary person's confidence in a shared religious language, or a way of articulating fullness."[35] For Taylor, it is the lives of Francis of Assisi, St. Thérèse

32. Ibid., 432.
33. Ibid., 431.
34. Ibid., 28.
35. Ibid., 729.

of Lisieux, Bede Griffiths, Vaclav Havel, Charles Peguy, Gerard Manley Hopkins, Mother Teresa, and Jean Vanier that lead one to make a confession of faith. This is, Taylor says, "part of what it means to belong to a church."[36] These people embody "new itineraries of faith," new ways of living out a response to the transcendent that can touch even those who do not believe. They are "perhaps the only irrefutable witness."[37]

Part of the authenticity of these lives can be discerned in their resistance to living their faith according to a code, but rather, according to a spirituality of *agape* that in turn spawns living networks of *agape*. A greater part of their truth, however, is that they are living according to something that is greater than themselves, and their lives refract some of the beauty and truth of that reality. They live beyond the borders of the immanent frame, choosing to see the world as more than the closed system that can be generated by a thoroughgoing naturalistic scientific picture, or one of human flourishing on human, temporal terms alone (exclusive humanism).

Taylor notes the power that a social imaginary exerts, and therefore the genuine challenge involved in stepping beyond the boundaries of the "immanent frame." Therein lies the admiration for such lives of self-transcendence and authenticity. Moreover, Taylor's foundational philosophical works emphasize the profoundly social, embodied, dialogical character of our existence, and the need of selves to experience recognition in order to become integrated, authentic persons. Indeed, it is important to recall some of Taylor's basic fundamental presuppositions about identity, authenticity, and the politics of recognition for we begin to see that Taylor may need to say more about both the challenge and the possibility of these lives of exemplary holiness in a secular age.

Interpreting Taylor—Synthesis and Critical Appropriation

Having outlined some of the ways in which Taylor has refigured the discourse about secularity and its implications for how to approach contemporary Catholic mission, the second half of the chapter will provide an interpretation of how Taylor's use of imaginaries, narrative, and overall attention to the languages of modernity comprise a significant

---

36. Ibid.
37. Kerr, "How Much Can a Philosopher Do?"

methodological proposal of how to raise the question of Catholic faith in the contemporary cultural context. I will then consider the merits of the content of Taylor's account of secularity, focusing on Taylor's final claim that faith remains possible in a secular age to see what it lends to my constructivist quest for clarity on the shape of Catholic mission today in the West. I will show that Taylor's proposal is finally limited in its value for Catholic mission because of its truncated notion of the Church and the way in which this latter poses a problem internally generated by Taylor's project. That is, Taylor would require a more affirming or affectionate account of the Church and its relationship to individual lives that show true conversion, given Taylor's earlier work on the relationship between horizons and identity. Finally, I will consider how several eminent arguments regarding Taylor's project are further reasons to understand Taylor's project as a contribution to Catholic mission but one, finally, whose proposal necessarily leads one to consider Balthasar's accounts of personhood and Church.

Interpretation

In chapter 1, we considered Taylor's critique of modernity, which he carries out through an experiential account of the gains and losses incurred through the development of modern selfhood. Two aspects of modern malaise that are particularly noteworthy for the purpose of this work are (1) the loss of ends and (2) the search for meaning and authenticity. In the first part of this second chapter, we considered Taylor's exploration of secularity as the sedimentation of five hundred years of developing and renegotiating the moral sources that shape us and that we ourselves fashion. A secular social imaginary that understands persons fundamentally as economic agents, members of the public sphere, and self-determining peoples is the result of historical developments spanning the Enlightenment and beyond.

If one takes a broad view of Taylor's project over the past forty years, a possible hermeneutic for it is a project of intellectual mission that undertakes, not unlike the tradition of critical realism, a retrieval of the reality of the transcendent in light of the modern "discovery" of the subject. Taylor's approach is phenomenological, however, and begins with the experience of the human person. Acknowledging the mutual implication of individual and culture, Taylor then moves to the level of moral ontology of the self through cultural analysis in *Sources of the Self* and *Modern Social Imaginaries*. By the end of *Sources*, Taylor arrives at the conclusion that theistic sources may contain the best hope for modernity's realization of its ideals and that its malaises are traceable to the loss of transcendence in our lives. Western modernity is rooted in Christianity, and *Sources* suggests mildly the value of retrieving its Christian memory. By the end of *Modern Social Imaginaries* and *A Catholic Modernity?* Taylor has shown with greater force the challenge of realizing what Taylor proposes as a solution at the end of *Sources*, namely, retrieval of some of the deeper moral sources in the history of modern identity, particularly theistic sources.

The secular social imaginary has its replacements for theistic sources. The shift to the cultural and how it shapes the experience of persons living in the modern West is further developed in *A Secular Age*. *A Secular Age* seems to be the final step in a long line of theoretical moves that proposes the possibility of faith again for persons living in a modern, secular age, but not without first acknowledging the pervasive experience of an "immanent frame," which can seem to tilt experience toward the secular. From his early works on the importance of language and dialogue to self-constitution to the history in which the modern subject is embedded that is elaborated in *Sources of the Self*, Taylor's method seems to proceed from verification to transcendence, from within, of the subjective turn in thought and in culture. Establishing his affirmation of this passage to modernity, Taylor's articulation of matters religious is automatically experienced as internal to modernity. Taylor's approach performatively validates not only fundamental and widely acknowledged principles of transformative communication but, one may say, an incarnational principle, and mission through dialogue.

Michael Gallagher, SJ, and others rightly note the significance of this project for those wrestling with the contemporary challenge for traditional religious faith to remain alive today. Few have articulated more succinctly the basic agenda of *A Secular Age*. Gallagher states, "*A Secular Age* is a complicated book with a simple core that seeks to dismantle various naïve interpretations of modernity as automatically irreligious. [Taylor's] constant desire in these pages is to deepen the argument about secularization and faith, and to make room for a more sophisticated reading of history."[38] This, one might say, is another reason why Taylor's

---

38. Gallagher, "Charles Taylor's Critique of 'Secularization,'" 433–44.

work can be read as both a guide for mission and as itself a form of intellectual mission.

At this point, I present a reading of *A Secular Age* in light of Taylor's earlier work on modern selfhood and modern malaise to show that, without explicitly drawing these connections, Taylor's reflections on modern selfhood and secularity can be read together in such a way that reveals, more forcefully than Taylor himself would ever express, the flawed understanding of personhood that pervades modern self-consciousness. While Taylor does not expressly claim to seek to retrieve *homo religiosus*, in many ways, this is the effective consequence of his work on modern malaise and modern selfhood in general, when refracted through his opus on modern secularity. With *A Secular Age*, Taylor clarifies the implications for personhood of refiguring time without God. He expresses the shortcomings of the modern social imaginary in terms of "fullness"; what we now suffer is a lack of "fullness," and Taylor seems to trace an argument in *A Secular Age* for the relationship between this lack of fullness and the loss of openness to transcendence.[39]

Philosophy: Articulating the "Unthought"

In order to understand the developments in *A Secular Age*, it is important to recognize that Taylor speaks not only of the vast expanse of historically significant intellectual movements, but that Taylor is deeply interested in a more tacit and thus ingrained understanding of the world, a pervasive understanding of life together that he terms "the social imaginary" (he acknowledges his debt to Benedict Anderson for this concept).[40] According to Taylor, a "social imaginary" is, of its nature, a concept that seeks to move beyond the false dichotomy of "theory" and "praxis." With it, Taylor aims for a conceptual tool that signifies what he calls the "background understanding" of our practices, something that captures a form

---

39. McEvoy, "Proclamation as Dialogue." James McEvoy has written lucidly on the way in which Taylor's account of personhood and the new social imaginary of the modern world help clarify the mission of Vatican II to be in dialogue with the world. McEvoy argues that Taylor's appropriation of a Gadamerian notion of dialogue helps the Church discern a new way of undertaking proclamation. He points out along the way that Taylor's approach brings attention to the rupture of common space in a pluralistic world, which can then only be restored by exploring the self-understandings and shared world of interlocutors.

40. Anderson, *Imagined Communities*.

of "rationality," but is more akin to a functional logic that underpins our practices. Taylor calls it our "naïve understanding," perhaps pre-reflective but not unreflective. The desire to be true to "lived experience" leads Taylor to speak at the level of "imaginary" rather than "theory" for understanding our activity and existence as social beings.[41]

Indeed, Taylor actively resists conducting his historical investigation through the lens of the elites of any given period, choosing instead to use as criterion of significance that which became the background, "ordinary" understanding of a culture, whether that culture be of the Enlightenment, Calvinist Geneva, or expressive-Romanticism or the age of authenticity. One of the advantages of the imaginary is that it highlights both the normativity and malleability of our social, historically contingent existence. In describing the discrepancy between sacred and profane in terms of social imaginary, Taylor demonstrates the historical enmeshment of church and culture and shows why they cannot be readily extricated from one another. Employing the past century's best insights on the narratival dimension of human experience, Taylor thus traces the "long march" toward secular time.

Examining the implications of Taylor's exposition of modern social imaginaries in the West holds some fecund revelations for the question of how the Church ought to conceive of herself in relation to the world in a modern and postmodern age. Taylor's description of culture in terms of a social imaginary certainly introduces some levels of complexity to the Church-world relation that seem to have been overlooked in the period of Vatican II: "The effect of the Christian or Christian-Stoic attempt to remake society in bringing about the modern 'individual in the world' was much more pervasive and multi-tracked. It helped to nudge first the moral, then the social imaginary in the direction of modern individualism."[42] His account of the social imaginary thus reveals that the modern social imaginary was not without Christian appropriation

---

41. Peperzak, *Reason in Faith*, 99. The "social imaginary" may be an attempt to move beyond the "boring" practice of contemporary philosophy as Adriaan Peperzak describes it: "The philosophy of Christians has assumed the form of a systematics in which the experience and meaning of a lived life hardly find a place. For non-Christians, philosophy could take root in what remained of Christianity or in other, non-Christian convictions, but for them, too, a sustained (and not only provisional or merely methodological) separation between fundamental convictions and experiences on the one side and scientific philosophy on the other side turned the 'love of wisdom' into a barren and boring activity."

42. *MSI*, 62. See also *Sources of the Self*.

and unwitting contributions to the historical emergence of modern secularism. Once we see that the Christian religion and its "cultural context" cannot be so neatly separated,[43] we are in a position, arguably, to better understand and accept responsibility for the existence and activity of our present-day economies, public spheres, and polities.[44]

I wish to draw attention to Taylor's approach to these shifts: he reads each shift as being attended by *moral motivation* and, ultimately, applies this same approach to frame our present time, which, he argues, gives us both the option for transcendence and the option for a rejection of the same. In noting the moral motivations that underlie the narrative shifts in social imaginary, Taylor demonstrates the significance of the *ethical plane* for the engagement between church and culture, particularly in a secular age.

The Appeal of Narrative: Resonance and Option

The narrative method of moral discourse assists the church in its engagement with culture insofar as it speaks to the norms and sensibility that Taylor recognizes as modern: namely, one that "affirms ordinary life" and the virtue of authenticity. The narrative method thereby meets its hearers and speaks in a medium that renders the message palatable, namely, the medium of choice. One can enter into the story that Taylor tells us at any point: recognizing oneself as secular because of lack of belief in a creator God deeply invested in a cosmos made in love; or seeing how one's desire to rebel and reform has led to a culture of nonreligious individuals, each of whom marches to his or her own beat. Where one finds oneself in the story activates a way of framing oneself, one's relationships and one's responsibilities, and one can begin to see where one's option for transcendence was a yes or a no.

The possibilities that Taylor's unique form of narratival method may offer to the question of church and culture are, then, as follows: (1) It allows people to see themselves in the narrative as atomistic, disembedded

---

43. Yet neither do they disappear into one another.

44. Christians are not to undertake as a mere human community, of course. William Cavanaugh's point about grace (*Theopolitical Imagination*, 47) becomes important and complementary here: "The Body of Christ which overcomes the scattering of humanity through Adam's sin is not enacted by any social contract but is always received as a gift; the 'free gift is not like the effect of the one man's sin' (Rom. 5:16). The Eucharist undercuts the primacy of contract and exchange in modern social relations."

individuals yearning for more, to see the moral sources for this reality, and to explore the real possibilities for another vision and experience of the world. The language of "buffered" and "porous" individuals, for example, is particularly helpful for understanding contemporary expressions of alienated humanity. (2) It helps people arrive at anthropological diagnoses without the burden of blame that can sometimes attend ecclesial receptions of right and wrong. Ronald Mercier has written helpfully on the importance of recognizing the distinction between responsibility and blame: "In a world of shifting moral horizons, where the self finds itself bereft of the social context that had previously rendered moral discernment and action much clearer, blame is not only unhelpful but also inappropriate." "Cultures once provided us with such horizons through strong and universally accepted narrations of the meaning of the cosmos; the Christian community had such an enduring cosmology. In the collapse of such communities, we lost not only the stories but the moral purpose or horizon they provided."[45]

> In the collapse of a context and horizon that gave moral certainty to us all, it can be comforting to see the point as simply one of individual failing, which can be counteracted by individual effort, as if the broader context for personal choice had not undergone radical change; indeed our current context virtually demands such an individualist reading of "the fault" . . . We need to attend, rather, to the ways in which the contemporary world—for reasons beyond our control—represents a much less stable and much more demanding moral arena.[46]

All of this is made possible by a discursive mode that acknowledges pluralism, fragmentation, creativity, and the enormous potential for both anxiety and hope in the midst of modernity, which Taylor exemplifies.

The hermeneutic of respect pervades Taylor's narrative mode, as D. Stephen Long underscores: "Taylor consistently opposes a 're-formed imposition of an ethic' wherever he sees it." The strongest and most consistent evaluation in *A Secular Age* is Taylor's opposition to "a disciplined society in which categorial relations have primacy and therefore norms." Yet even here Taylor, according to Long, balances this negative evaluation by recognizing it is not pure evil. *It arose from something good.* "But it

---

45. Mercier, "Holy Spirit and Ethics," 48.
46. Ibid. 50–51.

nevertheless all started by the laudable attempt to fight back the demands of the 'world,' and then make it over."[47]

Taylor believes that visiting history can thus be morally redemptive.[48] This is precisely what grounds his choice of narratival method. Taylor writes, "Our past is sedimented in our present, and we are doomed to misidentify ourselves as long as we can't do justice to where we come from. This is why the narrative is not an optional extra, why I believe that I have to tell a story."[49] The story is supposed to help us, I believe, along the way to recovering a renewed openness to transcendence.

The Missiological Significance of Taylor and A Secular Age

So where has Taylor's story of secularization brought us on the question of contemporary Catholic mission? Taylor's academic location as a social, political, and moral philosopher gives him an advantage of an audience that is likely not available to those in theology, namely, the cross-pressured believers, former believers, unbelievers of our secular age. Recognizing this ground, Taylor begins his account in *A Secular Age* in the language of philosophy and intellectual history. The first four sections of the book, "The Work of Reform," "The Turning Point," "The Nova Effect," and "Narratives of Secularization," comprise a creative narrative that uses critical analysis to uncover the conditions for the possibility of secularization. By establishing these "pre-reflective understandings," Taylor also sets out the immanent frame to lay the ground for his constructive project. By critiquing the current world-picture, Taylor again remains philosophical, but then come the burgeoning signs of theology in his turn to the language of "fullness" and "transcendence."

The language of ethics also plays an important role in inaugurating the shift. In "The Immanent Frame," Taylor portrays the various shifts in paradigm that led to the immanentization of transcendence as a result of certain *moral* preferences. Taylor asserts that the argument for childishness is one reason that belief in transcendence fell out of fashion. The ethical standard became, increasingly, a certain kind of courage and,

---

47. Long, "How to Read Charles Taylor," 101.

48. Taylor also acknowledges that judgments can be made and, in earlier works, articulates quite emphatically the possibility and veracity of transcultural values. (See, for example, his work on intuitionism.)

49. SA, 29.

specifically, the courage to overcome belief in a loving providential God. Taylor again uses his rhetorical strength as moral philosopher to good effect.

In short, one of the great opportunities that Taylor creates with *A Secular Age* is that he opens a space for faith, while nonetheless criticizing the codification of Christian morality. "If authenticity is being true to ourselves, is recovering our own 'sentiment de l'existence,' then perhaps we can only achieve it integrally if we recognize that this sentiment connects us to a wider whole."[50] Taylor helps the Church to see her need to speak into the vacuum left by modernity's implicit denial of transcendence and to speaking directly to the questions of personhood, identity, meaning, and value—without resorting to the language of 'code morality'.

Taylor and Theological Language

Taylor's choice of conceptual register, then, the social imaginary, may function to ground the ultimately similar theological point that lies at the heart of radical orthodoxy's critique of secularism.[51] Taylor, however, may not see himself as "doing theology"; he simply seeks to create an open space for the consideration of transcendence and a theological worldview in a secular age. In the final assessment it may be that he "enacts" theological speech only insofar as he wishes to exemplify to his readers that speaking of these realities in a discourse with secular academic disciplines such as sociology, philosophy, and history is possible.

Until *A Secular Age*, which we have considered more closely in this chapter, Taylor's recommendation has been that a retrieval of theistic sources can assist with the moral malaise of a modern Western culture striving for authenticity and benevolence. In *SA*, however, Taylor is moved to argue, ultimately, for a witness of faith, though a faith markedly different from that which characterized Christendom.[52]

---

50. *MM*, 91.

51. Indeed, Taylor himself acknowledges a qualified sympathy with the critical-historical method and aims of the radical orthodoxy movement at the end of *A Secular Age*. To present a substantial comparison of Taylor's account of secularity and that of RO, however, while an important future task, would exceed the bounds of this work.

52. It almost seems as if from *Sources of the Self* to *A Secular Age*, Taylor takes stock of the solution he proffers at the end of *Sources of the Self*, that modernity's ideals are, on the whole, best realized through a retrieval of theistic sources, but later, in considering the social imaginary of the West as it currently exists, recognizes that retrieval is

Moreover, Taylor employs the distinctive vocabulary of Christian theology throughout *A Secular Age*. From "eschaton" to "Eucharist" the language of theology certainly pervades the final chapter of Taylor's text. Its title, "Conversions," is itself a classic religious trope. Consider Taylor's evaluation of our present spiritual condition: "We have lost some of the communion, the 'conspiratio,' which is at the heart of the Eucharist. The spirit is strangled."[53] The language of "world structures," "frames," and "foundations" that shape our "consciousness" and "experience" is familiar to philosophers. The language of "secularization thesis," "population" and "demographic shifts," "youth culture," and "cultural symbols" is more aligned with the discourse in sociology. To these, Taylor adds the language of "eschaton," "kenotic self-emptying of God," "idolatry," and "agape," the language of theology. It is notable the way in which Taylor may be seen as transgressing disciplinary boundaries and perhaps even thereby breaking through the "immanent frame" of certain intellectual fields.

Taylor also offers a panoply of figures who have exemplified what he describes as "conversion." All of them are persons of faith. What begins as a negative argument by Taylor for the possibility of maintaining openness to transcendence earlier in the text culminates in the presentation of a multitude of spiritual exemplars to give hope and inspiration to a cross-pressured age seeking life beyond that of total immanence. Taylor could be seen as desirous of awakening in all who are still ambivalent an affirmation of the yearning for the "fullness" for which, he claims, every human heart yearns.

Michael Gallagher observes that "for Taylor, the challenge is to create new embodiments of faith and of spirituality in tune with the tone of the emerging cultural consciousness."[54] Taylor believes that "society will remain historically informed by Christianity, but it will be less common for people to be drawn into faith by strong political or group identity, but rather by forms of spiritual practice to which each is drawn."[55] Is this a prediction then that Christianity's thriving in a secular culture will depend less on the strength of the Church as it exists? Certainly, Taylor does not engage greatly with the Church on the ground except to present certain pointed arguments of indirection against a certain stance of

harder than he thought, and shifts, by the end of *A Secular Age*, to the need for saints, though not necessarily the Church.

53. SA, 739.

54. Gallagher, "Charles Taylor's Critique," 444.

55. SA, 514–15.

homogeneity, particularly around the moral norms governing human sexuality.

A central task of this work is to put forward an interpretation of Taylor's work as that of a phenomenologist whose philosophical explorations of the human person lead him to the question of spirituality. Importantly, Taylor does not make explicit the link between moral malaise and the loss of spirituality; he simply underscores that such loss exists in modernity and that there still exists an option to choose otherwise. In light of four suggestive works—*A Catholic Modernity?*, *Sources of the Self*, and *Modern Social Imaginaries*, but above all in light of *A Secular Age*—I read Taylor's larger project as one that is rooted in a concern for the rediscovery of the transcendent in modern life, a concern that renders Taylor a particularly important dialogue partner to theologians considering the evangelizing mission of the Church to the modern world.[56]

Functionally speaking, an argument can be made that Taylor introduces the question of religious experience and religious seeking to contemporary secular persons by demonstrating that the quandaries in contemporary Western moral, social, and political existence rest crucially on the loss of a transcendent horizon and a correlative lack of language for theological and spiritual existence. Taylor thus raises the question of transcendence and spirituality from within moral experience both implicitly and explicitly. A question this work raises is whether the Church may take this approach as a model for evangelization.

I have argued that *A Secular Age* is a culmination of Taylor's philosophical project on modern personhood and social existence and that it caps sustained reflection by Taylor on how it might be possible to retrieve Christian spirituality in the life of modern polities. In *SA* Taylor's Catholicity comes more explicitly to the fore, whereas it was largely implicit in his previous works. In some sense, we might see Taylor, with *A Secular Age*, responding most to George Marsden's comments on Taylor's *A Catholic Modernity?* Therein, Marsden challenges Taylor to lean into the particularities of Christian doctrine,[57] as he sees philosopher Alasdair MacIntyre doing, to form his case for the significance of Christianity for modern culture.

---

56. Fraser, *The Dialectics of the Self*, and Colorado, "Transcendence, Kenosis, Enfleshment."

57. James L. Heft, introduction to *A Catholic Modernity?*, 9, and Marsden, "Matteo Ricci and the Prodigal Culture."

And indeed, Taylor's Catholicity and his interest in the question of the possibility of faith in our time emerges in various ways in *A Secular Age*, particularly in the last chapter of the work, where Taylor points to several exemplary lives for the way in which they maintain openness to transcendence in cultural imagination by the very beauty of their own lives. Indeed, Taylor is really underscoring the beauty and attractiveness of the Christian life, though he might not put it in this way.

One of the key and most valuable insights of Taylor for the project and work of understanding the task of contemporary Catholic witness in a secular culture is his clear recognition of the disestablishment of Christianity.[58] He is aware, thereby, of the loss of certain "languages." This recognition of Christianity's existence only in the background, implicit consciousness of modern Western cultures guides his approach and work. While many others recognize the marginality of Christian consciousness today, few take the precise approach that Taylor takes, of appealing to the "Christian" element in contemporary culture in the precise form that it exists, that is, nebulously, at the level of imagination. Appealing to Matteo Ricci, Taylor can be seen as modeling his approach after the great missionary to China, allowing himself to be within and a part of the "alien culture," inculturating, empathizing, mediating.

A significant way in which this narrative of shifting social "ethoi" over time is important is that Taylor names the key desires of the "authentic subject" and speaks to them. Above all, Taylor's work on the moral ontology of the human person, from selves as self-interpreting animals, with horizons shaped by social, civilizational, and hence spiritual context, despite what modernity might claim, to the historical backdrop of the movement from porous, relational self to the "buffered" or "punctual" self of modernity, indicates a way in which Taylor's sense of persons and culture might open a path between the Church and the contemporary world and culture. Taylor's missiological dimension may also be seen in the intentional resistance he presents to "subtraction stories" of secularization: "The modern self does not arise because we moderns somehow faced 'stern realities' where previous eras were 'deploying comforting illusions.'"[59]

So, to state a theological interpretation of Taylor's work in its strongest form: the point of *A Secular Age* seems to be to effect a change. It can

---

58. *CM*, 84.
59. *SA*, 22.

read as a performative text that strives to effect an existential change in its readers. In order to do this, Taylor adopts the method of hortatory speech and rhetoric. One might go so far as to say that Taylor does this following the model given in the Bible: just as Jesus brought forth a call to conversion out of a story that was familiar to his listeners, out of *their* story (the story of the Jews and their covenant history with God), likewise, Taylor recognizes the need to tell a story that resonates with modern, secular selves who, without realizing it perhaps, nonetheless have a complex religious history. A Hegel scholar and an expert in contemporary philosophical hermeneutics and dialogue, Taylor understands that common ground is the foundation for receptivity to a call to transformation. While the theological *a priori* exists, to begin with the language of theology would be confusing and alienating; starting with conceptual underpinnings, pre-understandings and frameworks is more familiar to a philosophical audience. The importance of Taylor's shift into the key of imaginary is his naming of the horizon of modernity as tilted toward the immanent. Aiming his narrative at modern selves of the West, Taylor creates a space for considering the possibility of faith by pointing toward it as that which enables greater authenticity, a more profound freedom, a deeper relationality, and an enlarged capacity for love and personal meaning.

Critical Appropriation: The Church in *A Secular Age*

We have considered the possibilities of Taylor's narratives of the modern self and secularization for the church's encounter with culture. We now consider some possible limits of Taylor's proposal. These center mainly on Taylor's construal of the Church and how his diminished appreciation for the Church *as a shared horizon intrinsically open to transcendence* may run up against Taylor's own earlier accounts of the conditions of authenticity and his account of the challenge of contemporary secularity.

Long offers a richly discerned assessment of the significance of Taylor's *A Secular Age* for theology. To read Taylor, Long notes, is to appreciate the art of interpersonal, dialogical thinking. Taylor writes for real interlocutors and he writes with a hermeneutic of charity toward both subject matter and opponents. Taylor's method continually underscores, for example, that even when the result of a cultural shift was negative, the shift was always inaugurated by an impulse toward the good, a hope for something better. Long claims, however, that Taylor's account of secularity yields not only a wise discernment of the signs of the times, the seeds of the gospel and the transcendentals truth, goodness, beauty, but also a sense of how a transformation of culture may be achieved. Long shows that Taylor clarifies in a realistic fashion the implications of secularity for the reception of Christian doctrines. That is, the "new order," the modern moral order, will prevent people from seeing and understanding the dimensions of hierarchy, authority, clergy, worship, and the saints in ecclesial life. It will not be able to make sense of the Incarnation either. Finally, the usefulness arguments of ecclesiology fail insofar as they falsify the gap between time and eternity. In all these ways, Long reads Taylor as providing a charitable reading of modernity that also reveals the points of strong difference between Christianity and contemporary Western culture. Long states that Taylor "makes a case for the Christian faith and honoring what is good, true, and beautiful in the modern moral order."

While some of Taylor's most affirming theological interlocutors have felt that Taylor does little more than suggest ways in which culture contains seeds of the gospel, Long notes that there is something more, that Taylor also points to communion.[60] Indeed, Taylor points to the "eschatological banquet" and shows that "porousness to each other" is a condition for the possibility of arguing for what is good.[61] Taylor indeed moves into theological speech in the final pages of *A Secular Age*, from which Long quotes: "In the nature of things, Christianity offers no global solution, no general organization of things here and now which will fully resolve the dilemma and meet the maximal demand. It can only show ways in which we can, as individuals, and as churches, hold open the path to the fullness of the Kingdom." Long proceeds to note that Taylor's endorsement of forming a culture that is led by the lights of the exemplary lives of certain people and communities is not agape conceived as heroic, self-sacrificial love, but communion. Quoting Taylor again,

> If we think of ethical virtue as the realization of lone individuals, this may seem to be the case. But suppose the highest good consists in communion, mutual giving and receiving, as in the paradigm of the eschatological banquet. The heroism of gratuitous giving has no place for reciprocity. If you return anything to me, then my gift was not totally gratuitous; and besides, in the extreme case, I disappear with my gift and no communion

---

60. Long, "Balthasarian Theological Economics," 104.
61. Ibid., 106.

between us is possible. This unilateral heroism is self-enclosed. It touches the outermost limit of what we can attain to when moved by a sense of our own dignity. But is that what life is about? Christian faith proposes a quite different view.[62]

Long leaves us with several important questions, however. He asks, how particular are the theological events in Taylor's account of Christianity? Must doctrine always be code? Does it return us to a neo-Durkheimian dispensation? What is the Church for Taylor?[63]

Indeed, the question of Taylor's conception of the Church is of particular interest for the task of discerning Taylor's contribution to a vision of Catholic mission for a secular age (though all of Long's questions are truly the inquiries that a theologian must put to Taylor). In a foreword to a collection of essays on secularization in other modernities such as India and the Middle East,[64] Taylor proposes that perhaps the norm that pluralistic cultures might strive for is "liberty, equality, fraternity." The context to which he speaks in this volume is not an explicitly ecclesial one, the cultural shift Taylor envisions is conducted in the key of ethics for a political vision. While the norm Taylor suggests is certainly not inimical to an ecclesial vision, as Long notes, there seems to be something beyond this vision of striving that is needed for it to be seen as properly mediating ecclesial vision. This, in its simplest sense, would be the theological trope of "grace": the sense that all of one's work, including and especially one's ethical visioning and enactment, does not come about without the work of the Spirit in the world. Taylor acknowledges this in the final chapters of *A Secular Age*, but perhaps this is where some theological critique might arise from ecclesiologists who would find in Taylor too much of an af-

62. SA, 702.

63. In a conversation with Taylor once (during his November 2011 visit to Toronto for a speaking engagement on the future of religion in a secular age), I asked Taylor if he had a favorite theologian, to which Taylor replied, "Yes. Yves Congar." In an attempt to understand better the difference between Taylor and Balthasar on the Church, it is interesting to note that Balthasar has stated of Congar, "I must admit that in spite of my great admiration for Father Congar's magnificent oeuvre, I have always felt a bit uneasy when I came upon 'life and structure' or 'life and institution' opposing each other. I myself need to have an image before me: within the human organism the bones, too, are alive and indispensable; otherwise man could not stand straight and carry out an infinite variety of free movements. To repeat, the Church, living and official, is one single body, and any attempt to transfer this vitality to the particular churches and to decry Rome as mere structure, is destructive of *catholica*." Balthasar, *Test Everything*, 65.

64. Taylor, "Foreword: What Is Secularism?"

firmation of the humanistic, to the point where the spirituality to which he alludes disappears. With Long, however, I would argue that while it is true that both the richness and limitation of Taylor's work lie in his sensitivity and charity toward humanism, and his work on the human person, the lack of a substantive ecclesiology certainly opens the door for theologians to collaborate and complement the vision he presents.

In light of Taylor's astute reading of modernity and particularly Taylor's initial shaping of the question in the early 1980s through asking if the disengaged, atomistic self motivated by instrumental reason is indeed free and fully human, the groundwork for dialogue is certainly laid by Trinitarian theologians who seek to articulate the doctrine of person as relation in terms that speak to the values of production and reproduction that hold our attention today, and articulate a sense in which Trinitarian existence speaks to the longing for fullness that pervades our atomistic culture.

One may raise the question, for example, of whether Taylor's vision of the church in *A Secular Age* misses the notion of the Church as more than an institution. John Zizioulas and others reminds us that the Church is a "mode of existence," "a way of being."[65] In Zizioulas, especially, Taylor may recognize a profound possibility for the recovery of a sense of self that is not condemned to isolation or oppression, and indeed, is the condition for the possibility of a retrieved experience of embeddedness within a horizon that includes ultimate ends. Zizioulas does not "go back" to a time before the Enlightenment but helps us to see that ecclesial existence grounded in an ontology of personhood is precisely a possibility that offers a fruitful way forward. How we might "engage" theos, cosmos, and ourselves is through re-membering ourselves as the Church, through the embodied, other-centered response of liturgical existence.

We note the inherent antinomy in Taylor's own account of how new itineraries of faith are necessary to support the possibility of options for faith in a secular age, given his notion of identity as involving dialogue with others within a horizon of shared significance, the irreversible development of the secular horizon of our age such that most modern persons in the West frame their lives in profane time, and that his account does not seem to give much place to ecclesial community. More explicitly stated, it would seem that Taylor's account of moral development and the development of identity requires certain shared spiritual horizons,

---

65. See Zizioulas, *Being as Communion*.

which is often provided by a tradition. Without a tradition that understands openness to transcendence as constitutive of the human good, the question arises of where and how exemplary lives of agape will emerge. (As Taylor himself notes, benevolence is not the same as agape.) Taylor observes that the present lack of religious faith calls more than ever for lives that truly testify to agape, yet he also seems to overlook the deeply significant role of the Church, the whole Body of Christ in forming such lives.

All of this points to a tension in Taylor's account around the Church. On the one hand, Taylor makes clear time and again that he believes that the end of Christendom was on the whole a positive event that enabled the chief social and moral gains of modernity to be achieved. Taylor also notes that to some degree certain shifts into secularity, in particular the shift into Protestant reform, were the result of institutional Catholicism's own undue need for control. On the other hand, Taylor has traced a painstakingly detailed account of five hundred years that have gone into, unwittingly at times, the development of a distinctly secular social imaginary. Taylor believes that the best possibilities for modernity include some way of keeping faith alive, albeit fragilized religious faith. He believes that lives of exemplary love, or holiness, show that this is possible. What is missing in Taylor's account is an exploration of whether there is any generative connection between exemplary holiness and the Church. *Is it possible to affirm that itineraries of faith akin to those Taylor describes are possible without a concrete community of Christian faith in existence?*

As many contemporary interlocutors have done with Taylor's work, particularly Catholic interpreters, I argue that Taylor's account finally calls out for completion and gains greater coherence through recourse to a theological vision, which, I argue, can be best provided by Hans Urs von Balthasar. If we take what Taylor claims is true in the realm of identity formation and moral development, then there is some greater need for the Church, perhaps a renewed vision of the Church, than Taylor seems to indicate at the end of *A Secular Age*. Importantly, Taylor's method of raising the question of God outside of an exclusively theological and epistemological mode is, however, also a key aspect of Taylor's significance for mission in the Western world today. Taylor shifts the conversation about belief from the sphere of epistemic and theoretical debate to an examination of the lived social and moral shape of religious faith.

Taylor acknowledges that belonging to the Church is part of what it means to be a Christian believer.[66] However, Taylor is also deeply critical, in places, of Church authority and the Church in history.[67] This in itself does not show Taylor to be indifferent or opposed to the positive role that the Church plays in the lives of Christians. Indeed, it is possible that Taylor's criticisms are put from a stance of loving concern for the church. There is, moreover, a place for precisely such kind of critique in genuine ecclesial love. On the other hand, it is all too common in western modernity to hear statements about the authority of the Church that emerge from prevalent assumptions about the self, community, and authority. Without necessarily impugning Taylor's own treatment of ecclesial authority, it would seem that the modern malaise of subjectivism calls for a more fine-grained theological reflection on ecclesiology that Taylor's account can offer. Authority can have, after all, a role in teaching and forming a theological imagination that is not oppressive.[68]

Taylor has written explicitly on certain aspects of the Church that merit closer consideration and concern. In "Benedict XVI,"[69] Taylor provides a fairly forthright statement of his view on Pope Benedict. Taylor expresses concern that the papacy may lead the Church in the wrong direction in its aim to show strength on various issues at the heart of the culture wars of the West and fail to welcome plurality and the diversity of spiritual paths that is so deeply a part of religious experience today. The argument is, essentially, that a "smaller, purer" Church is not the way to deepen *catholica*; it simply repels those who might have been open. In "Magisterial Authority," Taylor notes, "Our notions of magisterial authority have been tainted by a failure to observe certain limits."[70] Taylor enumerates these transgressions as "false sacralization, legalism, and the refusal of contingent conditions and of the enigmatic."[71] Showing how certain moral issues, including abortion and homosexuality, require greater discernment and pastoral nuance, and that a greater toleration for spiritual ambiguity is needed in general such that an appreciation of other religions, for example, does not inherently signify a bracketing of

66. SA, 729.
67. See Taylor, "Benedict XVI", 7–9.
68. Thanks to Ron Kuipers for providing this helpful nuance.
69. Taylor, "Benedict XVI," 7–9.
70. Taylor, "Magisterial Authority," 262.
71. Ibid., 263.

one's own faith (Taylor quotes Benedict here), Taylor states that these infringements on Christian freedom amount to a harm to sacramental life.[72]

A risk of appropriating wholesale Taylor's vision of Catholicism for a contemporary, constructive vision of mission is that Taylor seems too dismissive of the role of tradition and authority in the Church.[73] His view seems limited by the horizon of modernity and, arguably, fails to be true to his own best insights on the relationship between tradition and individual freedom and virtue. That is, on the one hand, one of Taylor's foremost insights in contemporary moral philosophy is the degree to which larger horizons of meaning shape the moral understandings and actions of human agents. Taylor's arguments for the existence of hypergoods combined with the claim that human beings are fundamentally social and their horizons of meaning must necessarily come from a context beyond themselves converges in important ways to make an argument for the significance of moral traditions in human flourishing.

On the other hand, Taylor is not Alasdair MacIntyre. Where they differ, it seems, is that MacIntyre believes that tradition yields a sense of moral objectivity to a degree that certain modern ways of framing moral situations do not. Taylor, while affirming the means whereby tradition plays a role in the formation of moral consciousness, does not assert that a particular tradition has more of a hold on moral objectivity than others. While affirming the Catholic tradition, Taylor also frequently does so through an appeal to the modern ethos of pluralism. Thus, to perhaps put it too simply, Taylor allows his understanding of the Catholic tradition to be governed by his commitment to modernity, whereas for MacIntyre, the emphasis is in the other direction.

A potential problem with Taylor's ecclesiology is that it plays into and participates overmuch in the secular social horizon that, at some level, undercuts it. That is a key burden of Taylor's articulation of the "immanent frame": there is an inclination latent in the social imaginary of modern Western societies today that can systematically close individuals'

---

72. Ibid., 268–69.

73. This is not to say that Taylor lacks appreciation for the significance of tradition and authority and its role in constituting personhood. Taylor's strong criticism of contemporary ecclesial authority seems, however, to abstract from the cultural situation he has outlined in *A Secular Age*, from the notion that cultural shifts have affected and fragilized the condition of belief today, and to underemphasize the deep interconnection between authority, tradition, and the person-constituting character of the Church as community of faith.

vision and thereby orientation to transcendence. Taylor's import of the "democratic model" of harmony can short-change the Church's potential to provide an alternative formation and alternative imaginary to persons today.[74] While loving ecclesial critique is necessary, it is also important to consider the implications of vociferous critique within the context of an already secular social imaginary that often seems tilted toward atheism. Might it be possible that such criticism participates in the foreclosure of the tradition and horizon that gives rise to the exemplary lives of conversion that Taylor celebrates in his final chapter?

Taylor perhaps does not see the connection between these individual lives and the life of the institution, but that is then precisely where his argument falls short, namely, on his own terms. Taylor's argument for horizons needs to ask, I would argue, about the relationship between the existence of the Church and the lives of agape that can keep the option for transcendence alive in a secular age. While the lives of saints often do impact the world as "out of the ordinary," it is certainly not the case that they are extraordinary in the sense that they need no formation and no tradition to form them for their extraordinary holiness. It is indeed the Church that plays this role in the lives of most Catholic Christians. Thus, Taylor's own early work would challenge the way in which he treats the Church in his later works, that is, rather minimally, and as a broken institution if he does. It could be argued, however, that Taylor's critique of the present-day Catholic hierarchy cannot be equated with an overarching critique of tradition.

On Taylor's own account of how a social imaginary shifts, it seems that the Church needs to give a positive ideal that people will respond to in the same way as the development of exclusive humanism and secular horizon did. "The modernist retrieval of experience thus involves a profound breach in the received sense of identity and time, and a series of reorderings of a strange and unfamiliar kind. These images of life have reshaped our ideas in this century of what it is to be a human being."[75] We might say that Taylor shifts the challenge to the Church to be one of constructive response to the needs of the modern world rather than mere denial or rejection of its secular frame. In order to do this, however, Taylor needs to be clear on what faith is and to point in the direction of the Church who makes this clear. The problem is that Taylor

---

74. It is not that democracy is inimical to Christian life, but they are distinct and Christian existence goes much deeper than democratic principles of social life.

75. SS, 465.

is deeply ambivalent about such a move, thinking perhaps that it seems to trivialize individuals' search or reduce Christianity to a "code" because it proposes itself as "the answer." This is where Long's questions are deeply instructive. Is it the case, as Taylor seems to suggest, that doctrine must always be considered code? Is it not the case, rather, that this is a modernistic, secularist understanding of doctrine, rather than that of a Christian believer and of those who teach doctrine?

Balthasar eloquently shows how doctrine "accompanies us."[76] Taylor's reticence to assert that the Church proposes an objective answer in Jesus Christ that meets the quest of all subjects and enables them to get beyond individualism and to become persons shows the significance of Balthasar's constructive theological vision for Catholic witness and mission in a secular age. Balthasar will show that the horizon of the believing community is precisely that of eschatology, and the drama of salvation. This dynamic of love alone enables us to know who we are as selves if we are willing to be moved by the beauty of God's love into a relationship with him where we allow ourselves to receive who we most truly are from him.

Taylor's reticence concerning the Church is also lamentable since Taylor's narratives of modern identity, his articulation of the "landscape of the modern soul," and his account of the social horizon in which selves find themselves are so instructive and could be read as an invitation to look for transcendence and a way out of the immanent frame. However, Taylor seems to lack a clear articulation that the Church has answers for personhood and authenticity. (These answers in their simplest form are faith in the person of Jesus, who reveals God-with-us, and vocation, an invitation to enter the drama of salvation through the community of faith, the Church.)

Unlike moral theologian Servais Pinckaers, Taylor does not articulate clearly enough that there is something in the human heart that "knows" the triune God revealed in and by Jesus Christ:

> We have no need to fear presenting the Sermon on the Mount to nonbelievers, on the pretext that only a natural ethic is appropriate for them. Experience shows, and the reading of the commentaries confirms it: the Sermon touches non-Christians more deeply and has far greater appeal than any moral theory based on natural law in the name of reason. It is as if the Sermon

---

76. Balthasar, *In the Fullness of Faith*, 56–57.

strikes a human chord more "natural" and universal than reason by itself can ever do.[77]

Indeed, Taylor does not seem to possess a moral realism in a thoroughgoing way: on the one hand, he will insist on something like hypergoods which provide the criteria for strong evaluation and will even name theistic sources as the origin of some of these hypergoods, but, in the end, Taylor resists asserting in any but the most tentative way that there are "objective" moral goods and that some traditions will lead one in the direction of these more than others. Taylor does not also anywhere claim that the source of our authentic personhood is necessarily to be found in Jesus Christ. (As does Balthasar, as interpreted by David Schindler, who will say that Christ is at the heart of culture or "the world." This contrasts, too, with the options Niebuhr gives.)

The need to turn to a theological account of Church and personhood emerges finally from a sense that Taylor's concern for the concerns of modernity, namely, pluralism and a certain faith in dialogically mediated reconciliation, overrides the richness in his own account where he points to lives of conversion. Otherwise stated, Taylor would likely argue that the Catholic path is one viable option among many in a secular age and a very promising one at that. The question is whether Catholic ecclesial mission can be content to hope and to proclaim to be 'an option'. What follows is a consideration of four important critiques of Taylor's assessment of modernity and modern selfhood by Jean Bethke Elshtain, Alasdair MacIntyre, Fergus Kerr, and George Marsden. These, I believe, indicate the underlying theoretical limitation that emerges again in Taylor's approach to secularity and therefore limits its prophetic insight into contemporary Catholic witness and mission.

Taylor's Affirmation of Modernity

Elshtain's Critique—Is Taylor Too Optimistic about Modernity?

Speaking with reference to *Sources of the Self*, Jean Bethke Elshtain writes, "Taylor is surely right to suggest that the ground for controversy now is the manner of living that ordinary life which we would affirm."[78] However, Elshtain also states her opinion that "perhaps we have arrived at a

---

77. Pinckaers, *Sources of Christian Ethics*, 163.
78. Elshtain, "Risks and Responsibilities," 67–68.

subjectivist impasse in a more thoroughgoing way than Taylor allows or fears."[79] Taylor claims that "the moral conflicts of modern culture rage within each of us."[80] Elshtain avers that, unfortunately, they do not.

While Elshtain affirms the fundamental goals of Taylor's project and lauds him for repeatedly drawing attention to the importance of "believable frameworks and horizons of intelligibility,"[81] Elshtain's contention in this essay is that Taylor underestimates the degree to which both the sovereignty of the self and the sovereignty of the state pervade modern consciousness and existence.[82] Elshtain thus seeks to press Taylor on his claim that "contemporary affirmations and conceptions of freedom do not involve 'a repudiation of qualitative distinctions, [or] a rejection of constitutive goods as such,' and, second, that the forces of immanentization at work on so much of the moral horizon of late modernity yet retain, or bear within themselves, the possibility of 'the good.'"[83]

Her example is the affirmation of ordinary life that Taylor discusses as one of the key gains in modernity in *Sources of the Self*. Even as the affirmation of ordinary life may be a desirable good, Elshtain warns that this very affirmation is threatened by modernity's deep-seated narrative about state sovereignty in particular; its claim to be the guarantor of rights, the object of deepest allegiance and thus sacrifice (in war), is such that it in fact shows itself to be quite indifferent in profound ways to a true affirmation of the goods of ordinary life. Discussing sovereign selfhood, Elshtain notes the manner in which technology has been appropriated to support the myth of the unfettered freedom of the self. This radical subjectivity without any sense of limits displays itself in the logic that funds certain mindsets regarding the use of technology for various forms of "biosocial engineering"; everything that enables greater control of women over their bodies constitutes desirable reproductive "choice," and it is irrelevant whether this includes then choices against certain lives. Elshtain mentions persons with developmental disabilities and the problem of gender selection in particular.[84]

79. Ibid., 68.
80. *SS*, 202.
81. Elshtain, "Risks and Responsibilities," 80.
82. Ibid. 69.
83. Ibid., 68.
84. Ibid., 79.

To all of this, Elshtain proposes an ethic of responsibility, because finally we must answer to someone.[85] The affirmation of ordinary life is at risk if we do not take measures to understand the limits of both self and state. Elshtain claims to follow Vaclav Havel in this, and quotes Havel thus: "I feel that this arrogant anthropocentrism of modern man, who is convinced he can know everything and bring everything under his control, is somewhere in the background of the present crisis. It seems to me that if the world is to change for the better it must start with a change in human consciousness, in the very humanness of modern man."[86] The heart of the issue is that a real understanding of humanity is not readily evident and available in modernity's conception of either self or state, Elshtain seems to indicate. In a very subtle way, she notes that the rabid, totalizing desire for sovereignty was not a part of certain Christian instantiations of culture in the same way (she qualifies this claim, of course).

In all of this, Elshtain is in sympathy with Taylor. She acknowledges that there is, in Taylor, with his religious leanings, an intimation of where an answer might lie, namely, in his claim that Christianity offers some real possibilities for modernity in the face of the latter's challenges. "What Taylor offers to our rethinking of the sources of the modern self and politics is not, as some have suggested, a full embrace of the Christian moment but, rather, a canny re-interpretation of the profound challenge Christian theory and practice offers to any and all heroic construals and monistic constructions of political life and thought."[87] What I want to suggest is that Elshtain and others have found Taylor's account of modernity to be overly optimistic and not sufficiently faithful to the darker aspects of his own narratives of subjectivism, atomism, and instrumentalism in modernity. Though only very subtly hinting at where a valid subject of accountability may lie, Elshtain leaves it as a matter of ethics. I want to suggest that her critique is notable on two fronts: first, it enables us to begin to see that a stronger sense of reserve toward the culture of modernity may be needed than Taylor has because his account seems to leave out the pretenses of the state in modernity to sovereignty. Second, it can be seen to be a critique that Taylor addresses in his subsequent work on the secularity of the modern social imaginary. So, it gives us a sense of where Taylor seems to want to head.

85. Ibid., 80.
86. Ibid., 79–80.
87. Ibid., 71.

Elshtain's critique of Taylor's story of the self is similar to that of Alasdair MacIntyre, insofar as it could be construed that both express a desire for more objectivity in Taylor's account of the self and its ability to pursue the good in modernity without further discriminations than the ones Taylor has named. For MacIntyre, who has brought about in a singular manner a reconsideration of the importance of tradition and virtue and tradition *for* virtue in contemporary moral philosophy, Taylor's theoretical premises do not seem able to sustain the challenge Taylor himself poses in naming the quandaries that modern selves face. That is, although Taylor does not wish to be a relativist, as he knows well the problems that such a position entails, Taylor is also sufficiently "respectful" of all strong evaluations and subjectivity as to seem not to have enough foundations to avoid falling into arbitrariness and emotivism.[88] MacIntyre, commenting on *Sources of the Self*, notes that Taylor's acknowledgment of a wide range of goods and merely the criterion of reflexive learning from experience do not allow Taylor to establish objective judgments between those goods.[89] One could say that MacIntyre sees the objectivity of goods in Taylor's account trumped by Taylor's deference to selves as strong evaluators. MacIntyre contrasts Taylor's approach with the Thomistic approach to self-knowledge, which allows one to make an object of oneself "so that the inner loses Cartesian privileges."[90]

Indeed, MacIntyre's larger project, famously, spells out

> the kind of understanding of social life which the tradition of the virtues requires, a kind of understanding very different from those dominant in the culture of bureaucratic individualism. Within that culture conceptions of the virtues become marginal and the tradition of the virtues remains central only in the lives of social groups whose existence is on the margins of the central culture. Within the central culture of liberal or bureaucratic individualism new conceptions of the virtues emerge and the concept of a virtue is itself transformed.[91]

MacIntyre seems willing to go to the logical conclusion of Taylor's work on horizons and identity so as to make a judgment about the way in which the social horizon of modernity actually hinders the modern self's quest

---

88. MacIntyre, "Critical Remarks on *Sources of the Self*," 188–89.
89. Ibid., 188.
90. Ibid., 189.
91. MacIntyre, *After Virtue*, 225.

for virtue. In this, MacIntyre shows a willingness to make a judgment about the culture and politics of modernity that Taylor is unwilling to make. The problem is that it is difficult not to recognize the relationship between a culture's horizon and its malaises once it is established that there is indeed a causal connection between horizons and identity and that identity, particularly moral identity, is fundamentally constituted in and through communities and social existence.

Fergus Kerr also notes that Taylor moves in the right direction in seeking to articulate the possibility of self-transcendence but doesn't seem to go far enough.[92] Kerr acknowledges Taylor's work in trying to "enlarge, or retrieve, modes of thought that have been wrongly made to seem problematic,"[93] Taylor's insight that "reactions tend to be affirmations of a certain ontology of the human,"[94] that "minimizing human suffering has a source in Christian ethics,"[95] and "how religion can play a role in our moral lives."[96] He notes that Taylor is teleological[97] and affirms essences.[98] Yet, in debates with those who do not share his Christian theological or metaphysical presuppositions, such as his mentor and fellow political theorist, Isaiah Berlin, Taylor does not seem able to allow that his foundational commitments will lead to a rather different practical judgment about their situation in society and history.[99] Indeed, Taylor notes that they differ on the former but are quite similar in their assessment of their current situation. Kerr thereby challenges Taylor on his lack of recognition of the fundamental role that his Christian teleology and knowledge of theology would and ought to play in his understanding of social and political life.[100] That is, Taylor does not clarify Berlin's misunderstanding of Christian teleology or show how the latter consists in a fundamental sense that human beings, in God, are given a real participation in history.[101] Although Taylor includes a realist ontology of the human, an affirmation of ordinary life, religious belief as needing

92. Kerr, "Charles Taylor's Moral Ontology of the Self."
93. Ibid., 139.
94. Ibid., 140.
95. Ibid., 144.
96. Ibid., 146.
97. Ibid., 150.
98. Ibid., 151.
99. Ibid., 152.
100. Ibid., 154.
101. Ibid.

and having some interlocutor who is not ourselves, and deep ecology,[102] in the end, Taylor is simply not clear enough on the foundational truths of Christianity, and this does a disservice to the philosophical discourses in which he engages.[103]

George Marsden—Is Taylor Too Shy about His Catholicism?

Marsden's overall argument challenges Taylor's Riccian approach to engaging a secular academic configuration of moral truth and modernity. Marsden applauds, nonetheless, the basic task that Taylor undertakes, of engaging faith in perspectives on contemporary issues. A question at the heart of this work circles around precisely the problematic that Marsden raises: Taylor is a valuable Catholic thinker for what he seeks to do with his Catholic faith and philosophical work; whether his approach is the one that is finally most effective remains a question.

Working within Marsden's engagement of Taylor, we might consider the following question: Marsden claims that the appeal to Ricci is misguided insofar as the analogy between China's induction into the Christian worldview does not quite mirror the requirements of a secular Western culture's re-embrace of a Christian moral worldview. The chief element of difference is precisely that the latter's encounter with Christianity, by virtue of history, must be a re-encounter, a re-engagement, a recovery and a remembering. Thus, Marsden applies the metaphor of the prodigal son to contemporary secular culture, suggesting that what is needed is a call to repentance rather than a mere appreciation of a culture that has in many ways expressed its difference in the form of rebellion.[104]

SUMMATION

From a lifetime career devoted to questions of meaning and hope in modernity, Taylor deepens the Church's understanding of modernity (and lays out a path for mission in the West) in the following four ways:

1. Taylor highlights the complex history that has gone into the moral ontology of modern selves, emphasizing that much "suppression"

---

102. Ibid., 158.
103. Ibid., 150–55.
104. Marsden, "Matteo Ricci and the Prodigal Culture."

of certain spiritual sources has occurred in the process. Through a complex delineation of the various threads that have led to the making of modern identity, Taylor produces a moral map, in the hope of retrieving some of the theistic sources of contemporary moral understanding. Framing his moral ontology of the self in terms of helping modern culture achieve its highest ends and retrieving theistic sources to do so is Taylor's first main contribution. Taylor thereby shows consonance with the affirmation of the world that is so prominent in the work of the Second Vatican Council.

2. Taylor identifies forms of modern malaise—subjectivism, relativism, atomism, instrumentalism, loss of fullness, flattened horizons, excarnation, spiritual lobotomy—and the positive desires for justice, authenticity, and fulfillment in ordinary life—in modern culture that enable the Church to discern how, in particular, she might serve the culture.

3. Taylor outlines the social imaginary and hence understanding of personhood in Western modernity: namely, economic, public, and self-determining peoples. He underscores that this imaginary is decidedly secular in character, "unmoored from higher times and Great Chains of Being."

4. Taylor articulates the conditions of belief and unbelief through a detailed historical study of the development of secularization in the West. This last helps us understand how entrenched secularism is in our age, how Christianity has contributed to secularism, and that we cannot "go back." Taylor thereby enables the Church to learn how not to decry secularism as a starting point but attempt to understand it in a dispassionate way. He offers insight into how Christianity, and Catholicism in particular, may be lived in this age, and also what not to do. The former involves attending to lives that exhibit a true conversion (or re-conversion, Taylor says) and how they have shown that there can be new itineraries to the faith. The latter consists in a caution against repeating a mode of "reform," which has proven to be an ineffective and inauthentic way of living the gospel message.

Where does Taylor's account of secularity and Latin Christianity leave us? This might be another way of asking Fergus Kerr's question, "How much can a philosopher do?" The short answer, it seems, is that Taylor opens up the conversation about faith in a secular age in a way that acknowledges the historicity of religion and its limitations but nonetheless finds a way to vindicate religion in a new way for this age. That is, Taylor offers much in the way of highlighting and naming the many questions, doubts, and defenses at the level of background understanding that form a barrier to a proper conception of the possibility of a vibrant Christian spirituality and the meaning of Christian religion today. He gives voice to the critique based on excarnation, the challenge of religion's mingling with violence, the poor history and perversions of the Christian religion from within itself (from superstition to corrupt applications of power), and, above all, the reduction of religion to "code morality" and the drive to reform. This, coupled with an ongoing attempt to engage culture in a way that helps it reach its highest ideals, and a recognition of the ways in which modernity has led to a deeper incarnation of principles of equality and justice, is how Taylor helps the Church think more deeply about how she can serve God in and through genuine love and service to people, as she discerned was and is her mission at the Second Vatican Council. A good part of Taylor's answer involves challenging the Church to recognize the error of her ways in previous epochs and to be moved thereby to a sense of greater humility about the truth she bears.

Kerr is right, however, that as much as he seeks to move the culture into a horizon of deeper meaning—that of the poet (Hopkins) or that of the nun (St. Thérèse of Lisieux)—Taylor is not able to move us to contemplation. This is because Taylor's philosophy does not centrally and explicitly reveal the person of Jesus Christ, even as, compared to most, Taylor has made an inspiringly daring attempt to speak of Christ in his work on secularity.[105] A turn to Balthasar thus becomes necessary.

In short, Taylor's attempt to underscore the possibility of faith even in secular modernity leads the quest for a potential form for Catholic mission only so far. The limits of Taylor's proposal are related to a sustained ambivalence toward objectivity apart from strong evaluation for Taylor. As we saw already with Taylor's account of modernity, even as he began to make room for the possibility of retrieving theism with his plea for faith's consideration at the end of *Sources of the Self*, the challenge for theologians and moral philosophers who find an ally in his work is that they are finally unsure just how desirous Taylor is to allow the full impact of the gospel to permeate and norm his work. Elshtain, MacIntyre, Kerr,

---

105. References to Jesus Christ, his crucifixion, incarnation, and resurrection, appear almost seventy times in *A Secular Age*.

and Marsden all noted that Taylor's work could use more critical distance from the modern project and, with varying degrees of explicit critique, noted that that resource was there in Taylor's theological commitment. At the end of *A Secular Age*, we find Taylor's commitment to pluralism both promising and compromising; the promise lies in an awareness of God, who is part of the history that Taylor very compellingly lays out from within time.

Thus, in my view Taylor offers a highly nuanced history of secularization in the West and so a better understanding of the depth of the challenge of mission in this age. Through his works on modernity and moral ontology, Taylor provides an insightful picture of the way in which modern selves go about their lives and understand themselves today, namely, with concern for plurality, historical accountability, qualified hope about religion, and cautious permission of space for religious existence in the public sphere through a narrative of authentic searching. All of these are helpful in some way for understanding what some would argue are essential attitudes in approaching the task of Catholic mission today.

Taylor's limits are that he does not seem to realize how his narrative can impinge on the very possibility he seeks to raise up at the end of his work on secularity. If the immanent frame is the functional imaginary for most in our culture, criticizing those who are tradition is not the way to keep an already fragilized tradition alive for future seekers. Rather, it may be that what the Church requires even more at this time is a clearer inner narrative from the norm of Jesus Christ (the former approach may be also based on a selective reading of Vatican II). But it is also true that speaking of Christ may not be the way to begin a discourse about religion in our pluralist age. Indeed, Taylor's vision of Church as a social and political thinker arises from social and political considerations and implications more than ecclesiological ones. Herein lies the tension and challenge around how to proclaim the gospel in a secular age.

Taylor's account shows a working out of a Catholic response to modernity that rightly emphasizes openness to the world, the dignity of all persons, and a desire to help the culture achieve its highest possibilities. But Taylor does not provide or show recognition of the need to articulate the other horizon, the drama of human existence in God, of sin and grace and the otherness of God's world to counter the story inscribed in the modern moral order. This is what Balthasar's account offers. Balthasar's horizon of theodrama allows "God's world to meet humanity's world." Indeed, the Church needs to show the world what to aim for, a different kind of freedom, *theosis*. Balthasar elaborates the meaning of this with much more profundity and clarity.

As Kerr has asserted in another notable essay on Taylor, Taylor simply does not say enough to dispel the theological misunderstandings of eschatology of his opponents.[106] One could surmise that this is because Taylor's method proceeds, at times, too much within the horizon of modernity, which he himself has shown frames us, perhaps even "holds us captive." Rather than modernity's own understandings of justice and truth, precisely what Taylor needs to show is the nonrelative character of the Church (though not to the exclusion of its relative character vis. a vis. God) and the relative nature of modernity's social imaginary. Moreover, the critique of a certain style of presentation (code) can detract from recognizing the value of the Church's clear and profound articulations of doctrines of "person" and "Incarnation." In various ways, a two-pronged critique of Taylor fuses into one: on the one hand, Taylor seems to neglect admitting the serious lostness of this age; on the other hand, Taylor's perspective suffers from an impoverished view of the Church.[107] Taylor's modernism can be seen in the way he suggests that breaking out of the frame, or "paradigm shift," is the key to new life. Balthasar will show that that is simply another "move" within the immanent frame—that revolution is another way of describing collectivism or individualism, but not the redemption of the world through the conversion of persons.

Taylor's overly modern approach is most problematic in the way it can hinder him from discussing the Church as something other than an institution. That is, a deeper understanding of who the Church is and how, in her character as official and organic, she helps launch new itineraries of faith is lacking in Taylor's account. His strong critique of the Church can be particularly costly in a secular age, which, I argue, calls for greater communion than ever. The problem is that it undercuts the organism (as Balthasar would say) that gives life to those who ultimately bring life (back) to the world through the Church in a new way (such as Peguy, Hopkins, St. Francis, Mother Teresa). For this, Taylor requires a more robust understanding of both God and Church, which, as a philosopher, it is understandable he does not provide. For these reasons, the

---

106. Kerr, "Charles Taylor's Moral Ontology of the Self."

107. *Acknowledging both need not lead to a stance of triumphalism.* But to show how this is the case, we need to attend to Balthasar's retrieval of the Church as spouse of the Word.

question of Catholic mission today requires recourse to the revelation-centered theology of Hans Urs von Balthasar.

Interestingly, Taylor alludes to Balthasar twice in his work on secularity: once in a neutral affirmation that a theological aesthetic in modernity is still possible,[108] *pace* Balthasar, and again to express sharp disagreement with Balthasar's ontologization of gender difference.[109] Taylor unfortunately does not recognize the richness of Balthasar's articulation of the Incarnation for our time as that which most closely aligns to what Taylor himself recognizes as a central spiritual loss in our age: "We struggle to recover a sense of what the Incarnation can mean."[110] As we have shared, Taylor's inability to acknowledge in the Church the possibility of providing precisely that meaning to the age is where his account falls short.[111] It is certainly for the Church to recognize that it is to her that the gift of receiving the mystery of the Incarnation has been given.[112] Balthasar makes revelation the starting point of his theology, especially the Incarnation, and so it is to his work that we now turn to understand how the Church may meet contemporary secular Western culture on its way to God.

---

108. *SA*, 359. "If we reach our highest goal through art and the aesthetic, then this goal, it would appear, must be immanent. It would represent an alternative to the love of Good as a way of transcending moralism. But things are not so simple. God is not excluded. Nothing has ruled out an understanding of beauty as reflecting God's work in creating and redeeming the world. A theological aesthetic in von Balthasar's terms is still an open possibility after Schiller."

109. Ibid., 767. "We have to recover a sense of the link between erotic desire and the love of God, which lies deep in the Biblical traditions, whether Jewish or Christian, and find new ways of giving expression to this. And since the contemporary sexual revolution . . . has made issues of sexual identity central, this rediscovery or re-articulation has to explore once more the question of gender identities, male and female, and how they figure in the God-human relation. There are two ways of evading or short-circuiting this exploration: one is to consider the differences of gender identity as trivial, or quite malleable, or freely determinable by individuals; and the other is to fix on one, supposedly eternal and unchangeable, definition of the difference, which for instance von Balthasar seems to have done."

110. Ibid., 753.

111. It is not to be dismissed that Taylor might minimize precisely what "answer" the Church can give because of his awareness of its resonance or lack thereof to those who live already closed to transcendence. Nonetheless, this constitutes a limitation rather than appropriate pastoral sensitivity to my mind.

112. Though this is a potentially contentious claim, this statement does not in any way deny that truth and goodness exist in other faiths and faith traditions. In other words, this is not a statement on religious pluralism.

Conclusion

In this chapter, I have drawn on Taylor's work on the genesis of contemporary secularity in the West to deepen the Church's understanding of the secular cultural context. Taylor's narrative of secularity reveals five insights that I think have significant implications for the way in which the Church undertakes her discourse regarding secularism. First is Taylor's description of secularity as a condition of belief. Understanding the degree to which secularity shapes the possibility for faith shows that it will not be adequate to criticize secularism as ideology.[113] Second is that secularity is a cultural norm that has been generated over five hundred years based on myriad transmutations in values and theologies such that it cannot simply be "rolled back." Moreover, Taylor notes that Christianity is complicit in the genesis of secularity. Additionally, the contemporary situation is such that faith and unbelief are both fragilized because of cross-pressures from other positions and recognition of the optionality of one's own. Finally, Taylor ends with an affirmation of the possibility of faith in a secular age, and that the present context is one in which many and various itineraries to the faith should be welcomed.

Subsequent to laying out Taylor's account of secularity and the facets of that narrative bearing the most significance for the question of how to witness in such a context, I have articulated the way in which Taylor's body of work outlines a path of dialogue with culture through ethics and through an appeal to the experience of fullness. Taylor's language, particularly his use of narrative and his proposal of faith as an "option," are examples, in fact, of one approach to evangelizing a culture such as secular Western modernity. I have acknowledged the manner in which Taylor's approach may take the Church quite far in the directions of hospitality and openness to plurality, but I have noted finally that Taylor's approach requires a theological supplement on the fronts of ecclesiology and anthropology.

A possible limitation in Taylor's account illuminating a possible path for mission in a secular age is his thin view of the Church. I have tried in my own critique to note the inherent tension of Taylor's criticism of the Church with his own proposal. That is, I have outlined a critique

---

113. Or, perhaps it may be better to suggest that the Church's first "profile" in encountering secular culture ought not to be condemnation of secularism, unless that criticism can also be expressed—in a way that can be heard—with a true affirmation of modern persons. This is what Taylor richly models.

that is internal to Taylor's project even as I have tried to use the latter as constructively as possible. The difficulty in Taylor's proposal of the possibility of faith in a secular age is that Taylor has given an account of the profound degree to which Western modernity's social imaginary is secular, and he has also noted the tremendous importance of horizons to identity. If this is the case, it would seem reasonable to think that Christian communities should have, as their primary task, holding open the horizon of transcendence, through their witness. Criticizing the teaching church can have the effect of short-circuiting the process whereby those individuals whose lives show a genuine conversion or re-conversion are possible to the extent that it contributes to undermining the real authority of the Church. The question and challenge that remains is how to mount a critique of ecclesial authority that is loving and fair that does not undermine the unity of the people of God, which is the first sign of a joyful and compelling witness of love.

Ultimately, this critique draws on and is continuous with critiques of a MacIntyrean nature on the relationship between tradition, virtue, and modernity. It also concurs with Kerr's critique of what philosophy can ultimately do. Long's question regarding the robustness of Taylor's theological tropes (especially that of "church") and Elshtain's critique of Taylor's overly optimistic view of modernity are also the reasons why I believe the Church needs to look to the theology of Balthasar, finally, for a clearer vision of Christian witness and mission in a secular age.

CHAPTER 3

Balthasar's Theological Anthropology: Authentic Personhood and the Eschatological Horizon of Freedom

What is needed, then, is an anthropology which is both up-to-date and Christian, that is to say, illuminated by the light of revelation. There exist elements in the natural sphere . . . which reveal their significance only when touched by supernatural light. . . . Hence, we ought to be transposing "meta-physics" into a "meta-anthropology," without, however, neglecting the meaning of "meta" in any way.

—BALTHASAR[1]

"For 'In Him we live and move and have our being.'"

—ACTS 17:28

Our hearts are restless until they rest in You.

—ST. AUGUSTINE

IN THIS CHAPTER I show that Balthasar's theodramatic account of human freedom and his understanding of personhood in Christ are more com-

---

1. *Test Everything*, 24–25.

plete articulations of what enables faith to be possible, even in a secular age, namely, grace. Balthasar points to the face of Christ, the face of the love of the Father, as the one reality that clarifies the true nature of freedom and personhood. The loss of ends can only be met, as Taylor proposes, by the sense that the true end of human life is communion, a sharing in the life of the Trinity. In contrast with Taylor, however, Balthasar specifies the centrality of knowing Christ as the condition for the possibility of experiencing true authenticity. My contention in this chapter is that this needs to be the first horizon of Christian self-understanding if a life of genuine conversion and witness is possible. Balthasar's vision of the human person and, we will later see, more particularly his vision of the Church show that the Church's horizon of freedom, that is, the freedom of salvation history, is the deeper truth about personhood to which Christians must witness so as to address the desires for authenticity and freedom, recovering ends and meaning, that modern selves experience. Balthasar's account of the relationship between personhood and mission, existence as a gift, and prayer as the way in which persons participate in the drama of God's self-giving love provide, then, a fruitful response to Taylor's diagnosis of modernity and secularity suggest. It is certainly the case that Christianity can only be proposed, but, once it has been proposed, it must be lived. Balthasar, it seems, would be less inclined to go with Taylor's model (if one may be surmised) of a discourse that shows understanding of all positions and then attempts to express the persuasiveness of one's own through a confession of inexpressible experiences of "fullness." For Balthasar, true recognition of plurality lies in a single-minded following of the path of love marked out by Jesus Christ and enabled at every moment by God's Spirit.

To reiterate, the task of this chapter is to illuminate how Balthasar's theological anthropology provides the necessary Christian understanding of personhood that can address the desires and malaises of modernity that Taylor has discerned in a way that Taylor's account cannot. In the first chapter, I focused on the modern self's search for authenticity, freedom, and struggle with moral malaise that Taylor so eloquently articulates. The second chapter explored how *A Secular Age* develops a new discourse around religion as an option for modern, secular selves. I showed how Taylor's narratival approach attends to the ideals and the ethos of modern selves in the West and shows, through rhetorical literary performance, how Christianity may be a unique source of fulfilled personhood in a secular age.

I showed, in chapter 2, how Taylor begins to point out the way in which the Christian vision is implicated in the development of secularity, and how the former may also be the best possible way to live in a secular age. I indicated how a Christian theological appropriation of Taylor's account of secularity might indicate that the Church needs to understand her role in the processes of secularization in the West, and how she cannot engage in a dialogue with Western culture today without realizing the radical dissimilarity between the fundamental background understanding of the culture and that of the Church. Finally, I highlighted that Taylor's claim that "lives of conversion reveal the possibility of faith in a secular age" is deeply significant for the question of how to understand Catholic witness and mission in today's Western societies. Taylor clarifies that the life of which he speaks is the life of those who have shown a real conversion, the lives of the saints, whose orientation fully bespeaks love, and not "code morality." I ended the chapter with an affirmation of Taylor's intuition regarding exemplary lives of *agape*, but also with a critique that Taylor's own account of the sedimentation of secular humanism in cultural imagination together with his explicit critique of the Church does not get us to the desired end. Rather, given Taylor's past work regarding horizons and identity formation, it seems that one of Taylor's questions might have been, "What are the shared horizons today that generate 'a saint'?" My claim is that his discussion of conversions requires the strength of a theological anthropology rooted in Christology if it is not to remain within the immanent frame of modernity that he so critiques.

I thus turn to Balthasar's theological account of personhood to show how there are further resources in Balthasar for understanding the potential shape of effective Catholic witness in a contemporary secular age. Whereas Taylor underscores the challenge of certain existential problems, of purposelessness, meaninglessness, and atomism in light of an increasingly flattened horizon of social and individual existence, Taylor only gestures, I argue, toward the possibility of fullness of life through the option of religious belief. As much as Taylor moves the conversation forward in moral and cultural philosophy so as to generate a clearer vision of the present and future of religious faith in contemporary Western societies, Taylor's account is troubled by an inability to be clearer about how modernity's need for an alternative horizon of transcendence can only be achieved through a community that witnesses to such a horizon.

Balthasar traces out a theological understanding of personhood that firmly underlines the possibility and *necessity* of finding one's personhood in Christ for fullness of life in time. The aim of this chapter is to show, then, that while Taylor takes us a certain distance toward understanding the modern subject in terms of her poverty, the "seeking" of modern selves can only be met, finally, by receptivity to the gift that comes from God. Balthasar's answer to modern malaise is to live life conceived as *theo-drama*, that is, life lived as a response to God's beauty, through which we find our true freedom. I will consider how Balthasar portrays authentic personhood in the biblical terms of an encounter with Christ and, in particular, how the personal-ecclesial relationship enables true authenticity.

Balthasar's treatment of human freedom and personal fulfillment will be presented as one crucial way in which Catholicism in a post-Vatican II era may renew its understanding of mission. While there are other proposals in modern Catholic theology that have sought precisely to renew the cogency of revelation to the modern human subject, whether through transcendental method parsed through an existential theological anthropology (Rahner) or cognitional theory (Lonergan), Balthasar's proposal is unique[2] in that he does not seek to translate revelation into the idioms of modern subjectivity but begins with the revelation of the triune God in Jesus Christ. It is precisely Balthasar's approach of elaborating with glorious vividness the drama of divine and human love that is needed to not only supplement but to transvalue the modernistic overlay of Catholic sensibility. This is a renewal from within that enables the Church to move in the direction that, according to Taylor, is most deeply sought "from below."

As with all of Balthasar's work, the fragment is in the whole. Each piece is continuous with the larger aims of his project. His account of personhood is no different. In his essay "On the Concept of Person,"[3] Balthasar clarifies again the way in which the retrieval of Christ is crucial for the ends of Vatican II to be realized, namely, modern persons' genuine encounter with a Church that radiates a spirit of love. He is clear that his anthropology is inextricably bound with a mission Christology:

---

2. Cf. Edward Oakes' extraordinary overview of Balthasar's unique theological approach in Oakes, *Pattern of Redemption: The Theology of Hans Urs von Balthasar*.

3. Balthasar, "On the Concept of Person," 18–26.

> What de Rougement calls "vocation" I have named "mission" in my definition of the person in the truly Christological context. "As the Father has sent me, so I send you," Christ says. Here we can presuppose, with St. Thomas, that in a Trinitarian sense *missio* is the economic form of the eternal *processio* that constitutes the persons of the Son and of the Spirit in God. Participation in the mission of Christ (or that which in the building up of the church Paul calls "charisma" and which is given to each as his eternal idea with God and his social task)—that would be the actual core of the reality of the person.[4]

The essay shows what is gained in retrieving the "unique theological meaning of personhood" by tracing the concept through its history. Balthasar acknowledges that there is a general understanding of personhood, which he distinguishes from mere individuality, but that this general sense of personhood, as signifying the uniqueness, incomparability, and irreplaceability of an individual, can slide into mere individuality—the identity of human nature, which includes dignity as a spiritual subject, but not more—without the Trinitarian and christological doctrines. Recounting the history of the concept of person from its earliest roots in ancient Greek and Roman understandings through its various significant medieval and modern transpositions, Balthasar highlights how Trinitarian doctrine brought about the development in the concept of personhood of relationality:

> With the transfer effected at Chalcedon (431), the concept's philosophical determination as noted above makes itself felt for the first time in Christology. In establishing that in Christ two natures, the divine and the human, are united in one (divine) person, has one paid sufficient attention to the fact that this divine person can, as such, exist only in a (trinitarian) relation, for otherwise we would end up with a doctrine of three gods?[5]

The next step came, ironically, through modern atheism, and it was the recovery of the I-thou relationship through Feuerbach and then Jewish and Christian personalism. Balthasar asserts, however, that forgetting the biblical, Christian view within these philosophies will only ever lead to "personless collectivism or individualism" and, indeed, "the world situation today shows [this] clearly enough."[6]

4. Ibid., 25.
5. Ibid., 21–22.
6. Ibid., 25.

Balthasar's Attunement to the Secularity of Western Culture

In many ways, Balthasar's "answer" consists in a gestalt that is markedly different from Taylor's, primarily because he begins his engagement of history from the reality of Christ, while Taylor reads history, at least putatively, from the purview of modern man. This chapter aims to show that Balthasar's account of God's action as dramatically involved in the genesis of free, authentic persons allows the gospel's perennial message to speak to the world, as clarified by Taylor's account of modern secular existence. Balthasar's theological vision "breaks in" to the seemingly closed frame of exclusive immanence and undoes the latter's inner logic even as it attends to the key questions for secular humanists: freedom, beneficence, and authenticity. This chapter attends to how Balthasar's christological and Trinitarian approach furnishes an account of the form of human existence that most deeply engages the questions of modern secular identity in the West and offers a salvific intellectual and existential possibility for modern selves. It does so by first highlighting the fundamentally divine and divinely given foundation of human freedom.

We may glean that such is Balthasar's approach to Western modernity from his appreciative work of interpretation on the corpus of German poet and novelist Reinhold Schneider. In *Tragedy Under Grace: Reinhold Schneider on the Experience of the West*, Balthasar receives the insight from Schneider's work that Christian history in the West can be read finally only through the refracted light of the Cross, and that light indeed casts a shadow on Christian existence, such that it may be said that in the world, Christian existence is indeed tragic. Quoting from Schneider's *Das Heilige in der Geschichte* (*The Sacred in History*), in words that could be Balthasar's own,

> The Christian stands in a thoroughly dramatic, indeed, tragic relationship to the world: he must represent in the world something that is not of the world. The truth into which the life of the Christian is to enter has been crucified: it cuts across the course of the world and man, and yet it addresses the course of the world and man, and these are related to it; the Christian has experienced, and will continually experience, that to the extent he genuinely tries to do the truth, and the truth acts through him, he will become a tragic person; the truth that is life in eternity can take on the form of death in time. The same is true of the historical image of the Christian, in whom those values are

the highest that count for the least in the world or are hated by it. Thus it is not correct to say that Christianity has abolished tragedy through the proclamation of grace. Nevertheless, this Christian (and perhaps intensified) tragedy is not an inextricable contradiction. In the death on the Cross lies the victory, the explosion of the contradiction. This is no natural law but the miracle of grace. And the world stands upon the miracle of the Cross and the Resurrection. The tragic net has been opened. "This drama, which is concerned with the salvation of man's soul, is no tragedy but rather a mystery play."

It is tragic because the world does not recognize the nobility of spirit that is characteristic of the Christian heart. Indeed, this is the linchpin of Schneider's insight into Europe's modern history. What he displays according to Balthasar in his works on Portugal, Spain, England, and Rouen is attention to the way in which, at one point, there was truth in the phrase "the divine right of kings." This right or righteousness, rather, of the holder of political power in the world originated from a sense in particular kings that their life was, at its heart, a life of service. This total embrace of the form of service—which Schneider highlights in, for example, the life of King Philip II of Spain—is that which fully echoes the descent and total self-gift of the Son to man. The other portraits of Europe's climbs and falls are all iterations of this same theme: of how modern man images the kenotic Godhead in the use of power. The glory of Rouen is such because it reveals the fullness of total love that reveals, too, the depth of divine suffering for the sake of love of humanity. The guilt of England lies in its struggle and failure at various points to remain true to the noble spirit of kingship. The renunciation of Rome is seen in the unwillingness of some popes to allow the holy Church to manifest itself in the office of the Church, which, Balthasar believes, has less to do with individuals but more their susceptibility to the real demonic power that forms the other pole of the spiritual warfare that pervades the drama of history. In speaking of the tragedy of Pope Celestine, the contemplative monk who had to flee the office to save his soul, Balthasar puts it bluntly:

> It is not the fault of the saint that the Church of the office and the Church of the saints diverge so terribly.

In this chapter, I begin to draw out how Balthasar may enter into conversation with Taylor on the topics of modernity and modern selfhood as there is little, if any, material charting their potential engagement.

The first sections of this chapter function as a kind of transition to establish Balthasar's own consciousness of secularity and its implications for human fulfillment. Looking at Balthasar's approach to modernity,[7] I show that, like Taylor, Balthasar recognizes both the need for change in the Church as well as the need to recover an approach to mission that emphasizes proclamation through one's life in Christ (proclamation of the *theodrama*) rather than argument, and engages modern selves' questions concerning personal freedom and authenticity. This will be followed by an elaboration of a key modern category, *freedom*, which Balthasar transforms and illuminates through his theodramatic approach to Christian doctrine. For Balthasar, human freedom cannot be conceived apart from divine freedom; the fullness of personhood requires engagement with God, who alone confers mission, the embracing of which constitutes the beginning of authentic existence. In the final section of this chapter, I consider the implications of Balthasar's refigured notion of human and divine freedom for personhood and ethics, which moves us toward a deepening of the question of Christian witness and mission in a secular age.

We begin by drawing out the connection of a shared recognition of secularity and its implications for Christian believers by both Taylor and Balthasar. Our focus on their convergence arises from exposing Balthasar's own clear awareness of secularity in modern culture and in modern philosophy. Like Taylor, he recognizes the Christian roots of secularity: "So Christianity today, borne along by the secular impulse *to which it itself largely gave rise*, has to live out in an exemplary way that fundamental dynamism which sets out to embrace the future that is in store for the world."[8] Notably, he also describes the future in hopeful and affectionate terms.

Much of what Taylor has articulated about the Church in its engagement with the modern world can be found in the work of Balthasar. For example, Balthasar agrees that modernity has been, in some sense, a great boon and purifier of the Church in her own sense of mission: "Without doubt, the unifying movement of the modern world was the occasion

---

7. With reference to *The Moment of Christian Witness, Razing the Bastions, Love Alone: The Way of Revelation, Engagement with God,* and "The Fathers, the Scholastics, and Ourselves."

8. "Trends of Modern Theology: 'Futurism,'" in *TD* I, 41.

for the theological breakthrough and for this (re-)discovery of the true essence of the Church."[9]

Awareness of Secularity and Its Implications for Human Fulfillment

My treatment of Balthasar will be guided by my appropriation of Taylor's account of secularity and his treatment of the spiritual longings and challenges of Christians in a secular age. Taylor's assessment is that the development of the modern moral order leaves persons with a loss of meaning, a persistent sense of an existential lack, which Taylor describes in terms of "fullness." Taylor notes the important step of providential deism in the genesis of the modern moral order, through which God becomes remote—the one who is responsible for bringing the created order into being but who then retreats and allows the world to run according to its own natural laws. Taylor also describes the experience in which time and the whole of reality with it becomes increasingly flattened; this, too, contributes to a seeming diminishment in depth and a sense of ends. A secular culture is left with an ongoing residual sense of fragilization both in the options of belief and unbelief. Yet it might be helpful to realize simply that new itineraries to the faith exist and are necessary in contemporary Western culture. Balthasar, who has given equally serious reflection to the question of Christian witness in a secular age, provides an approach to secularity that is more distinctly theological. His theology proceeds methodologically from contemplation, is refracted through the revelation of Christ, and is rooted explicitly in Trinitarian understandings of reality.

Balthasar's theology of human freedom, time, personhood, and the Church aid the Church in her engagement with culture insofar as it provides an objective pole[10] and counterpoint to the ongoing problems of subjectivism, atomism, and instrumentalism in contemporary Western culture. It is Christianity's understanding of these foundational dimensions of human existence that the Church offers the modern world. If

9. "The Council of the Holy Spirit," in *ET* III, 247.

10. See Schindler, "The Significance of Hans Urs von Balthasar in the Contemporary Cultural Situation" and Potworowski, "An Exploration of the Notion of Objectivity in Hans Urs von Balthasar." See also Schindler, *Heart of the World, Center of the Church*; Schindler, *Ordering Love*; Healy and D. C. Schindler, *Being Holy in the World*; and D. C. Schindler, *Hans Urs von Balthasar and the Dramatic Structure of Truth*.

Taylor helps pave the way for fresh consideration of the possibility of a revitalizing faith in our time, and believes that the cultural tendencies toward subjectivism, naturalism, and exclusive humanism are not entirely hopeless, Balthasar's theological vision expounds the possibility of *how* a secular age might be transformed, by Christians, from within. The latter transformation would occur through recognition that the situation of subjectivism, individualism, instrumental rationality and alienation in the world is related to a fundamental *denial of the reality of the triune God*[11] and the ability to perceive that God's incarnation and redemption alone breaks open the horizon of closed immanence. The full meaning of life and truth can be found, ultimately, only in the love that shines forth from the revelation of God in Jesus Christ. Indeed, Balthasar shows the limits of finding truth elsewhere—in the cosmos, or in the human subject, anthropos.[12] Simply put, this chapter will demonstrate Balthasar's understanding and transformation of the subjective turn of modernity. The metaphysical underpinning of Balthasar's account of human authenticity is the doctrine of the analogy of being, which grounds Balthasar's claim that humans may participate in divine life.[13] Indeed, Balthasar's sense of objectivity thoroughly accounts for the truth of subjectivity, without leading to the perilous path of thoroughgoing subjectivism. What Balthasar helps to show is that the objectivity of human subjectivity, in a word,

---

11. "The claim, then, is that our cultural crisis turns on the reality of God in our lives. . . . For Balthasar, therefore, the crisis of the present time likewise concerns the absence of God in the dominant patterns of our cultural life and thought. For Balthasar, the death of God in the cosmos leads, logically and over time, to the death of love and beauty in the cosmos. There is a mutually causal relation between the two events—the absence of God and the absence of love and beauty—even though, within this mutual causal relation, the absence of God has an absolute (ontological) priority." Schindler, "Significance of Hans Urs von Balthasar," 19; first published as "Modernity, Postmodernity, and the Problem of Atheism," 563–79.

12. *Love Alone: The Way of Revelation* outlines this succinctly, and this claim is worked out over the course of Balthasar's trilogy, *A Theological Anthropology*, and elsewhere.

13. Moreover, this analogy of being is *concrete*: "The divine Son who becomes man is 'the concrete *analogia entis*' . . . It is only because the Son in very truth possesses the 'form of God,' and hence the divine pole of the *analogia entis*, that he can 'empty himself' and take 'the form of a servant.' The creature cannot do this, for it always comes into being *in* this state. Here we can see, incidentally, that when Marx and Nietzsche dream of a true, positive humanity as the self-positing of freedom, their dream-like illusion carries them outside the real *analogia entis* in which the Son's infinite freedom is realized solely in the Eucharistic movement back and forth from and to the Father" (*TD* II, 267–68).

personhood, is found in Christ's action, and that the Kantian problem of the diremption between subject and object is not the final word.[14]

Awareness of "Post-christian Man"

Consider Balthasar's query regarding "post-Christian" man:

> What then if man, no longer accustomed to taking his standard from the cosmos (now emptied of the divine), refuses to take it from Christ? This is post-Christian man, who cannot return to the pre-Christian fluidity that once existed between man and the cosmos but who, in passing through Christianity, has grown used to the heightening of his creaturely rhythms and wants to hold on to them as if they are his personal hallmark, a gift that now belongs to him entirely. This will be the general characteristic of the post-Christian era, however manifold and contradictory its concrete expressions may be.[15]

There is something reminiscent in Balthasar's observation of Taylor's account of the transitional process in modernity that Taylor, following others (notably Weber), terms the disenchantment of the world. "Post-Christian man, who cannot return to the pre-Christian fluidity that once existed between man and the cosmos" sounds very much like Taylor's account of the "buffered self" who has lost his relation of "porousness" to the world enchanted by spirits of the medieval worldview. Similar, too, is Balthasar's remark on such a man's tendency to have "grown used to the heightening of his creaturely rhythms and wants to hold on to them as if they are his personal hallmark, a gift that now belongs to him entirely." This echoes Taylor's critique of the ethos of exclusive humanism that colors modern consciousness. In short, a shared awareness between Taylor and Balthasar exists regarding the profound transformation of the relationship between man, cosmos, and their creator and the loss incurred with the rise of exclusive humanism.[16]

14. One needs to consider of course the important epistemological work of Bernard Lonergan in association with this issue, but we would like to maintain that Balthasar's work is as important in this respect, and perhaps even more so, in that Balthasar's theology operates at the aesthetic/affective level in a profound manner, such that it retrieves the Christological centre of theological reflection: "Were our *hearts* not burning when he spoke to us?"

15. "Man Without Measure ('Post-Christian')," in *TD* II, 417.

16. Louis Dupre's *Passage to Modernity* also underscores the challenge of ontological fragmentation.

Subjectivity, the Immanent Frame, and an Alternative—*Theodrama*

Recognizing the problem with the subjectivization of the world and all of human experience, Balthasar also perceives the loss of the framework of drama, which is "a shared spiritual horizon."[17] Insofar as Balthasar believes that drama still has the capacity to awaken persons to truth, however, he aims to create precisely such a drama. His voice is thus particularly cogent for the shifting conditions of faith that Taylor terms "secularity." Such conditions of change call for a re-establishment of a shared spiritual horizon and the coherence of a narrative by which to structure existence.

Balthasar understands all too well the condition of postmodernity and the fragmentation that colors modern Western consciousness, such that even the potentially healing capacity of a dramatic enactment of the beautiful, the good, and the true may seem impossible. That is, the condition for the possibility of drama, a shared spiritual horizon and faith, seems no longer to exist. Yet Balthasar believes that there is enough of "an openness" in the horizon of certain human dramatists (he cites Brecht and Wilder, for example), such that it is still possible (in theater) to express "Christian dramatic tension."[18]

Balthasar notes that even in Brecht's and Wilder's use of subversive methods of throwing ordinariness into relief—that is, in their "use of 'alienation effects' and desacrali[zation of] theatre, [their works] manifest theatre's intrinsic function, namely, to be a place where man can look in a mirror in order to recollect himself and remember who he is"[19]—there remains promise for the dramatic form to reveal the salvific nature of Christ's person and mission anew. While Balthasar acknowledges theater's ambiguity, he believes in it still, arguing that "existence has a need to see itself mirrored, and this makes the theatre a legitimate instru-

---

17. "What [also] dramatists of classicism (since Lessing) and romanticism (like Shelley) had wanted: instead of a court theatre they wanted a national theatre, educating the people toward an ethical consciousness (Schiller). This is no longer a serious proposition today, however, when we have come to think in terms of 'one planet.' This loss of an audience united in faith and *Weltanschauung* corresponds—we are deliberately avoiding the terminology of 'cause and effect'—to the more or less evident disappearance from the stage of that spiritual horizon which, for Hegel, was still the precondition for a meaningful play, whether it was tragic, comic or simply dramatic" (*TD* I, 71).

18. Ibid., 86.

19. Ibid.

ment in the pursuit of self-knowledge and the elucidation of Being—an instrument, moreover, that points beyond itself. As a mirror it enables existence to attain ultimate (theological) understanding of itself; but also, like a mirror, it must eventually take second place to make room for the truth, which it reflects only indirectly."[20]

Awareness of the Church's Complicity with Secularism

In *Bernanos*,[21] Balthasar notes with the author the Church's complicity in her own demise in the eyes of the world, her own lack of conviction, her own lack of a sense of the mystery at the heart of Christianity. He follows Bernanos where Bernanos takes the part of "the world," asking the Church what she has done with the sublime mystery with which Christ has entrusted her. Bernanos, not dissimilar to Nietzsche in this regard, points out the cowardice and weakness, the "hidden faithlessness" that has been the chief source of the decay of Christianity. Balthasar completes Bernanos' thought that where Christians have failed is in their own lack of faith in being able to restore the order of Christian faith and their incapacity to assent to the "sacrifices necessary for such a restoration." That loss of an attunement to the mystery at the heart of Christian faith reduces the faith to

> a ready-made, self-contained and self-evident affair, which is therefore devoid of any mystery, existing "alongside" the world as a "perfect society" parallel to the other, imperfect one—in the end, Christianity as one idea among many other ideas, no longer the leaven and the grain of wheat, the active principle that, in order to have its effect, must enter the world, die there, and dissolve within it, so that, once it again bursts through to new birth like an ear of corn, it will be both things beyond distinction: the field of the world but transformed into the power of the Word.[22]

Balthasar prefaces his reference to Bernanos' insight into the Church's responsibility for the world with another reference to Bernanos' observation that the Church is not only a failure at living out the mystery with which she has been entrusted, but that she also lacks awareness of the world's perception of her: "Pious persons doubtless have a lot of things to

---

20. Ibid., 86–87.
21. Balthasar, *Bernanos: An Ecclesial Existence*.
22. Ibid., 252.

say to unbelievers, but often they could also have a lot of things to learn from these unhappy brothers, and they risk never knowing what those things are because they never stop talking."[23]

Balthasar possesses an attunement, like Taylor, to the peculiar struggle of the modern self; he thus offers a theology that addresses the modern malaises of a loss of ends, meaning, and embodied community. He provides an articulation of revelation that engages the challenge of having a firm sense of identity, the shape and texture of true personal freedom, and to what goal one's personhood should aim. It is arguable that his theology, portrayed in terms of drama and starting with the experience of being moved by beauty, is precisely for this age, with its emphasis on experience, action, and authenticity. Balthasar is as aware as Taylor is of the shifts in the horizon that have arisen with modernity and that, as Taylor has compellingly argued, have brought about the malaise of instrumentalism, a loss of a sense of the chief ends of life, and an erosion of an habitual way of thinking toward such ends as one proceeds to action. He goes beyond diagnosis, however, to invite attention and then participation in the beauty that is Christ's unique glory.

Balthasar's theodrama is a key for our culture, then, to the Church and the world at this time because it recalls us to a lost context within our very situation. As in the famous Heidegger quotation of Hölderlin, "Where the danger lies, there grows the saving power,"[24] so too Balthasar's "solution" to the problems of modernity take place within the experience of modernity's "post-Christian" fractured horizons. Balthasar shows the depth of the problem of framing time, personhood, freedom, and holiness, without God. It may be said that Balthasar reinscribes modernity with a Christian horizon that offers once again the possibility of God through locating *the loss of God* at the very foundations of human self-consciousness. In recognizing the shift in consciousness, he responds to the age of heightened attention to the aesthetic dimension of life and to experience with an account of Christian life that highlights the beauty of theodramatic existence. Balthasar's signal contribution with *theodrama* is his ability to articulate the central theological doctrines of the Christian faith through a form that underscores the movement and dynamism of

---

23. Ibid., 251. It should be noted, for example, that the Church needs to attend particularly to the justifiable moral offense and horror of those who have left the Church on account of the scandal of sexual abuse by clergy that has been uncovered in recent years.

24. Heidegger, *Question Concerning Technology*, xxxv.

Christian life.²⁵ We thus attend to Balthasar's retrieval of personhood, time, freedom, ethics and the Church in light of this awareness. Balthasar's articulations of personhood, time, freedom, and ethics are a direct consequence of a keen understanding of the reality of contemporary secularity and, ultimately, directly illuminate the mission of the Church.

Theology is "faith seeking understanding." Balthasar's faith, we might say, seeks to understand and to "perform" how we might "redeem the time" of a secular age. That is, his portrayal of Christian life as a *theodrama* is crucially aware of the secularization of Western culture and aims to reconnect time and eternity through a drama that draws persons into intimacy with Christ. His answer is, at core, "Only in Christ, only in Christ's Spirit, in the Church, can the world be saved." *Theo-Drama* has often been considered the "ethical" piece of his theological trilogy,²⁶ and indeed, it aims to clarify the transcendental of the Good in the way that the theo-aesthetics sought to elucidate Beauty and the theologic, Truth, respectively. The *theodrama* shall frame our discussion of Balthasar's contribution to a deeper sense of human freedom, time, and personhood, in such a way that it speaks to the current questions of contemporary culture, and in particular, those malaises and challenges that Taylor has outlined in *Sources of the Self, Modern Social Imaginaries*, and *A Secular Age*.

Human Freedom in Balthasar

Attuned to the modern search for freedom, Balthasar retrieves the centrality of Christ and the doctrine of salvation. That is, his theodrama can be understood as a direct response to the deism that Taylor describes. Emphasizing the asymmetrical relationship between infinite and finite freedom, the kenosis of Christ, and how infinite freedom is the ground of all finite freedom, Balthasar invites selves into awareness of the participation

---

25. Cf. Healy, *Church, World and the Christian Life*, and Wells, *Improvisation: The Drama of Christian Ethics*.

26. Works focusing on the ethical dimension at play in Balthasar's theodrama include Samuel Wells' *Improvisation: The Drama of Christian Ethics*, Christopher Steck's *The Ethical Thought of Hans Urs von Balthasar*, and Melanie Barrett's *Love's Beauty at the Heart of the Christian Moral Life: The Ethics of Catholic Theologian Hans Urs von Balthasar*. For an excellent defense of the existence of a social ethic and political theology in Balthasar, see Casarella, "On Frederick Bauerschmidt's 'Theo-Drama and Political Theology,'" 553–57.

in God's drama that God offers. While discussion of Balthasar's aesthetics would lead quickly beyond the purview of this work, it is notable that Balthasar's theological aesthetics underscores that engagement with the Christian God begins with an experience of the beauty of God that is manifest in his act of total self-giving love, Jesus Christ.

Importantly, Balthasar is aware of the false foundations of human freedom that attempt to locate its ground in isolation from God and as competitive with God. He names deism and idolatry as the results of such problematic understandings of God and man.[27] The parallels with Taylor's critical account of secularity as being bound up with the rise of exclusive humanism are evident here. Balthasar's account of human freedom thus grounds all freedom in Christ. Balthasar outlines a theological program that begins with a sense of God as one who conducts a lawsuit, is moved from wrath to the sacrifice of his only Son, his own self, such that the very depths and abysses of creation are redeemed through his own presence therein, and finally a new judgment that wills to save the world.[28] The love that overcomes the pain of rejection to love infinitely through total self-gift is the difference Christ makes to freedom. The Incarnation must be confronted, as it is the basic confrontation that every person experiences at the root of his or her existence, Balthasar avers. Beginning with the objective reality of Christ leads Balthasar to note that one may reject the reality of the divine invitation to fullness of life, but one cannot deny it.[29]

One of the problems in modernity is, however, the temptation to do precisely that. Just as Taylor has shown in his analyses of Western modernity, *The Moment of Christian Witness* highlights Balthasar's awareness of what has transpired in Western thought regarding metaphysics. Balthasar recognizes that a key distinction has been set aside and a new system of thought erected based on a fundamentally different platform. The overlooked distinction is that between existence and essence, and the map of being has been reworked such that only the horizontal axis between matter and form remains under consideration.[30]

From the question of creator/creation, and the corollary reflection on why it may be said that we exist in the best possible world, as Leibniz predicated, "today" we begin with the belief that we have only this

---

27. Balthasar, *TD* II, 313.
28. Balthasar, *TD* I.
29. Balthasar, *TD* II.
30. *MCW*, 68.

world for human destiny; the new options of what becomes of humanity ultimately in this frame of the human situation is either Hegelianism or Marxism. Balthasar notes that both fail to accurately account for the human situation: "For Hegel has sacrificed him as an individual to the idea in its realized state, and Marx has continually sacrificed him to an idea that has to be realized." Balthasar contends that to abide by the system that modern philosophy has erected in place of Christianity involves the acceptance of a paradox, of both Hegel's already and Marx's not yet, which is a contradiction "because there can be no question of immortality or resurrection."[31] Moreover, Hegelianism ultimately involves a sacrifice of man the individual for humanity that amounts to a "kind of altruism, demanding an absolute love for the All (God as a realized idea) as for any fellow creature, and a willingness on the part of the individual to blot himself out and perish in the interests of the fellow creature who represents this idea." In short, the problem with Hegelian philosophy is that it reduces and belies the truth of man's destiny, by claiming that man as an individual must now only hope to fulfill his existence through this idea of totality.[32]

This is Balthasar's recognition of the implications of modern system philosophy. Like Taylor, he has an analysis of how this situation came to be. As a theologian, however, Balthasar also discerns the theological transmutation in Christology that plays a role in the development of secularization. Without going into atheism as a way of thinking and being,

> It will be necessary to discuss in more detail the "anthropologizing" of Christology, because it deserves special attention as the piece de resistance of the whole process. It provides the bridge between the most authentic Christian thought of the New Testament and atheism, which passes over the bridge without being aware of it, having a share in the central truth of Christianity. It is here that the vital, moving contact point has long existed between the so-called Christian orthodoxy and all the liberal forms of Christianity.[33]

While Taylor conducts his analysis of secularity by combining his knowledge of the history of Western thought with the depths of sociological and historical detail on the ground, however, Balthasar presents a description

31. Ibid. 70.
32. Ibid.
33. Ibid., 86.

in broad strokes of the kinds of metaphysical and theological shifts that have led to the predicament of many modern Christians today. His description restricts itself to the new transpositions that have occurred in the philosophy of the modern era; it begins with an analysis of what happens with Kant. The relationship between the limitation of reason and the absolute or infinite character of freedom has changed because Kant highlights the importance of the self-criticism of such finite reason, an importance that becomes foundational to all knowing, and becomes the foundation for many variations (including Schelling and Sartre) of a thesis which generally claims that "essence becomes the function of existence freely outlining itself."[34]

Then there is the thesis that freedom is found only speculatively as an intra-subjective phenomenon, and since it is found in the dialogical realm, this realm must be extended without condition. Balthasar ascribes this sensibility to Marx, as well as to Fichte and to Feuerbach. He writes, "Every creature who has a share in the uniquely precious essence of autonomy and emerges from nature into the realm of freedom belongs, as an inhabitant of this dialogical spirit-world, to the realm of the absolute and has a claim to the protection afforded by the rights of man. This is the ethic of humanism."[35]

In addition, modern shifts in thought lead to the purpose of nature being reduced to that of a standing reserve for the development and flourishing of man: "Because man is seen as the center and aim of this process, nature itself loses its aura of a mediating agency for the divine purpose and is reduced to being a 'worldly world.'"[36] And so man stands self-sufficient in his freedom, apart from God:

> But the freedom of man (dialogically interpreted as love) is self-creating and requires no aid outside itself. With this explanation all proofs of God's existence—cosmological or otherwise—are found to be invalid and removed from even the "contingent" position to which they had already been relegated.[37]

Balthasar makes the assessment that "ever since Descartes, Bacon and Hobbes, all philosophical thought has been an attempt at some kind of control."[38] The system is closed and is becoming increasingly

---

34. Ibid., 63.
35. Ibid., 64.
36. Ibid., 65.
37. Ibid., 66.
38. Ibid., 67.

self-contained.[39] In the face of the system, Balthasar proposes three points to consider, prefaced by two pieces of counsel for the Christian. The first word of counsel is discernment. Balthasar refers to the traditional exhortation "Examine it thoroughly and retain what is good in it."[40] The second is recognition that we cannot go back: the philosophies of Hegel and Marx have had their effect and, indeed, *a new kind of human being has emerged in the process*[41] who cannot think of himself apart from his ability to function with complete autonomy and self-legislation. We have changed in light of the modern philosophies that have taken root; Balthasar's awareness of modernity, like Taylor's in this regard, does not require a shift in the mandate of Christianity to become something other than it is, something other than faith in the love of God for humanity and the call to respond to this love as transformative and indeed redemptive for the world. Thus, Balthasar ultimately contends that one cannot forsake the challenge of *Ernstfall* to follow Christ's example for the sake of an *aggiornamento*.

This work shows the clear and striking parallels between Balthasar's analysis of the gestalt of modernity, with its shifts toward the subject and tendency toward control, and that of Taylor. Balthasar underscores the increasingly closed character of the system, our intellectual frame of reference, which is remarkably similar to Taylor's conception of the immanent frame of the secular age of today. Importantly, Balthasar also notes with Taylor that "going back" to a previous age philosophically and culturally is not an option. Like Taylor, Balthasar reads history, though in this case theological history, with appreciation: "The course of the history of theology from the Fathers to the Scholastics to the Moderns very well might represent the progressive waning of mental and synthetic powers. But that would in no way affect our point, that the sequence of the formal laws of these periods has brought what is distinctively Christian to more and more clarity."[42]

---

39. Ibid., 70.

40. Ibid., 71.

41. "The epoch-making changes in thought brought about by Hegel and Marx have had their effect, and they cannot be reversed. By detaching philosophy from its speculative beginnings, these changes have produced their own type of human being and molded him in such a way that he has accepted the idea of intellectually controlling his own destiny, as if it were second nature to him, and has adjusted himself without a murmur to the paradoxical ethic described above." Ibid.

42. "Fathers, Scholastics, and Ourselves," 385–86.

Balthasar underscores that a true freedom entails the aid of God.[43] Indeed, Balthasar, as much as Taylor, shows a keen awareness of the importance of freedom as a theme and concept of modernity:

> In modern times, human freedom is a theme which preoccupies both Christian and non-Christian, and there is a kind of competition as to who can understand this freedom more profoundly, who more effectively put it into practice. Atheism is wholly preoccupied with this theme: the freeing of reason from the fetters of faith (the Enlightenment); the freeing of the economically enslaved humanity from the nightmare of a concept, namely God, which is no longer believed and which has been dragged like a corpse through world history (Nietzsche). Everywhere at the very portals of freedom the human being seems to be chained to some past, to a traditional custom, to a moment in history made absolute, or to some forbidden totem in the realm of nature or culture. And yet human beings only become truly human when they have chosen and actuated themselves in freedom; when the "nature" in them has been totally and freely appropriated and responsibly worked through. So long as Christianity appears to be principally a matter of traditions and institutions, the emancipatory movements of modernity will have an easy time of it.[44]

At some level, the cultural issue that manifests itself in a secular social imaginary, and a picture of persons as buffered selves ultimately striving to do good together because of a fundamental sense of mutual benefit through such a program, is underwritten by a certain metaphysics and, too, a particular anthropology. Balthasar notes that the problem of positivism is ultimately traceable to "blindness to the primal value of being"—that is, loss of recognition of the giftedness at the foundation of one's experience of reality and, in theology, loss of a sense of oneself as addressed by God.[45]

---

43. Ibid., 386.

44. Ibid., 308; Balthasar, *Engagement with God*, 6.

45. "We have to feel our way back; we have to overcome a certain blindness to the primal value of being. This sick blindness is called Positivism, and it arises from regarding reality as raising no questions, being 'just there'—for the phrase 'the given' already says too much, since there is no one who 'gives.' In fact, the only question that arises is: 'What can we do with this material?' When men are blind to the further question, it signifies the death of philosophy and even more the death of theology. For philosophy begins with the astonished realization that I am this particular individual in being and goes on to see all other existent entities together with me in being; that is, it begins with the sense of wonder that, astonishingly, I am 'gifted,' the recipient of

While Taylor alludes to the problems of positivism and behaviorism, and gestures to faith to support the sense that there must be "something more," his account does not provide the explanatory power that Balthasar's theological account of human freedom and authentic personhood provides. Balthasar begins by resituating the question of human (finite) freedom within the drama of salvation. He shows, ultimately, that it is only in Christ that human freedom can be fully realized. Christ is the one who reveals to us that God gives himself as a total gift to us. Christ reveals the truth of God as the Other who is not-Other except within himself. Christ reveals that we are the "others" to God who is One; Christ, through God's kenosis, allows us to call God "Thou" through the act of worship.[46]

> The competition will only begin in earnest when the Christian undertakes to show in theory that God's free opening of himself in Jesus Christ is an invitation into the realm of an absolute and divine freedom, in which alone human freedom can be fully realized. Nor is this just an invitation, but through God's becoming human in Jesus Christ, which is an exemplary fulfillment for all, there is a breakthrough and entry into the sphere of precisely that kind of freedom which is so feverishly sought by the moderns but which, without the opening of God, they cannot find.[47]

"One thing we can say in advance: from the true Christian there radiates the kind of freedom that is always the first thing to be sought after by the non-Christian."[48] While trusting that an answer to human fulfillment

---

gifts. As for theology, born of the knowledge that eternal freedom eternally gives itself away and thus generates the Son, it begins when, addressed as 'thou,' I hearken to the One who thus addresses me" (*TD* II, 286).

46. "Only on the basis of this miracle can finite freedom, endowed with the gift of self, know itself to be addressed as a 'thou' and so designate itself an 'I' vis à vis the Giver. Indeed, it must draw the appropriate conclusion from being thus addressed and go on to call infinite freedom 'Thou.' This is an astounding word to use here, for God in himself is no one elses's 'other': he is the All-embracing One (Non-aliud). Left to itself, in the face of the Ground that calls into being and upholds all things, the finite could at most worship this overall reality and extol it as the Ultimately Precious in its unconditioned self-affirmation. It can only dare to call it 'Thou' if, in doing so, it is answering to a 'thou' that comes addressed to itself from the inner nature of the Absolute—from the divine Trinity. The two things affect each other: I only appreciate fully that God is my 'highest good' when I learn (in the Son) that I am a 'good' to him, affirmed by him; this is what guarantees my being and my freedom" (*TD* II, 287).

47. Balthasar, *Engagement with God*, 21.

48. *MCW*.

lies in the truth of revelation as mediated by the tradition, Balthasar is also explicitly unwilling to go back to a narrower conception of "outside the Church, no salvation."[49] He simply sees that anonymous Christianity and the problem of the Church's external form or "carcass" are quickly becoming the only things left in view and that neither in fact meets the challenge of bettering the world. For Balthasar, the freedom of Christ is the thing that will most draw modern persons into the kind of freedom, integrity, authenticity, and goodness they seek.[50]

Balthasar's attention to the problems of subjectivism and the related development in theology of the reduction of Christology to anthropology reveal Balthasar to be a valuable interlocutor and supplement to the quandary with which Taylor's analysis of secularity leaves us. Taylor's argument, both a critical and appreciative stance of modernity's losses and gains, is the culmination of, we have tried to show, an ongoing attempt to reconfigure and to retrieve the importance of the spiritual dimension in contemporary cultural experience in the West. Indeed, while *A Secular Age* comes at the end of a body of work that begins with philosophical questions on the deeply problematic assumptions inherent in behavioral moral psychology, the question of how we might get to the origins of human crisis and fragmentation, how we might plumb to the "something deeper" that modern moral philosophy belies, seems to characterize Taylor's project as a whole.

Balthasar's commitment and deep interest in drawing attention to the transcendentals in their unity is not radically distinct from Taylor's deepest spiritual concerns. Above all, a point of convergence seems apparent when Taylor begins to speak of the possibility of faith in a secular age, and how conversions, and new and diverse forms of spirituality, must be the witness of faith that shows the resilience of religious experience in any time.

Balthasar's account of the Church speaks to this amply, particularly the idea of new forms of spirituality (cf. Balthasar's work on secular institutes) and possibly more so than other theologians of the contemporary period. He stands out among them as having realized that *aggiornamento* is a choice of attitude that must remain contextualized within an ongoing and more pressing commitment to love Christ and his mission. Balthasar's configuration of the dramatic character of Christian and ecclesial existence, the clear sense of meaning and beauty that this existence possesses,

49. Cf. *The Church Today*.
50. *EG*, 1–7.

addresses the larger ambiguous questions that moderns face, according to Taylor's account of modern selves in a Western context, namely, the question of the ends of our freedom, and the question of how to attain personal integration in a postmodern culture.

We can characterize Balthasar's rejoinders to Taylor in three chief ways:

1. Balthasar clarifies the nature of the *human person* in the light of God in a way that neither dismisses nor unduly reifies a secular culture's emphasis and need for an *aesthetic* and affective dimension to faith. He does this through his articulation of human freedom and the Church through the analogy of a theodrama. This rejoinder clarifies and addresses the malaises of subjectivism and instrumentalism (problem of ends) in human freedom, in particular.[51]

2. Balthasar's *idea of the Church*, while orthodox and supportive of hierarchy, shifts its central trope from a linear, top-down modality to one of circles of perichoretic existence, which places the heart of the Church in the heart of the saints, indeed, in the heart of Christ, and emphasizes a spirituality of communion. This, in many ways, addresses Taylor's naming of the modern challenges: atomism in social life and soft despotism in political life. Balthasar's ecclesiology and christological, ecclesial anthropology stands as a significant alternative to the state's imaginary, which reifies economic agency, collective action without shared belief, and self-determination without any sense of shared tradition or history—an immanent horizon to social life, which forecloses openness to transcendence.[52]

3. Balthasar's idea of *ethics*, while acknowledging the value of natural law, underscores that Christ is the concrete norm of Christian ethics, which dramatically transforms the meaning of Christian self-understandings of moral existence in terms of mission and discipleship. His emphasis on holiness as the goal of Christian existence helps resituate Christian identity from the realm of universal ethical

---

51. "To center Christianity in anthropology and thus turn it into a pure ethics would be to eliminate its theo-logical dimension." Balthasar, *Love Alone Is Credible*, 107.

52. "The sole credibility of the Church Christ founded lies, as he himself says, in the saints, as those who sought to set all things on the love of Christ alone. It is in them that we can see what the 'authentic' Church is, that is, what she is in her authenticity, while she is essentially obscured by sinners, and turned into a useless enigma, which as such deservedly provokes contradiction and blasphemy." Ibid., 122.

norms that may tend to moralism to authenticity that includes right action, but also elevates such action to the dramatic witness to love.

The recognition of the meaning of Christian life as arising from one's relationship with God, nurtured through prayer and participation in the loving communion of the Church, not only has then the potential to reveal the possibility of faith in a secular age but also to evangelize, to transform, and, ultimately, to "save" the present.

One of the upshots of reading Balthasar in light of Taylor's analysis of modern selfhood, Catholic modernity, and secularity is that it allows us to appreciate the manner in which Balthasar's theology emerges from beyond the limits of a certain first reception of Vatican II rather than a reversion to a pre-Vatican II church. It is less a reactionary and defensive posture of identity than it is a rallying call for modern persons in the West to base their identity in Christ, and in doing so, find a place in the Church from which to meet the hearts of those who seek God today. This recalled sense can then transform the Church's sense of mission to renew the world through an ecclesial identity of love (of which a key mark is *unity*).

Balthasar's insight is that "Jesus for today" is the Jesus Christ for always. The Church for today is not one that begins and ends with the Second Vatican Council but one that affirms the truth of that council and the truth in all the councils before and hereafter that reveal the work of the Spirit.

Balthasar and Post-christian Man

Balthasar states explicitly that the problem with conceiving of the human person apart from the person of Christ is that it burdens itself with modern starting points that are untenable, because the philosophy of modern autonomy and subjectivity have no inner path to God:

> This notion fails to take these essential implications into account and—ever since the Enlightenment—starts with an inert "autonomy" of the "subject"; this "autonomy" has no inner path to God (let alone Christ), and this "subjectivity" has no access to authentic personhood. From this inert autonomy, the watchword of the so-called modern "history of freedom," there is no path to the religious dimension in general, nor to the christological and trinitarian religion in particular. Nonetheless, at its

origin, [the human person's] actual experience of freedom still contains these elements, though they have been consigned to neglect and oblivion; they are still there, latent. It only requires their traces to be uncovered, and man can once more be put on the path of genuine religious awareness, from which he can go on to seek the true religion.[53]

A Theodramatic Account of Human Freedom

Balthasar's theology emphasizes the way in which divine freedom is the condition for the possibility of human freedom. Discussing human freedom in terms of a *theodrama*, which centers principally around what the person of Christ reveals about God's relationship with humanity, Balthasar significantly shifts the field of vision on human freedom. The theodrama is an attempt to show how the world of God is directly involved with the world of man, a relationship born out of the total self-divesting love of the triune God. It is thus an antidote to the modern, deistic conception of God that has translated the Incarnation out of its view of God (as Taylor has shown). The remoteness of modernity's God is such that humans and God are understood as distinct and mutually exclusive. The modern conception of human freedom apart from divine freedom is theologically problematic insofar as it fails to take account of the person of Christ, who, for Christians, Balthasar underscores, is the starting point for understanding the possibility of divine and human interaction and their respective freedoms. That is, Christology is the proper context within which to understand human (finite) freedom:

> Anyone who reflects on the revelation in Jesus Christ must take this inherent philosophical thinking beyond itself, in two directions: he must heighten the contrast between infinite and finite freedom and reveal the abyss that opens up between the holiness of infinite freedom and the plight of finite freedom that has fallen into sin, which can only be redeemed by the healing succor of God's holy freedom.[54]

To understand human freedom accurately is to first situate it within the drama of salvation. The relationship between infinite and finite freedom is utterly asymmetrical. But it is also the case that the holiness of infinite

---

53. *TD* III, 457.
54. *TD* II, 194.

freedom is such that God in his freedom, which is to say God in his love, chooses to redeem finite freedom from the depths to which it has fallen. Far from being a relationship of competition, Christ is the existence that reveals God's will for human salvation. The language of "the abyss that opens up between the holiness of infinite freedom and the plight of finite freedom that has fallen into sin" demonstrates the foundation of revelation in Balthasar's understanding of human freedom, which, first of all, reveals the necessity of recognizing sin prior to any real understanding of the relationship between God's freedom and human freedom.

Christ, the "Acting Area"

For Balthasar, the person of Christ is the one who forms the "acting area" for all human beings. Christ is the "way" into the drama in which God and humanity are engaged because of the free, initiating love of God the Father. That is, the true horizon of human existence and where one's "itinerary" flows is from and toward divine life, infinite freedom. We know this to be the case because of the revelation of Christ, who is the gift of the Father to the world so as to draw the world and finite freedom back into the fullness of life that characterizes the Trinity.

All of this is of course clarified by the eschatological reality of the drama. There was a fall away from infinite love, which we call original sin, but the Father, because of his nature as infinitely free, which means infinitely loving, chose to save humanity by becoming human, becoming finite. The person of Christ is precisely the full form of God's love and the dramatic apex of God's relationship with humanity. Christ "opens up" humanity to the divine life of the Trinity, showing us our origin and true end. He is in his person "the path"; in him there is a clear *egressus* from the Father and *regressus* to the Father. But the path is not his alone. The drama is between God and humanity precisely because Christ comes to make a way for humanity to enter into divine life once again.

What happens through this redrawing of the full possibility of human freedom within a theodramatic horizon is that it clarifies that we are all already within God's divine life. Christ alone helps us to see this, and to see that infinite freedom is in fact the ground of finite freedom. Once we begin to see that our lives are the result of the gratuitous love of God, it is clear that the fundamental ontology of all created existence is gift. All is given; reality is pure gratuity. Reflection on the experience of the gratuitous nature of the world inevitably leads to the question, who is the source of this gift? Balthasar notes that any philosopher thinking about existence would have to acknowledge first the wonder of existing, its sheer givenness.[55]

Yet it is a drama because God through Christ does create a "role" on the stage of life for finite freedom.[56] There is something for humanity to do in the midst of the givenness and giftedness of existence. Christ not only shows us who the Father is, he invites humanity into divine life precisely in the same way that he loved us. The Word is God become man, the Word is the Father loving the world so much that he emptied himself of his divine form and took the form of a slave. As kenosis is the way in which God gives himself to us, so our path to infinite freedom and our way to true personhood is likewise kenotic. It is in our self-emptying that we become truly divine. For the logic of love is self-gift, extension beyond oneself for the life of the other.

Just as Christ reveals his Sonship in the fulfillment of his mission, so all persons are called to participate in the redemption of the world through a similar response: a response of ongoing obedience to the Father, a willingness to receive one's mission and to live one's mission for the redemption of the world. This entails a consciousness that is ever in unity with that of the Father. In this regard, Christ, as God himself, was unique. Christ's consciousness could be described as being at every moment a unity of will with the Father through prayer: "Nothing in the life of Jesus is separate from God's involvement."[57]

Christ shows us, thereby, the way to be in unity with the Father, namely, a moment-to-moment consciousness of unity with the Father, and the Father's will, comes through prayer. Christ can only live what he lives because he lives his life as one who is ever aware that he is sent and ever allowing himself to be sent. The fullness of one's identity as a person in Christ will be revealed to the degree that one hears and responds to one's call, consents to one's election, and undertakes one's mission. Balthasar's reception of St. Ignatius of Loyola's understanding of freedom is evident. The Ignatian emphasis on a total surrender of one's will explains Balthasar's critique of any kind of Christianity that seems to have understood God's total will for oneself or, more specifically for

---

55. This is not to say that Balthasar found Marion's phenomenology problem-free.

56. For an excellent account of the relationship between finite and infinite freedom in Balthasar, see Dalzell, *The Dramatic Encounter of Divine and Human Freedom in the Theology of Hans Urs von Balthasar*.

57. *EG*, 43.

the community of faith, the Church, too comprehensively, for the drama of life in God is truly a drama (not an epic), and this means that one is called to attend to the Lord at every moment, rather than leave him "in the rear" or far ahead. The mystery of the Incarnation means that we too can be sent, we too have a mission, and in fulfilling it, we too participate in the redemption of the world.[58] Peter, who came into his true identity, finally, as a person of authority and unity, exemplifies what it means to encounter Christ and to allow the encounter to comprehensively shape his existence.[59] This path of glory and to glory involves self-denial, certainly, but it finds its fullness in this self-denial precisely because it is love's wont to spend itself out of love for the other.

> The significant factor in being a Christian is that he does all with reference to and in dependence on the ultimate source of his action, through loving first and above all things, the God who loves us in Christ in order that he may then, by means of and together with love, turn his attention to the needs of those who are the object of the love of God. Only if we start from this "Alpha" will our involvement lead us to the "Omega" of the man who is loved, only thus will we succeed in caring for him inwardly, in order that he may find his true destiny, only thus will we achieve that solidarity with him which is only possible in God.[60]

Balthasar notes that God is the source of all Christian action not only as an inspiration and as a model to imitate, but as the One who guides and enables all acts of love for every suffering and disenfranchised person. "Jesus Christ, in his role as mediator [is] the everlasting midpoint in whom the love of God for us shines brightly and in whom our love for God and for our neighbor is gathered together into a unit."[61]

> Similarly, Jesus of the Johannine writings demands that we love him, since the whole essence of the faith is simply that we should understand that the love that characterizes the life of the Trinity has been manifested in him, and in him has been abundantly proved. To say that love is the communion of Christians is not simply to enunciate an abstract principle; rather in the Christian communion of love we share in a personal act of God

---

58. The influence of Ignatian spirituality is highly evident in Balthasar's theological anthropology.
59. Balthasar, *Who Is a Christian?*
60. *EG*, 40.
61. Ibid.

himself, the tip of which may be seen shining in the person of Christ, but which in its depth contains the interpersonal life of the Blessed Trinity and in its breadth embraces the love of God for the whole world.[62]

In Christian love there is an experience of Christ, and thereby, of God's own inner life as a community of loving, totally self-giving persons.

Challenging the Modern Understanding of God: Beyond a Zero-Sum Conception of Infinite and Finite Freedom toward an Ontology of Gift

If God's holy freedom redeems finite freedom, it is not in a manner that renders finite freedom autonomous insofar as finite freedom is capable of giving itself its own law, but in a manner that allows finite freedom to achieve fullness in the act of self-gift, a self-gift that is only possible in, through, and as response to the initial self-gift of God in the Incarnation.[63]

---

62. Ibid., 41.

63. In speaking of the stage of heaven and earth (presupposition of the drama) as, following Barth, a metaphor for the God/man, Creator/creature distinction (*TD* II, 177), and of how the earth is "endowed with its own power of conception and fruitfulness," Balthasar elaborates, "In its higher potency, grace endows the one who receives it with a special receptivity: he is enabled to conceive, to be a womb; he is enabled to bring to maturity the fruit he has been given; so much so that heaven becomes dependent on earth, earth seems to give birth to heaven" (ibid., 184).

Again, "God interprets himself to man as love in the same way: he radiates love, which kindles the light of love in the heart of man, and it is precisely this light that allows man to perceive this, the absolute Love: 'For it is the God who said, "Let light shine out of darkness," who has shown in our hearts to give the light of the knowledge of the glory of God in the face of Christ' (2 Cor 4:6)" (*Love Alone Is Credible*, 76). And following, "Had the love that God poured out into the darkness of nonlove not itself generated this womb (Mary was pre-redeemed by the grace of the Cross; in other words, she is the first fruit of God's self-outpouring into the night of vanity), then this love would never have penetrated the night and it would never in fact have had the capacity to do so (as a serious reading of Luther's *justus-et-peccator* theology illuminates in this regard)" (ibid., 78).

Finally, "Gratitude for the gift of self means 'owing oneself.' Finite freedom, genuinely set free and equipped with its own sphere of freedom, cannot set itself off in just any direction but must pursue the path of self-realization, that is, toward absolute freedom. Its coming forth (*egressus*) from its origin is the beginning of its return (*regressus*) there. And, as we have seen, this is not heteronomy but the only possible way in which finite freedom can imitate the perfect identity between divine freedom and divine being. This identity—the absolute affirmation of the absolutely Good or Holy—is its watermark, in virtue of which it *is* freedom. The watermark starts to become visible when finite freedom affirms itself, as a result of being addressed as 'thou'; it can only be perfected when it has become 'thou' in God's sight in its fully divine,

For Balthasar, revelation is the fullness of human understanding of freedom; the incarnation of God in man in Christ enables us to understand divine and human freedom properly. Understanding finite freedom to be independent of God is ultimately inadequate, on modernity's own terms, as it requires an affirmation of contradiction: Balthasar observes the strange separation between the understanding of human freedom in terms of the individual and then in terms of community.[64] Moreover, such an understanding of finite freedom reveals an incomplete understanding of *God's* freedom apart from man:

> A purely theological doctrine of God that did not arise out of a theology of God-made-man would fail to present the full dimensions of the divine freedom: it would not set forth the true relationship between God and created freedom. The nature of both of them is only revealed in their dramatic interplay which comes within our grasp in the Christ-event.[65]

Balthasar underscores that finite freedom only exists within, though it is distinct from, the reality of infinite freedom. Otherwise stated, infinite freedom "guarantees" finite freedom. Showing the distinctions between Christian revelation and non-Christian philosophical understandings of infinite freedom, Balthasar notes that the nature of the Christian God, as tripersonal and self-giving, revealed in the person of Jesus Christ illuminates for us that it is the nature of divine freedom to make space for human freedom. Underscoring the foundational *pro nobis* of divine freedom, and the development of true human personhood through a relationship of responsive self-gift to the divine, it becomes clear that God gives "the self" to us as gift. Speaking of the transformative power of Christ in terms of his atoning death, Balthasar clarifies again the liberating character of Christ's mission: "Not only does this new orientation of the entire human existence of believers, on the basis of Christ's act on their behalf, not interfere with their freedom (something that is denied from Kant up to Hegel); it actually sets it free to journey toward God."[66] The lives of theological persons, with their rootedness in the person of Christ, reveal this truth.

---

absolute manner, when it has become identical with the 'idea' reserved for the finite 'thou' within the infinite 'Thou,' within the eternal Word and Son" (*TD* II, 291).

64. That is, one can only attain a conception of man merely as an individual or merely as a community. *TD* II, 205–6.

65. Ibid., 196.

66. *TD* III, 245.

Autonomy is entailed in the full realization of one's mission.[67] Yet Balthasar clarifies and corrects the modern notion of autonomy in emphasizing that a genuinely human action is one that originates from the "autonomy" that is grounded in and guaranteed by the grace of infinite freedom. Balthasar does employ the term "autonomy" in his description of the appropriate action of a Christian, yet he speaks about human freedom ultimately as the freedom that arises from chosen unity with the divine will and actualizes itself through giving itself back to the divine: "What the Father gives is the capacity to be a self, freedom, and thus autonomy, but an autonomy which can be understood only as a surrender of self to the other."[68]

In *The Christian State of Life*, Balthasar writes more concretely about mission in its various shapes or "states." Balthasar highlights the way in which mission finds its roots and exemplar in the person of Christ and thereby involves a thorough-going self-understanding as moving ever within the ambit of the will of God the Father:

> But the Christian does not take his stand in some external—as it were geographical—location, but in the personal divine-human reality that is Christ. "To take one's stand in Christ" means so to take one's stand in this reality that one is thereby fashioned and marked as what one will henceforth be by nature. For in Christ, in the Word, is to be found the very idea of the Christian. . . . The '"where" of the Son is the Father. . . . He cannot be more perfectly with the Father than by proceeding from the Father in order to return him in love. . . . The Son's state is so securely in God that he can, at the same time, perform actions outside the Godhead; for every distancing of himself from the center has no other purpose than to show how immovably he has taken his stand on this center.[69]

---

67. "It may be difficult for us to bring both things into harmony: on the one hand, the presence, from the beginning, of the full mission in the small Child, who can envision it in its totality in a genuine, even if childlike, manner; on the other hand, the human process of maturing and the ever-deeper understanding of this totality, until the total mission has attained, within the adult human consciousness, the plenitude that will allow its autonomous and responsible execution" (Balthasar, *Unless You Become Like This Child*, 35).

68. Ibid., 44.

69. *Christian State of Life*, 185–86.

A Theodramatic Account of Personhood: Personal Identity and Mission

One of the chief lacunae that Balthasar notices in much modern Catholic theology is the aim of translating the Christian message into a common, that is, secular idiom. Balthasar observes that "the aim of 'greater intelligibility for modern man'" cannot be the ultimate criterion, "particularly as what Jesus *really* meant then, even clothed in the conceptual garb of the time, cannot be limited to these concepts."[70] The anthropological focus of modern theology has resulted in the rejection of such distinct theological concepts as salvation and mission, key dimensions of Balthasar's Christology. By recalling the modern Catholic tradition to the person of Christ and re-establishing the centrality of Christ to our understanding of human action, Balthasar takes vital steps toward refiguring our concepts of freedom and time, and our movements and weak gestures toward the good.

Christ, Time, and Theological Anthropology

As we have noted, for Balthasar, the person of Christ forms the "acting area" for all human beings. In Christ alone is there the true possibility of becoming a *person*, rather than a mere "conscious subject." Balthasar sees that the profound conceptual and existential shift away from a divinely created cosmos and man understood as the creation of a God who is love requires a dramatic retelling of time and personhood whose center is Jesus Christ.

Part of Balthasar's critique of the contemporary trends in modern theology includes a challenge to the tendency to reduce the meaning of things to the horizontal dimension:

> But whether the historical is seen as rooted in God or in man, the mere category "history" is insufficient to grasp what is distinctive about biblical revelation, what sets it apart from other forms of religion and world models. Now it is the horizontal that absorbs the vertical. The eschatological dimension, present in the early Church in the categories of apocalyptic and the expectation of the Second Coming, is assimilated into the continuous stream of a time that is somehow "heavy with salvation," yet without leaving a recognizable trace in it. The form (*Gestalt*)

70. *TD* II, 98.

which slowly arose out of the Old Testament and is brought to fulfillment in the event of the Cross, Good Friday and Resurrection is subordinated to the overall category of "history."[71]

By establishing Christ as the foundation of human identity and by establishing this not as a theologoumenon for reflection but writing in such a manner that moves one to contemplation, Balthasar sets in swing two motions: the transformation of knowing and the transformation of doing. These two movements are inseparable. From the pole of knowing, Balthasar's contemplative writing persuades us to encounter Christ and to begin meditation on human freedom from the space of unity with the person of Christ, and, more than this, from a space of holy intimacy. From the pole of acting, Balthasar moves us toward an action premised on the horizon of known reality that is revealed in prayer, namely, a horizon of freedom that experiences its source and ground in divine freedom.

Both of these transformations have significant ramifications for ethics, and Balthasar makes these clear.[72] We shall look at this later, but first we attend to the primary address of the dilemma around conceiving freedom for the Christian—and, in particular, for the Christian living within the conditions of modernity—and Balthasar's retrieval of a notion of freedom in light of revelation.

---

71. Balthasar, "Trends in Modern Theology," in *TD* I, 29–30.

72. Balthasar clarifies the manner in which ethics is transformed into revelatory acts (eschatological, even) of divine glory when, in acting, we direct our action to God in praise and thanksgiving: "For no one but Christ alone succeeds in directing his action entirely to God; and thus, if we live in loving faith, our ethical standard is in the end taken from our hands and placed in the love of God" (*Love Alone Is Credible*, 111).

"The people who live entirely for love are not merely 'moral examples' of Christian action, but, because they have handed themselves over to the fruitful love of the Redeemer, they are also our intercessors and chosen helpers. In the place that has been designated for them, however, they no more than point to the total reciprocal integration of the deeds of all those who love; in the infinite, their lives and deeds open up to one another and mutually interpenetrate (the 'communion of saints'). From this perspective, every Christian encounter is an event within this community, and there is always a responsibility (*missio*), given as much by Christ as by the Church, to enter every situation as a representative of the whole and of the comprehensive idea of love. This is the Christian version of the categorical imperative, by virtue of which absolute love, as a 'duty' that transcends every individual 'inclination,' is elevated and ordered to itself, with the implacability of the Cross of Jesus Christ, and with the severity and burning flame of the living Christ himself, who seeks to set the whole of world history aflame with the fire of his love" (ibid., 119).

Person

Balthasar's anthropology is christologically focused, which transfigures the modernistic notion of freedom as pure choice. Freedom, and moral freedom, in particular, is often characterized as the human situation whereby one may choose between options; in the case of theological ethics, the option is cast as a choice between acting according to God's will or according to one's own will. Balthasar, in contrast, underscores the aspect of *readiness to respond*[73] as the meritorious aspect of Christ's obedience. The merit of obedience lies in the willingness to risk intimacy through trust and love rather than in the rejection of the choice to disobey.

> Although he [Jesus] cannot sin, his obedience is meritorious. His merit is that he himself anticipates nothing; thus no particular success can obscure the mission's universality. In this way,

---

73. McIntosh takes pains to emphasize the active dimension of obedience and seems to stress the ongoing willingness and constancy of a listening response as characteristic of Balthasar's sense of Christian obedience, which leads, ultimately, to a missional and hence authentic form of life. I see McIntosh's account of obedience in Balthasar as a maximal account of obedience, in contrast to what may be considered more minimalistic conceptions of obedience, which construe it implicitly as mere avoidance of a sinful option. E.g., "At the heart of Balthasar's myriad discussions of obedience there lies his belief in the forward momentum bestowed with every mission. He sees every disposition to authentic self-surrender as bearing within it the seeds of certain charisms which must come to fruition if the mission is to thrive. In von Balthasar's view, one's mission is only made known by revelation, that is, by finding one's place in the mission of Christ. As we saw above, a mission is never, therefore, adequately pursued by a purely self-transcending ascetical ascent toward higher levels of being but comes to fulfillment in a concrete historical apostolate; its direction is not to be found purely in an inspection of the unquiet longings of one's own heart but in obedience to externally manifested counsels and guidance. Indeed von Balthasar specifically credits Ignatius of Loyola for the evolution of *apatheia* into active obedience. The self-surrendering availability of the believer 'can no longer remain at the level of indifference in the sense of merely letting things happen; no, the particular will of God, which is to be actively grasped and carried out, must also be actively pursued.' He points out that whereas the Rhineland mystics place abandonment at the end, 'Ignatius transfers it to the beginning'; it becomes more and more a prelude and a prerequisite for the active cooperation of humanity in God's work" (*Christology from Within*, 75–76).

Also, "Certain idiomatic features stand out in von Balthasar's discernment of the experience of love: specifically Christian love is always a response to the drawing near of God in Christ and is marked chiefly by a *readiness for service* that could as easily take the form of darkness as of illumination. In his important essay 'On Defining the Place of Christian Mysticism,' von Balthasar propounds the view that what sets Christian mysticism apart from mysticism more generally conceived is not simply its external forms or theoretical apprehensions—which are often shared with other religions—but its irreducible character of being a response to God's approach" (ibid., 115).

> Jesus is the perfect example not only of the fundamental Christian virtue of patience, but also, equally, of faith and hope.[74]

Within the Christian tradition, Balthasar recalls modern persons to the centrality of the theological virtues of love, faith, and hope to the expression of Christian personhood. The love, faith, and hope of Christ in his Father reveal the heart of the incarnation to be Christ's perpetual willingness to remain in the Father. This becomes the chief act of redemption, and the condition for the possibility of becoming truly human. That is why Mark McIntosh says that the choice to be obedient to God *is* the choice to *become a person*:

> Drawing on the insights of a spirituality which shares in Christ's obedience to his divine mission, von Balthasar has highlighted the interior freedom of obedience. He characterizes it *not only as a response to love but as a discovery of one's truest self and therefore as a fulfillment of one's own being.*[75]

What McIntosh underscores is the theological work that is carried by Balthasar's notion of obedience in Balthasar's Christology and, thus, anthropology.[76] It is not only a "response" that may be parlayed into a theological ethic of divine command; it is also, and perhaps more centrally, a term of personal, ontological, and soteriological significance. Obedience is the manner in which redemption and transformation are effected—first through Christ, then, by Christoform discipleship, in us.

Obedience, at the heart of Christ's fulfillment of his mission and his identity as Son of God, is only possible through prayer. Prayer, as Balthasar elucidates it, discloses in a particular manner the way that divine freedom seeks the fulfillment of human freedom. Prayer that requests accompaniment by God on one's path is answered; indeed, God seeks to accompany every person on their personal path to wholeness:

> Insofar as every individual endowed with freedom has his own, personal path disclosed to him, this path will look different in God, depending on whether man walks along it or refuses to, pursues it eagerly or lethargically, directly or by a roundabout route. Through prayer—expressly formulated or inarticulate—a man can request that he or others may be accompanied

---

74. *TD* III, 200.

75. McIntosh, *Christology from Within*, 87.

76. Balthasar is emphatic that anthropology can only be understood in the light of Christology.

along life's path. The man who does not pray will not be thus accompanied.[77]

As is God's way, human freedom is honored; God does not impose his presence where it is not sought. Emphasis on the sensitivity and responsiveness to the Spirit of God, of living a life of holy intimacy with the divine, can be seen again in Balthasar's reminder to not only live the moments of Christ's life in the liturgy but to allow the liturgy to shape one's daily life: "The cyclic commemoration of the most important events of our salvation ought to become an exercise in the Christian way of life. To practice Christmas means to carry the spirit of Christmas into our lives."[78] Thus, in addition to observing the communal, "social and predetermined paths of the Christian year," the Christian truly practices the command to love God and neighbor in the midst of his or her own everyday existence, in the "unknown and unordained paths of his [or her] own destiny."[79]

To some extent, the qualifier "ecclesial" is unnecessary when one is discussing Balthasar's notion of personhood. For a person is one who becomes who she is by virtue of consent to her mission, which, presupposes one who sends, God, and one who by human energies carries out her mission. Insofar as the Church, the living Body of Christ, and his spouse, is the mediation point of the encounter between God and man, as per Catholic tradition, the Church mediates the human encounter with Christ. If personhood is defined as the living of one's mission, and mission comes about through an encounter with Christ, then personhood must necessarily pass through the "role" of the Church.

Balthasar himself does not employ the term "ecclesial person." Balthasar treats simply "personhood" in *Theo-Drama III: Dramatis Personae; The Person in Christ*. However, he does this within the context of Christology and, by way of Mariology, shows its outworkings in ecclesiology. In other words, Balthasar's anthropology is rooted in Christology, of which ecclesiology is an indispensable corollary. Thus it is reasonable to imagine that "person," in light of Balthasar's christological and ecclesiological assertions, involves the Church as an implied and essential horizon to this reality. (Recall that with respect to Christ, the basic characteristic of the Church is receptivity.) Balthasar does use the terms "theological existence" (*TD* III), "ecclesial existence" (*Bernanos*), and "anima ecclesiastica" (*Sponsa Verbi*), all of which get to the heart

---

77. *TD* II, 293.
78. Balthasar, *Who Is a Christian?*, 100.
79. Ibid., 101.

of what is being explored when we consider "ecclesial person," as such. Stephan Ackermann's phrase is "realsymbolic persons,"[80] and he notes that "persons in this sense are above all the saints."[81] Thus, in this section we shall consider the question of who is a person for Balthasar, and the importance of the ecclesial dimension with respect to personhood.

As Victoria Harrison observes, for Balthasar, true theological personhood does not coincide with birth. Balthasar asserts that there exists a great distinction between the being of a conscious subject and the being of a person. He observes that while it is common to use the two interchangeably in colloquial speech, "person" means more than mere consciousness, and Balthasar seeks to reserve the term "person" for all that a human subject comprises, beyond mere consciousness. Balthasar notes that we are, in some sense, always on the way to personhood, for we come to consciousness through the recognition of ourselves as beloved. Famously, for Balthasar, the paradigmatic moment of experiencing personhood lies in the experience of an infant of her mother's smile. Importantly, Balthasar names love and not knowledge as the primordial experience of subjective consciousness. Kenneth Schmitz highlights the transformed meaning of personhood if Balthasar's view is adopted: whereas with Descartes, according to many, we received a tradition in which "I know" becomes the condition (premise) by which we may say "I am," Balthasar offers a different understanding, almost diametrically opposed to the modern sense: "I am known, therefore I am." More than that, as Christophe Potworowski shows,[82] Balthasar's "epistemology" is underwritten philosophically, by a phenomenology of receptivity, and deeper than this, by an ontology of love. Simply put, the order of love is the order of being and the order of being exceeds the order of knowing.[83] Thus, our experience of being loved is more basic to human consciousness than our experience of ourselves as knowing subjects. This experience of being loved is that which raises us to consciousness and, if we respond and choose to participate actively in receiving love, enables us to become persons. Thus, in a profound and privileged fashion, the smile of a mother is of deep theodramatic significance.

For Balthasar, a mother's smile to her child reveals the scope of theodramatic meaning. The smile of the mother begins to raise a

80. Ackermann, "Church as Person," 242.
81. Ibid.
82. Potworowski, "Christian Experience in Hans Urs von Balthasar," 107–17.
83. Ibid.

consciousness in the child as one loved, yet, Balthasar notes, "the most emphatic affirmation can only tell a conscious subject who he is for the one who values him or loves him. And as long as the conscious subject cannot discover his qualitative identity, he cannot find any absolute meaning, either, for his existence, for his task in the world and for the existence and tasks of others."[84] According to Balthasar, such an individual may know that he is a unique subject; the "what" of his or her existence is not insecure, but the "who" remains a question.[85] Only God can give this answer: "It is when God addresses a conscious subject, tells him who he is and what he means to the eternal God of truth and shows him the purpose of his existence—that is, imparts a distinctive and divinely authorized mission—that we can say of a conscious subject that he is a 'person.'"[86]

Jesus Christ, receiving his identity and name as God's "beloved Son," is the archetypal "event" of personhood. "Others can claim to be persons only in virtue of a relationship with him and in dependence on him."[87] Yet Jesus is the only case where person and mission are identical. However, by our participation in Christ's mission, through our "analogous, unique, personal missions," we, too, may become persons.

Our participation in Christ's mission, to be "personalized and socialized," is in fact the ultimate "end" of the soteriological drama. Christ's coming allows humanity to be dramatically included in the Trinity's eternal life of self-giving love. By this participation we become persons; by giving ourselves—which is always the form of mission—we receive who we are.

Thus, an important aspect of "personhood" is that it is inextricably linked with God, for personhood arises through the gracious receptivity of one's mission, a response of "yes" to God's invitation to participate in the life of love. Mission as a way of articulating personal identity means that God is necessarily involved, for a key element of mission is that it is not self-initiated or conferred. By definition, one cannot send oneself; one must be sent. Potworowski's phrase "active receptivity"[88] is helpful here. Personhood is a challenging, demanding act that is belied by modern prejudices toward "activity." Balthasar notes that even as Christ may

---

84. *TD* III, 205.
85. Ibid., 206.
86. Ibid., 207.
87. Ibid.
88. Potworowski, "Christian Experience in Hans Urs von Balthasar," 112.

have known who he was in the eternal consciousness of God the Father, as a human being he had to "consider, plan and test" the particular carrying through of his mission. His temporal existence was not docetic: it was lived, experienced. Balthasar notes thereby that Christ not only makes possible the illumination of humanity with God's glory ("dramatic inclusion"), he also refracts the "face" of God in new ways for humanity: Christ reveals the "grief, tears, and *pathé* of God for those who sin"[89] and the challenge of what it means to surrender to the point of "drinking the cup."

Personhood is, above all, a gift: Kenneth Schmitz notes the self-donative element of personhood, in contrast to the self-referential and authorizing character of selves. He acknowledges that in our broken humanity both of these elements exist: the self-donative and the self-referential. It is the exemplary person, namely, the saint, who participates in life with such commitment to her mission, who then becomes characterized by her gift. Her life is, in fact, gift for the Church. This is another characteristic of ecclesial personhood: through one's receptivity to one's mission, which begins in responding to the call of God by a total gift of oneself, the saint thereby becomes transparent to the life of God. Her participation in self-giving, self-emptying love is apparent (a mark of sanctity, as Victoria Harrison notes, is that it is always outwardly evident in fruitful action) and, as such, becomes gift through and to the Church.

While Taylor indicates at the end of his opus on secularity that the persistence of faith in the West will depend on exemplary individuals whose lives attest to a real conversion to *agape*, Taylor stops short of explicitly naming conversion in traditional religious terms, such as "conversion to Christ." He alludes, however, to the "communion of saints."

The centrality of sanctity in the theology of Balthasar is indisputable. As Harrison states,

> Reappearing again and again throughout the broad range of von Balthasar's works are two themes: prayer and mission. . . . Yet the place that prayer and mission occupy within his theological philosophy is determined by an even more central feature of von Balthasar's thought: his notion of human holiness.[90]

According to Harrison, Balthasar's notion of human holiness organizes his thought on prayer and mission. Indeed, Balthasar, a former Jesuit, for

---

89. *TD* III, 225.
90. Harrison, *Apologetic Value of Human Holiness*, 1.

whom mission is the heart of one's identity in God, would hold holiness to be fundamental to any meaningful action in the world.[91]

Significantly, exemplary, holy persons cannot become holy without the objective holiness of the Church. This was a trust that Balthasar felt the author Bernanos gave expression to in an incomparable fashion: "For Bernanos, the saint—which means the subjective following of Christ and the realization of his holiness within the sphere of the human person—is simply unthinkable without the objective holiness of the Church."[92] Sanctity was his "central concern": "In a time when the Church's official and organizational aspect appeared continually to gain the upper hand, Bernanos campaigned for the Church of the saints with all the energy and spontaneity native to him."[93] Yet he recognized that if sainthood is a transposition in subjective human existence of the objective holiness of office and sacrament, these latter are necessary, even as they are for the "subjective sanctification of Christians in general."[94]

Ultimately, the ecclesial person is characterized by receptivity of mission, obedience, and ecstatic existence—saints are often mystics. Ecstatic underscores that the center of their lives is elsewhere; it is not in themselves but in God. Their lives yield transparency to the glory of God. Notably, the total self-giving of those persons who are holy coincides with "an ever deeper ecclesial obedience."[95] Balthasar notes that the life of an exemplary ecclesial person, namely, a saint, can only be "launched" by the Church. He acknowledges the limits of the verb "launch" as it implies a trajectory, and the lives of the saints are not thus predictable by the Church.[96] Yet, the Church certainly begins all saints on their way, even as they go into terrain hitherto unforeseen; again, their existence is ecstatic, they risk with their lives "crossing over into the sightless and the pathless."[97]

Now some might raise concern and even doubt that claiming that the Church is the only source of authentic personhood[98] is a good way to

91. Ibid. See also the many instances where Balthasar critiques activism, contrasting it with true *action*.
92. Balthasar, *Bernanos*, 260.
93. Ibid.
94. Ibid.
95. Ibid., 267.
96. Ibid.
97. Ibid.
98. The gendered aspect of Balthasar's anthropology is also a well-known source of

hold a conversation with people who are disinterested or opposed to the view that the Church is a source of meaning and value. However, let me clarify that I do not see making the distinction between a person and a conscious subject as Balthasar does as an *ad extra* conversation but as a conversation, and a theologoumenon-ordering practice, that should take place *ad intra*. It is only in being convinced of the difference God makes to the community of those who believe in him that this message can be revealed to others.

Ethics

Balthasar shows that the moral life of the Christian is ordered in a way that cannot be encapsulated in a moral code but, rather, in a posture of openness to the One who orders. Here again we can see the consonance between Taylor and Balthasar on authentic Christian existence. The latter is the dynamic relationship with the divine that grounds a life of goodness and gives it holiness, rather than principles and structures in and of themselves.

In a word, Balthasar seems keenly aware of the manner in which the sphere of ethics can become a sphere of temptation for the Christian: "Modern man is more aware of his share of responsibility for the whole of creation than were his forebears, and, seeing himself as the divinely appointed steward of the world's affairs, is more easily tempted to regard himself as the ultimate truth of the cosmos."[99] Rather than the deepening of virtue, ethics can reveal a misplaced emphasis on human will and human achievement to the effect of blindness to the grace that first calls us and gifts us with a mission in and for the world. The orientation to the divine mystery is, however, the first and only means whereby the Christian lives an authentic moral life, that is, life within that of Christ.

It all begins with a conception of human freedom in a radically secularized sense: divine freedom is not presupposed as the foundation that is woven into the fabric of human freedom. Finite freedom cast in such a light allows for the emptiness arising from the plight of human freedom without orientation to manifest itself. God's freedom has nothing

---

criticism. While a valid critique—though there is also a defensible counter to it—this work proceeds with a focus on the equivocation between a modern notion of person and Balthasar's Trinitarian rendering.

99. Balthasar, *Prayer*, 65.

to do with human freedom, and so, human freedom has no anchor or direction. The question that is seldom asked is whether human freedom needs a foundation and an orientation. The assumption of modern secularization stories is that human responsibility has grown in a desirable fashion, not a hubristic one. In light of the temptation of a new sense of responsibility, the human person, Balthasar shows, "is doubly in need of persisting in the contemplation of the word of God, so that [he or she] may bring [him or herself] and all other things to the genuine, definitive truth."[100] Without recognizing the priority of prayer, there develops in contemporary ethics the tendency to conceive of the good as an act to be effected by the human moral agent, rather than as a reality that exists prior to human actualization. Balthasar points out, however, that

> The question is not how he can realize the good by his own power, but how he is to realize himself by the power of the good and according to the law of his own reality which is already there. In this perspective, Christian existence is the reversal of all natural ethics. Contemplation serves this reversal; it is indispensable to it.[101]

According to Balthasar, Christians have become profoundly mistaken about what it means to be a Christian. To be a Christian is not to achieve the good by one's power but to allow the power of the good to be the fertile soil that gives rise to a true, full self. Goodness is not the goal of capable, autonomous man; rather, it is the gift, should one desire it, that is given so that a man or a woman may become a *person*.[102] In this way, Christian existence turns natural ethics on its head. Rather than an autonomous striving, it is a practice of surrender to relationship with the divine. Contemplation "serves this reversal" because in contemplation one discovers that prayer is not a monologue but a dialogue with God, and moreover, the dialogue *begins* with God.[103]

Contemplation

Balthasar recognizes that signaling Christian contemplation as a key activity of Christian moral life seems counterintuitive in light of many

---

100. Ibid., 65.
101. Ibid., 61–62. Emphasis mine.
102. McIntosh, *Christology from Within*.
103. Balthasar, *Prayer*, 14.

contemporary understandings of moral activity: "Many people go astray here; they feel that Christian contemplation is obsolete and imagine they can re-invigorate it by turning to the values of the world."[104] Balthasar emphasizes, however, that Christ is the true "end" of human existence: "It is only 'in Christ' that things can attain their ultimate goal and meaning, and the man who wants to help them thither must himself be 'in Christ,' striving his utmost to achieve the supreme freedom which alone can lift things into the sphere of freedom."[105]

In *Prayer* Balthasar describes mission as "the form of the Christian," the "shape of man's existence as a member of the mystical body of Christ." Pointing to the example of Peter, Balthasar describes "Peter" as the form of Simon and claims that it is only and precisely in this form that Simon was able to know Christ. That is, one comes to discover one's identity only in responding to Christ's *call*. One's true identity is bound up in one's mission in Christ. This latter is achievable only in response to God, in obedience to the call to participate in the life of Christ.

This "form" of the Christian, which is at the same time pure grace from the Father, the shape of man's existence as a member of the mystical Body of Christ, and ultimately the human being himself in all his concreteness, we can speak of in the context of redemption as *man's mission*. He is to commit his entire nature to the service of this mission; here, in this dedication, this worship ("divine service"), it will enjoy its particular, its absolutely personal fulfillment quite beyond its natural and imperfect abilities. It is this mission that, without fail, enables man's nature to go beyond its own powers and yield much fruit. It enables man at last to come to an understanding of himself (in faith).[106]

Human freedom, human fulfillment, and salvation arise from one's commitment to the mission given one by God. Thus, in the end, Balthasar's great concern is the mistake of taking as the object of contemplation the words of creaturely nature rather than the Word of God. Noting the penchant to rely on human will and interpretation in contemporary ethics and the development of theologies as agendas of praxis, Balthasar challenges the notion that contemplation is irrelevant to the "active" life of mission. The hearing of the Word of God is necessary at every step of one's enacting of the mission. Balthasar notes, "Christ's

104. Ibid., 65.
105. Ibid.
106. Ibid., 59.

mission presses him forward, toward its fulfillment, and its contemplative component does not imply any interruption in his life of mission; rather, it enables him to persevere in it."[107] One might say that Balthasar "upends" the modern emphasis on ethics through his focus on contemplation. Balthasar also challenges the "ungraced" concept of nature that is often assumed and operative in theological ethics today. Following de Lubac (and, of course, Aquinas), nature always builds upon grace,[108] for there is no nature that is unaffected by grace.

The World

The world, for Balthasar, is not the object of mission, but is transfigured through mission. Rather than a picture of holiness divided into members of the Church and those outside the borders of the Church, Balthasar's "schema" for missionary activity remains within a metaphysics of radiance; that is, holiness is grounded in Christ. Because the Church exists explicitly to reveal this relationship of Christ, between God and man, it has a particular vocation to incarnate the presence of Christ in the world. In the revelation of human "answers" to love, through the formation of persons, theological persons, the Church then indeed sanctifies the world, but this same love may also be found beyond the borders of the Church, and Balthasar makes clear that this possibility exists:

> The range of Jesus' eschatological work is such that he can operate directly, outside the Church; he may give grace to individual persons, and perhaps to groups, enabling them to act according to his mind; the Church must allow for this possibility. The special vocation of Christians is explicitly to adopt his standpoint (Mk 3:14) and to receive the fullness of his power so that they can continue his work in the world. Through the sacraments, Christ opens up whole realms to the Church; these the Church herself has to open up to others through her sacramental life. She is commissioned to stand close to Christ's center of operation, to be the "light of the world" together with him (Jn 8:12; Mt 5:14). Yet she is not identical with his light: it can happen that, bringing her light into some new area, she finds his light shining there already.[109]

---

107. *TD* III, 196.
108. "Gratia non tollit sed perfecit naturam."
109. Balthasar, *TD* III, 282.

Thus, Balthasar does not deny the holiness of non-Christian persons in the world, yet neither does he deny that that very holiness is rooted in Christ and given by Christ. Indeed, Balthasar's concern is less to deny the existence of holiness outside of the Church than to argue—in this age it seems necessary to make this argument anew—for the presence of holiness in the Church. Balthasar maintains that the mission and task of the Church is to be a witness to Christ even as she is clearly not identical to the light of the world, but receives her light from Christ himself.

The Upshot of Balthasar's Theological Engagement of Modernity

According to Cyril O'Regan, Balthasar's weakly epochal scheme of succeeding cosmological, anthropological, and post-anthropological regimes is intended focally as an account of different theological habits in the Western tradition, but also, perhaps peripherally, of the different metaphysical habits, given the chronic interlacing of philosophy and theology.

> If Balthasar finds in the retrieval of a scriptural view of reality the definitive postmetaphysical posture, then this does not prevent him from issuing more nearly metaphysical challenges to the Heideggerian *"phainesthetics"* that presents itself as an alternative to the premodern and modern metaphysical tradition. One form the challenge takes is the more or less systematic preference for Thomistic *esse* over Heideggerian *physis*....[110]

In his essay on Balthasar's engagement with modernity,[111] O'Regan clarifies Balthasar's theological retrieval of beauty in the face of Heideggerian tendencies toward nihilism.

Balthasar's *theodrama* is an attempt to recall Christians to a radiant life that reveals Christ to a world that believes he no longer exists. The beauty that is possible in human life through the form of Christ, refracted through the saint, who may be a religious or may be "an ordinary person of the street," is what Balthasar seeks to retrieve for, arguably, a post-Christian world. However, for the world to receive this beauty, the Church must first receive the beauty of Christ herself. The underlying concern of Balthasar's work on the radiance of Christian life seems to be to clarify for Christians of this age in what precisely the beauty of Christ consists.

---

110. O'Regan, "Von Balthasar's Valorization," 147.
111. Ibid.

O'Regan's summary of Balthasar's program with respect to beauty and his response to Heidegger in particular illuminates the synchronicity between Taylor's articulation of the genealogy of modern secularity and his ongoing concerns with modern malaises—and Balthasar's deep hope for Christian theology to renew the world.

In the final analysis, O'Regan claims, "von Balthasar is less interested in burying Heidegger than correcting him."[112] O'Regan's view is that Balthasar both shares sympathy with Heidegger's critique of ontotheology yet remains more sanguine about classical and modern theology.

> Conceding that throughout history, and especially in the post-Reformation period, theology can function nihilistically, von Balthasar believes that most of the classical, and a significant part of the modern, theological tradition not only does not erase epiphany but rather represents privileged sites.... On von Balthasar's view, then, Christianity, Christian theology in particular, is a *pharmakon* in the double sense of poison and cure made so current by Derrida.

It, too, is poisoned and poisonous to the degree to which it is tempted to overconceptualize Christian mystery, to fall in love with system, and to misidentify itself in scientific and/or psychological apologetics. Yet by and large Christian theology is medicine against occlusion, and perhaps even inoculation against epiphanic loss. Balthasar believes that Christianity can be a safe haven of the epiphanic and the bastion against nihilism in the modern world.[113]

While this chapter has touched in only a cursory way upon the key loci of Balthasar's vision of the transformation of modernity that may be effected by theology of Christian life in a different key, that of drama, I hope to have moved into a space in which it becomes ever more interesting to consider Balthasar's theology of holiness and its theodrama for the Church in a secular age. Balthasar's concern, as O'Regan notes, is, in a very direct way, the lives of Christians in a modern world that have grown too accustomed to system. Without using such vocabulary, Balthasar seems to recognize what others will describe as the "inauthenticity" of the Church, or its lack of resonance with the Western world of his time. Yet where others might locate the problem with the Church qua institution, Balthasar's understanding of the challenge of witness involves a sense

---

112. Ibid., 146.
113. Ibid., 154–55.

of the deep levels at which consciousness has been refashioned upon a Christ-less foundation both outside of and within the Church. His desire to retrieve metaphysics speaks to the truth, underscored one might say by the modern period's emphasis on subjectivity, of *personhood*. Balthasar attempts to transform the Church from within, by calling Christians to recognize that personhood in the Church, ecclesial personhood, entails being born of God, putting on the "mind of Christ" a mind that uniquely and incomparably enacted the identity of person and mission.

Looking at the way in which Balthasar refigures "person," "freedom," "Church," and ethics leads us to argue for a kind of "epiphanic ethics" of which holiness is the chief criterion. Balthasar's answer to formalism due to the emptying of metaphysics in philosophy[114] is, similar to Taylor's, attuned to the truth available through the medium of art ("drama," "story"). Moving away from aestheticism, however, both Balthasar and Taylor recognize that *human lives* of beauty, namely, the lives of saints, are, as they ever were, the form that God's Word takes in the world to transform it: *persons*.

In the next chapter, we consider the manner in which Balthasar articulates the tasks of the Church, the importance of holiness, and the particular role of the secular institutes. All of these lead, I argue, to a clearer sense of Catholic mission and witness in a secular age through argument for a lived theology of authentic personhood in every member of the ecclesial body and, additionally, to a theology of ecclesiality as intrinsic to such a concept of personhood.

---

114. Should one perceive a tension between O'Regan's description of Balthasar's stance as 'postmetaphysical' and Balthasar's concern about the emptying of metaphysics in philosophy, one way to make sense of both is to point to the way in which Balthasar argues for the reality and power of beauty. See Anne Carpenter's *Theo-Poetics: Hans Urs von Balthasar on the Risk of Art and Being* (Notre Dame: University of Notre Dame Press, 2015).

CHAPTER 4

Balthasar's Vision of a Witnessing Church: The Holy Church, Possibility of a Genuine Christian Inspiration

WE COME, FINALLY, TO Balthasar's vision of the Church. We have seen that there exists a connection between the longing of the modern self in the West for something beyond the merely horizontal, flattened sense of time, moments that characterize our contemporary technologized, digitized, self-determined lives, and the presence of Christ at the heart of one's identity. This chapter underscores the relationship between Christ and the Church. It looks in particular at the following features of Balthasar's conception of the Church: the Marian dimension of receptivity at the foundation of all profiles of the Church including the Petrine, institutional dimension; the Church as the community of friends who loved Jesus; and the *anima ecclesiastica* which reflects the deep intuition of the Church as both soul and structure. What we gain from this interpretation of Balthasar's ecclesiology, which some may say minimizes the importance of the official Church for Balthasar, is a reading of the Church that may both speak to and ultimately transform the logic of anthropocentric modernity. I suggest, in my reading, that Balthasar retrieves the relationship between the institutional church (the "objective holiness" of the sacraments and of office) and the personal holiness of individual lives ("subjective holiness"). This last becomes primary for understanding how the Church may be considered an alternative social imaginary that enables the path toward transcendence in every age. It also names her missional task in this one.

In the previous chapter, I considered Balthasar's conception of time and personhood, underscoring that Balthasar's articulation of authentic personhood demonstrates how true personhood and freedom exist in the life of Christ and in the Church. I showed that his portrayal of human existence as dramatic, dynamic, and as having its source and summit in the mystery of participation in divine life is rooted in a profound understanding of contemporary secularity, as well as the situation of modernity with the latter's emphasis on the freedom of the subject. Balthasar, it was argued, offers a constructive response to the theological losses incurred with the "flattened" horizon of which Taylor spoke. The modern self's muted sense of ends and "deep time" (arising from the development of new moral sources beyond those of theism and the rise of exclusive humanism) may be recovered through a sense that Christ is the starting point of history, its origin and its goal. Authentic personhood and freedom in contemporary Western experience are related, then, to a retrieval of christological eschatology in Christian theology. In many ways, the chapter worked to suggest that Balthasar's anthropology, as unfolded through the *theo-drama*, proposes for Christians the embodiment of a new social imaginary, one that is rooted in the doctrine of the Church, and shaped to speak to a questing, aesthetically focused modern sensibility.[1]

In this chapter, I hone further a sense of how the Church may understand her mission today as being responsible for the formation of saints. Both Balthasar and Taylor, with their readings of secularity, underscore the power of authentic, self-transcending persons, or, in the words of both, the saints, to inspire faith. While Taylor has outlined the ways in which Christianity lost its true power in trying to marry a univocal vision of codified morality to whole social orders, Balthasar retrieves a vision of the Church that can sustain the lives of holiness the secular age so needs. This vision has five essential parts: (1) a refiguration of the common identification of the Church with her hierarchical structure, showing instead the various profiles of the Church, foremost of which is the Marian profile of receptivity; (2) the true identity of the Church

---

1. That is, Balthasar's theological vision of personhood provides a remedy for the challenges of living in a secular age that Taylor's philosophical analysis of secularity both diagnoses and begins to propose.

as the holy Church, as a communion of saints; (3) the relationship of dependence between the Church and Christ with the priority of Christ to the Church; (4) the primary function of the hierarchical Church to be the formation of saints; and (5) the Church as united and scattered in the world like leaven, that is, the Church in the form of the secular institutes. All five aspects of Balthasar's vision of the Church work together to move toward a self-understanding of the Church as the humble handmaid who nonetheless does not view ecclesial office as mere superstructure. The centrality of having an ecclesial soul (*anima ecclesiastica*) in Balthasar's ecclesiology will also be examined.

A New Vision of the Church

The vastness of Balthasar's theology of the Church will be limited by the criterion of how Balthasar's understanding of the Church sheds light on the shape and priorities of Catholic mission and witness in a contemporary, "post-Christian" age.[2] First, Balthasar understands the real, empirical Church as the Church of the saints. We will explore in detail Balthasar's analysis of the works of French Catholic writer Georges Bernanos to mine from it what Balthasar considers an important understanding of ecclesial existence in the contemporary, "post-Christian" world. The significance of Balthasar's treatment of the Church by way of the literature of Bernanos is that Balthasar's account of the Church through the French writer attends particularly to the complexity of the relationship between holiness and hierarchy, giving attention to both the Church of the saints and ecclesial office, and bringing to light the necessary role of the hierarchical Church to authentic and vital ecclesial existence or sanctity.

2. The choice of Balthasar's ecclesiology and my particular appropriation of it for its potential resources for the contemporary mission of the Church in the West should not be taken to mean that I see Balthasar's reading of all ecclesiological issues as problem-free. To the contrary, certain elements of Balthasar's theology more generally indicate that there would be some real challenges in mining his work for questions of interreligious dialogue or intercultural theology and the world church. Karen Kilby, in *Balthasar: A (Very) Critical Introduction*, has criticized Balthasar for taking a "God's-eye view of the world." While the criticism might be considered simply as an occupational hazard plaguing all theologians, there may be some substance to this challenge where Balthasar's theology of other religions is concerned. It would not be sufficient to ignore Balthasar's provocative depictions of the axial religions, but that is a separate book, as is Balthasar's lack of engagement with the cultural diversity of the Church, particularly the Asian and African churches. I address the latter in two forthcoming articles on intercultural theology and the world church.

Locating *Bernanos*, with its meditations on sanctity, modernity, and the Church, within Balthasar's larger corpus, we consider the pillars of Balthasar's conception of Church, namely, the Church as Body and Bride of Christ, her Marian profile, and the christological constellation at the origin of the Church. We consider, from there, Balthasar's proposal that the most vital face of the Church today is the servant Church, "buried deep" as the "yeast" of the world, in the form of laypersons who choose to live a life of radical commitment through consent to the evangelical counsels, all the while living in the secular world and serving it with their expertise and experience. What may be gained from exploring these areas—(1) the Church of the saints and the hierarchical Church; (2) the Church in her relationship with Christ, the Marian profile and the christological constellation; (3) the Church of the vanguard, the secular institutes—is a kind of razing or deconstruction of the Catholic Church in Western culture's "social imaginary" as hierarchical Church or the official Church, reducible to a set of moral teachings, *tout court*. Balthasar refigures the hierarchical aspect of the Church as one necessary but not totalizing dimension of the Church. One of the chief implications for the life of the Church is a sense of radical freedom and responsibility in the life of all her members, which begins with a foundational sense of unity through mutual self-giving that invites others to participation in Christ's life, rather than a truncated obedience to norms that can be perceived as moralism or Christianity as "code." This sense of responsibility does not denigrate the hierarchy or focus on the self-understanding of each individual Christian apart from the whole Church. Simply put, Christianity becomes more than an ethic (even a socialist or personalist one), and becomes instead a question of a way of life, a shared life of discipleship and, ultimately, a life of mission in and through communion.

The aspect of the Church that Balthasar is most interested in highlighting is the Church as a mystery. To that end, Balthasar reintroduces the conception of the Church as Bride and Body of Christ. The mystery of the Church is revealed, at bottom, in reflecting on her relationship with Christ; the Church as institution can only be truly affirmed in light of a deeper sense of her essence as mystery, participating, through the triune God's divine initiative, in the activity and cosmic story of redemption. Focusing on the identity of the Church as a communion of saints is one way of showing how the Church exceeds her image as institution. Clarifying this mystery in a manner that is more resonant with the contemporary awareness of personal relationship, Balthasar describes the Church further in terms of the christological constellation, that is, the group of intimate friends in Christ's life that, with Christ, helped inaugurate the life of the Church.

Mary, Christ's mother, is preeminent in this regard, and much can be drawn from Balthasar's consideration of Mary in conjunction with Balthasar's affirmation of the Church at her most authentic as a communion of saints. Disponibility and full self-surrender are the mark of both the communion of saints and of Mary, in particular. Balthasar's ecclesial vision culminates in a constructive vision of the Church that has at its heart a Church that includes all Christians:

> There exists a Christian order. . . . This order is the order of Christ, and the Catholic tradition has preserved its essential principles. But the temporal realization of this order does not belong to the theologians, the casuists, or the doctors, but to us Christians. And it seems that the majority of Christians are forgetting this elementary truth. They believe that the Kingdom of God will happen all by itself, provided they obey the moral rules (which, in any event, are common to all decent people), abstain from working on Sunday (if, that is, their business doesn't suffer too much for it), attend a Low Mass on this same day, and above all have great respect for clerics. . . . This would be tantamount to saying that, in times of war, an army would quite fulfill the nation's expectations if its men were squeaky clean, if they marched in step behind the band, and saluted their officers correctly.[3]

Balthasar's portrayal of what most Christians believe to be an adequate life of religious fidelity complements the story that Taylor tells of the eclipse of a genuine religious sense by a horizon of pre-understandings that define ultimate ends in terms of economic existence (abstaining from work on Sunday "if their business doesn't suffer for it"), general beneficence (obedience to moral rules that are "common to all decent people"), and the rights of a people to democratic self-rule (attending a "Low Mass" on Sunday). Although writing a generation before Taylor's, Balthasar senses the despair of Christians, which manifests itself in the form of a compromised Christianity. Ritual practices are observed, but the substance of one's life remains free from divine "interference."

---

3. Balthasar, *Bernanos*, 555.

At the heart of Balthasar's critique is certainly the bourgeois Christianity that Nietzsche, too, trounced famously. As David Schindler notes,[4] the parity between Balthasar and Nietzsche is that both realize the truth of "the death of God"; however, Nietzsche believes that the answer is to absolutize human creativity, whereas Balthasar senses that the problem requires a retrieval of the desire for the truly beautiful and can be solved by humanity only through a receptive creativity to the creative genius of God evident throughout the cosmos and through a self that is constituted in and through the other. Without making an appeal for the Christendom of ages past, Balthasar contends that full self-surrender of human hearts to the reign of Christ is not an optional mission for Christians, but a task and goal for the Church, as much today as it ever was.

Balthasar recognizes that Christianity today is, so to speak, in crisis (likening it as he does to a "time of war" in the quote above). He thus exhorts the "ordinary" Christian to lead the charge for the order of Christ in the temporal world, though he does not have in mind a revolution that would pit "the people" against "the hierarchy," nor does he endorse a return to historical Christendom. Balthasar sees, on the contrary, that all Christians play a vital role in the realization of the kingdom of God but that, ultimately, the Christian order or *catholica* is realized by the surrender of every person to God's being in them. This order will be led, in an exemplary but not exclusive way, by the radical witness of those called to live according to the evangelical counsels, and who thereby inspire in all around them a sense of what the "reign of God" truly means in the world, a sense of the triumph of total self-gift in a world that claims persons other than the one who undergoes utter kenosis to be the face of true power.

Interestingly, however, Balthasar acknowledges the "double-movement" by which God fills the world with his presence: through those who have renounced the world for him and those whose existence is raw to the transience of this world,[5] and who embrace the world for God, living as if in exile, seeking him from within the world. Showing the misplaced emphasis on the thinkers and "rule-makers" of the Church, Balthasar will nonetheless suggest, through the example of Bernanos, that there exists an unmistakable relationship between the ministries of the Church, a certain radical ecclesial obedience, and the holy, exemplary lives that will

---

4. Schindler, "The Significance of Hans Urs von Balthasar."
5. Balthasar, *Laity and the Life of the Counsels*, 181–82.

shine Christ's light in the world. Balthasar's understanding of ecclesial mission opens up, indisputably, a central role for the laity.

Through well-formed laity, filled with *anima ecclesiastica* and knowledge in spheres of worldly concern, the Church may reveal herself as being for the world in a way that the world may receive. Indeed, Balthasar believes that the challenge of the unbeliever to the Church today is that she "has failed to tell us about the saints."[6] According to Balthasar, the saints reveal a fullness of life in the present that comprises the authenticity, the objective subjectivity, so deeply craved by modern man.

Balthasar is consistently emphatic that the reality of the Church is that she exists for the redemption of the world, and he is not afraid to call the Church to awareness of what she might "learn" from the world. But he is also clear that authentic Christian existence entails being in the world but not of the world. In the following chapter, we attend to each of these dimensions of Balthasar's portrayal of the Church: (1) the Church in the world, that is, the Church as members of a secular society and economy—persons as workers and citizens; (2) the Church that is not of the world, that is, the Church of the saints, or holiness; and (3) the Church as for the world, otherwise described as the Church as representation for all and as sacrifice, that is, the secular institutes. We come to see that each of these dimensions of a Balthasarian church point the mission of the Church in the directions of humiliation, simplicity, and humility. Taken together with Taylor's insights into the secularity, struggles, and hopes of modern persons, it becomes clearer that the mission of the Church today requires, more than the theological work of "translation" for encounter and resonance with the world, *prayer* and the *formation of anima ecclesiastica*, the formation of *saints*, for encounter and resonance with the world. There is a knowability to love that exceeds articulation. We know love when we see it. We know love when we hear it.

Balthasar's concept of mission shares the attunement of Taylor to the colonization of the socially imagined horizon by rationalism and moralism. This chapter will continue to bring to light Balthasar's awareness of the loss of a horizon for authentic human existence. Rather than push a kind of new morality, or even a new kind of society, Balthasar expounds on the power of the saints, looking to them as models and exemplars of the living Church, the Church at her best and most vital.

6. Balthasar, *Bernanos*.

However, Balthasar is not interested in a spiritualization of the Church; he thus emphasizes the concrete path of sanctity in its relationship with the institutional church, in her ministers and her sacraments. The official Church is deeply involved in the formation of saints, Balthasar claims, drawing on the works of Bernanos to show this. (That Balthasar's theology passes through literature shows insight, again, into where post-Romantic modern man looks for wisdom: in artists rather than in ecclesial authority.) Balthasar's project thus opens up a fresh form of communicating the gospel today, of being the living Church: first and foremost through retrieving a sense of the Church for Catholics as mystery and forming a new relationship with her of holy intimacy; as being called as a body and as unique persons to join the communion of saints, rather than a dis-embodied activistic or pietistic Catholic. Such an approach highlights the urgency of prayer and acquaintance with the Church in her sacramental life.

Mission follows this in the form of working in the world with *anima ecclesiastica*, as one whose life is mission to and for Christ—in short, daily kenosis. Art, particularly literature, infused with a spirituality of communion, is the reflexive, more explicitly linguistic counterpart of this concept of mission. But, at its most basic level, mission must be carried out at the level of existence, that is, existence *in Christ*. Secularity, in this sense, has brought about the great good of raising the stakes of discipleship. While Balthasar may not go so far as to consider it purifying, his theology of the Church is clearly written from a space of *hope* on the far side of despair over a post-Christian world. Saintly individuals in the world become Balthasar's revisionary proposal of the Catholic Church; these individuals, Balthasar asserts, following Bernanos, do not come to be without the office holders and sacraments of the Church.

Recovering the Church as Mystery: Person, Body, and Bride

Church as Person

In attempting to understand how Balthasar preserves the significance of the official Church even as he emphasizes the Church as communion of saints in his portrayal of a Church for the present, we need to attend to how Balthasar delineates the role of the Church in the formation of authentic or theological personhood. This involves, first, a sense of the Church as herself a mystery.

The first and most important way in which Balthasar describes the mystery of the Church is through her relationship with Christ. In "Who Is the Church?"[7] Balthasar notes that his approach to the Church is as to a "who" rather than to a "what." For a culture more prone to seeing the Church as an institution as a social body emblematic of the organized religion of Christianity, and as the organized religion *par excellence* of the West, reference to the Church as a person is provocative at the least. Balthasar, however, sees the Church as a person, with all the dynamism and complexity that the word connotes. "The Church is [more than] a 'structure' set up by Christ, an institution designed to shelter and sustain a multitude of believers in Christ, as a formal element enclosing a material one."[8] The Church as mere institutional structure is one of the misconstruals arising from the Church characterized as Body of Christ, a metaphor that Balthasar will both affirm, in certain aspects, and bypass. Balthasar's concern with the Body of Christ metaphor is the way in which it was used by some theologians to reduce the sense of the wholeness of body through which the glory of God may shine, by minimizing one part at the expense of others. In this, he followed and contributed to the work of Henri de Lubac.[9]

Shifting the terms of ecclesiological exploration from object to subject, Balthasar considers who the Church is and in what her nature consists. Balthasar moves gradually from subject to nature, clarifying first what it means to consider the Church as a *subject*. He notes that there is legitimate ground linguistically for describing the Church as a subject, since the notion is already operative in the language we use in liturgy. We say, in liturgy, that the Church prays for, suffers, offers up, praises, etc. The Church teaches, nurtures, feeds, and so on.

Balthasar clarifies, however, that the Church is more than a collective subject in the manner that a nation, people, race, or "humanity" can be seen as a collective subject. The irreducible distinction between the Church and other collective subjects is that the Church, by definition, has no identity apart from Christ. Balthasar even uses the term "parasitic" to describe the relationship between the Church and Christ. By

---

7. See *ET* II, 143–91.
8. Ibid., 154.
9. Balthasar, *The Theology of Henri de Lubac*.

this, Balthasar means that *the Church truly has no life of her own; her very life depends on the life of Christ*. The biblical foundation for this, to which Balthasar adverts often, is the Johannine text describing water and blood emerging from the pierced side of Christ, which has been used to interpret the origin of the Church. Insofar as the life of the Church is continuous with and, in some sense (namely, in the Holy Spirit), shares the very same life as Christ, we may say that in its simplest form, the *subject* of the Church is *Christ himself*. In short, what characterizes the Church is an inextricable relationship to Christ; her life flows from the life (and death) of Christ.

The Church as *Totus Christus*, most famously associated with Augustine, holds to this view. In this characterization, the Church is the Body of Christ and Christ is the Head of the Church. The priority is clear: the Head may exist without the body, but the body may not exist without the Head. While Balthasar embraces this ecclesial metaphor, with the elements of vitality and intrinsic relationship to Christ that it captures, he prefers the metaphor of the Church as Bride of Christ. Balthasar believes that the *nuptial metaphor*, like Church as Body of Christ, captures the dynamic or "event-like" character of the Church,[10] as well as the Church's love relationship to Christ. Balthasar also sees, however, that the Bride of Christ metaphor may be open to distortion, as is the Body of Christ metaphor. For example, Balthasar sees the temptation of overly subjectivizing one's "bridal" relationship with Christ, or the risk of misunderstanding the idea of "alter Christus."[11]

However, dimensions exist within the nuptial metaphor that bring out more clearly the nature of the Church in her relationship to Christ; most significant among these is her nature as feminine and, hence, as *receptive*. For Balthasar, femininity and receptivity go hand in hand. Receptivity is a term of highest praise, for he considers receptivity to be the true measure of personhood. Personhood is the fruit of an attitude of deepest receptivity to God's self-revelation, which then becomes the form and norm of one's life, a life transparent to the glory of God. If the vocation of all of humanity is to become persons, and the transformation of one who exists as a conscious subject into a person comes from God alone, then receptivity to his call to be a person in him becomes paramount. The Church as person who radiates the glory of God and attracts

---

10. Balthasar, *The Laity and the Life of the Counsels*.

11. These ideas are explored in *Explorations in Theology*, for example, in "The Mass, a Sacrifice of the Church?" (*ET* III, 185–243).

the world to him with her beauty will require, at heart, a total receptivity like that of Mary.

The Church as Bride: The Church as a Unity Based on Receptivity

Because of the radical and utter dependence of the Church on the life of Christ, Balthasar notes that the Church has no authority to define herself or to organize her activity apart from Christ. She is in no way autonomous from Christ: her offices are not her own, and she has no power to confer office. Office, call, and charism are the domains of Christ's authority. The Church, Balthasar asserts, can claim no power to determine these, and she belies her own existence when she takes such power as her own. This is so because the Church's character is, again, one of receptivity, an attitude best exemplified in the person of Mary.

Importantly, Balthasar's description of the Church in a Marian vein is not an attempt to "present an ontology of Church as Body or Bride which underwrites a sociological understanding of the Church." To do so would depart from Balthasar's approach to characterizing the Church, for it is, above all, a sense of the Church as personal mystery that Balthasar wishes to convey. If personal (and preexisting: "The Church is a 'someone' whom the Lord loved and for whom he delivered himself up"),[12] we may also say that the Church is the totality of persons living in and through her, the life of Christ. Balthasar notes, "Once one takes seriously the question 'Who is the Church?' . . . the only satisfactory answer is that she consists of *real subjects!*"[13] Balthasar distinguishes again any sense of the Church as comprised of real subjects from the sociological sense of the Church as a collective subject. The difference is *the love of Christ*, which is the "real interconnection" that distinguishes the Church from the biological or sociological arbitrariness that "unites" members of other collective subjects hitherto named. As Stephan Ackermann elegantly sums up, "The Church in her deepest reality is the *unity* of those who, gathered and formed by the . . . limitless assent of Mary, are prepared to let the saving will of God take place in themselves and for all their brothers [and sisters]."[14] This saving will needs, of course, to be seen not only in the light of creatures that need to be redeemed, but in the sense

---

12. Balthasar, "Who Is the Church?," in *ET* II, 147.
13. *ET* II, 179.
14. Ackermann, "Church as Person," 247.

that even once that work of redemption is "done," creatures continue to be "saved" by it since the dynamic of redemption is the same as that of the divine life itself: the relationship between the persons of the Trinity into which we are called.

The Marian receptivity of the whole Body that is involved in the Church truly being the Bride of Christ cannot be overemphasized.

> If the Church, as institution and sacrament, cannot be designated in the proper sense as bride of Christ, then the Church fully constituted (of form and matter) can rightly bear the personal name of bride only insofar as the people of the Church, coming under this form, receives it into itself and lets it work there—as a community, in other words.[15]

The significance of the nuptial metaphor is threefold: (1) it names the reality of two *distinct persons* coming together without dissolving their distinction; (2) it names the fruitful result that underscores the *unity* of two persons; and (3) it expresses the significance of sexual difference whereby the relationship is characterized by complementarity: Christ's masculine initiative is complemented by the Church's feminine response of receptivity. The author acknowledges that there is much debate and critique of Balthasar's conception of gender and sexual difference. The work of Linn Tonstad and Karen Kilby is notable on this front. The point here, however, is to underscore the centrality of ecclesial receptivity to Christ in Balthasar's ecclesiology. While there are no doubt legitimate challenges to be raised on the feminist front to Balthasar's gendered conception of receptivity, the author holds the view that Balthasar's conception of receptivity is active and is upheld as a model for all persons, and thereby defensible to that extent.

Finally, as Balthasar consistently emphasizes the personal character of the Church, it must be stressed that the Church lives in concrete persons and thus in their missions. So, one may say that the Church according to Balthasar is characterized by Christoform lives marked by Marian receptivity, who allow the self-gift of Christ to be the form of their lives as well. This then brings us to a consideration of Balthasar's notion of the "ecclesial person."

---

15. "Who Is the Church?," in *ET* II, 155.

The Church as a Communion of Saints:
A Communion of Missions, Holiness, and Receptivity

This highlights the deeply important characteristic of Marian receptivity. Mary, as the exemplary personal, human response of receptivity in the life of Christ, is the overarching characteristic of the Church. With her "yes," Mary's well-known fiat gives birth not only to Christ but to the New Covenant.[16] Through her completely receptive existence, Mary is most truly a person and becomes *realsymbol* par excellence, the Church. In other symbolic persons of the Church, whom Balthasar calls "realsymbols,"[17] the aspect of receptivity, disponibility, utter obedience to the will of God and the living out of their mission is thus the overarching hallmark of the way in which they all share in the existential "yes" uttered in Mary's life. Their missions all involve, thereby, an expropriation of their lives for the appropriation of the same by God, by *love*, but they are expropriated in unique and characteristic fashions. Peter is the realsymbol of the Church in her official and institutional character. Balthasar underscores the self-emptying expressed by this life, which undergoes the anonymity of impersonal "office" for the sake of mission.[18] The Johannine "principle" of the Church is that of the one who loved the Lord, and who mediates between the Marian principle and the Petrine principle of the Church. Finally, there is the Pauline mission of the Church, which is the life of discipleship whereby one is sent as individual, holding the tension of Catholic unity in the midst of diversity. All of these ecclesial lives are archetypal for the variety and forms of mission that the life of discipleship then takes within the Church. Notably, these missions are not exclusive of one another. Balthasar notes the clear interweaving of each mission in the others, and its needfulness to the others: of Peter's for John's, of John's for Mary's and Peter's, and of all of them for Mary's mission.[19] Here then, we see the manner in which the *perichoresis* of the Trinity and the *communio* existing in and among these lives characterizes the Church in Balthasar's writings.

We may say then that the Church, for Balthasar, is characterized by a life of dependence on Christ and, more particularly, by a nuptial

---

16. As Thomas Norris reminds us, Mary's fiat is "the very first moment of the New Covenant" ("Symphonic Unity," 244).

17. Balthasar, *The Office of Peter and the Structure of the Church*

18. Ibid., 293.

19. Ibid.

relationship with Christ that is marked by a grace-gifted receptivity to divine life in the person of Christ and Christ's Spirit. The Church is a person insofar as she is living and dynamic, in light of her life in Christ. The Church is also characterized by objective holiness (or "following") and subjective holiness. The former is concretized in the structural and sacramental orders of the Church, including the office of Peter; the latter is the holiness of which these structures and sacraments are in service. Importantly, Balthasar does not consider the hierarchical structure of the Church and the sacraments she administers to be purely instrumental; yet he is clear that the mission of Christ, and thus of his bride, is to bring to fruition the enjoyment of divine life, of love, to all, that *God* may be all in all.[20]

Refiguring Hierarchy: The Church as Christological Constellation

Balthasar pursues the dramatic line in his treatment of the Church as personal in terms of the relationship of Christ with those who loved him, chiefly, Mary, John, Peter, Paul, and James. In addition to Mary's "yes" as an incomparable human response that gives rise to the Church, Balthasar's notion of Church is that of a mystery born of a drama of personal relationships with Christ, the "christological constellation" of Peter, John, Mary, John the Baptist, Paul, and James.

The person of Christ and his life within a constellation of relationships of mutual self-gift and faith are normative for all Christians.[21] Our experience of freedom depends, in Balthasar's vision, on the degree to which we participate in the person of Christ, who expressed complete obedience to the Father in the breadth and depth of his existence as man. The form that freedom takes in our lives must likewise involve total receptivity to the will of the Father.

Mary, Peter, and the other persons within Christ's existential constellation exist to show us what it means to allow Christ to be the concrete norm of one's existence. It entails a kenotic trust in God, a willingness to "let it be done according to your will," that is, the self-surrender of Mary. Each disciple chooses to consent to the mission that God alone confers. Agency and receptivity are inseparable, an existential principle

---

20. As Balthasar has famously expressed, the truth is *symphonic*.

21. Cf. "Nine Propositions for Christian Morality" and *The Office of Peter and the Structure of the Church*.

that Balthasar derives from the Spiritual Exercises of St. Ignatius.[22] Thus, genuine Christian action is only possible through a fundamental and ongoing self-surrender to God.

It is only in and through such a relationship of self-surrender, which epitomizes trust in and with Jesus Christ, that Peter's life fulfills its eternal significance. It is only through Jesus that Peter receives a way to give himself totally to God and to others. Through his earnest yet muddled following of Christ, Peter becomes the man whose mission it is to "shepherd Christ's people" because he "love[s] Christ more than these."[23]

Balthasar's aim with his theology of the Petrine office is, analogously, to retrieve something of the personal mystery that lies at the heart of ecclesial authority. In attempting to do this, Balthasar's notion of the Church as a living organism, as a body, stands out. Balthasar looks back to the theological origins of the institution of the papacy and considers the *relationship* between Peter and Jesus. He observes that Peter's call does not exist in isolation but participates in the constellation of relationships that surround Christ and Christ's mission. Peter, Mary, John, James, and Paul *together* form the christological constellation. Office (Peter) cannot do without love (John); yet office is not the primary emblem of love, or of tradition and law (James), or of the freedom of the individual charism (Paul). Office is just one aspect, though a crucial aspect, of the Church.

The relationship between Peter and John and the relationship between Peter and Mary are particularly instructive for our understanding of Balthasar's ecclesiology. The love of John is, in a manner of speaking, more important than office is to the Church; and, for Balthasar, Mary's total self-surrender is even more characteristic of the Church than the Church's character as institution. Because of the centrality of Mary's disponibility, and John's love, there exists a certain paradox in the prominence of ecclesial office, yet Balthasar sheds light on the consistency: it is the nature of love to yield. In an excursus on Peter and John at the tomb of Jesus, Balthasar notes how John arrives at the tomb first, but lets Peter enter before him. Love always lets office proceed before it.[24]

Thus, Balthasar's privileging of the Marian principle does pose a challenge for approaches to the Church that take office to be the dominant feature, if not the whole identity, of the Church. For Balthasar, it is

---

22. Balthasar, *TD* III.

23. Balthasar, *The Office of Peter and the Structure of the Church*; "Christology and Ecclesial Obedience," in *ET* IV.

24. Balthasar, *The Office of Peter and the Structure of the Church*.

the willingness of Mary to participate in Christ's mission that governs all missions in the Church, including the vocation of ecclesial office. Rather than a one-sided approach to receptivity, everyone in the Church, including the hierarchy, according to Balthasar, must embody the Marian profile of receptivity to the will of the Father. Balthasar's approach has the advantage of being a truly organic ecclesiology based on human relationships[25] that avoids the binary oppositions that seem to divide an all-too-human Church, with authority on one side and those who advocate for the laity on the other—commanders on one side, receivers on the other. In short, office is not totalizing for Balthasar but is, rather, an essential aspect of the Church. While necessary, his elaboration of the various other profiles of the Church shows how he considers it to be far from sufficient.

This characterization of the Church as a living organism which includes diverse missions, foremost of which is that of Mary, demonstrates, among other things, the potential of Balthasar's organic ecclesial vision to yield a path beyond certain conceptions of the Church, often configured in terms of dualistic conceptions of authority: between those who hold office and those who do not hold office. Balthasar's emphasis on the Marian principle of receptivity and the Johannine principle of love indicate that the center of Balthasar's sense of the Church is that of witness to the authority of love rather than witness to authority *tout court*. The Church that emanates from love entails an acceptance of authority, but the former circumscribes the latter. Indeed, the Church of love entails not only an acceptance of authority but *a desire*, in love, to submit to that authority as is love's wont. Likewise, ecclesial authority is itself viewed and exercised as love—imperfectly by the fallen creatures who exercise that office, but perfectly by God, whose prerogative it is to complete all that is lacking in the exercise of that office so that it can be called a perfect instrument of God's will. Persons holding highest authority in this Church are the saints, both those with offices and those without. The authority of holiness and, by extension, the authority of holy laypersons highlights the distinction, moreover, between Balthasar's affirmation of ecclesial obedience and any support of authoritarianism. Indeed, Balthasar's is a theology of obedience that furnishes an alternate route to authority by way of a thoroughgoing sense of the Church as a living organism with an ecclesial spirituality in all her members.

---

25. Saward, "Mary and Peter: The Christological Constellation in Balthasar."

Bernanos: Church of Christ in the World

Solidarity With the World

Ecclesial existence according to the model of Bernanos means the choice and enactment of a kenotic existence that sees the Church as existing in solidarity with the world, rather than over and against it. Part of Balthasar's choice of Bernanos as a Catholic author who exemplifies a deep attunement to the truth of ecclesial existence seems to be Bernanos' sense of the world, temporality, the human challenge of freedom, and his recognition of man's confrontation with death.[26] In short, Bernanos highlights an existential approach to ecclesiology. Bernanos, Balthasar seems to show, understands that Christians are no longer at liberty to consider the world as a problem for the Church. Indeed, "Bernanos' first concern was the world, not the Church.... The Church exists for the sake of the world."[27] Bernanos thus emphasized the need to listen to the world and named the Church's betrayal of Christ "from the inside."[28] Ecclesial existence refracted through Bernanos means the world's disappointment with the Church must be attended to, and heard.[29] Bernanos criticized the notion of Christianity as "a ready-made, self-contained and self-evident affair, which is therefore devoid of any mystery, existing 'alongside' the world as a 'perfect society' parallel to the other, imperfect one."[30] In contrast to a sense of ecclesial transformation of the world through a heavy-handed "pure moralism" in the key of "America or the Puritans,"[31] Bernanos' ecclesial sense was attuned to the character of Christian truth as "a leaven activating mankind's every major awakening to salvation." Bernanos saw, according to Balthasar, that "the weakening of the Christian spirit is catastrophic for both: we are *in solidarity* in the face of the peril threatening us. Whether we and the world save ourselves or perish, it shall be together."[32] "To be Christian can be nothing other

---

26. Balthasar, *Bernanos*, 217–44.
27. Ibid., 248.
28. Ibid., 250–51.
29. Ibid.
30. Ibid.
31. Ibid., 247.
32. Ibid., 249.

than to accept from grace, in union with Christ, the responsibility for the non-Christian world. Such responsibility, moreover, can only be love."[33]

The question of the world and how to transform it is nothing less than the question of how Christians are to live in the world as followers of Christ. It crystallizes the question of mission, then, as an experience of discipleship. The Church *is* her mission, just as Christ is the Christ in the becoming, in the following through of his mission. In her book, *The Apologetic Value of Human Holiness: Von Balthasar's Christocentric Philosophical Anthropology*, Victoria Harrison's exploration of Balthasar's conception of holiness helpfully shows that holiness is not to be conceived of as a "gold star" that is awarded at the end of a successful completion of mission; rather, holiness is the daily working out, the ongoing attempt to live according to the mission given one by God:

> Human holiness is not to be regarded as an ideal which is achieved at the end of a successfully completed mission—a retrospective assessment of a human life. Rather, the holy life is something that can be lived. To be precise, living a life of human holiness is the process of following one's mission.[34]

If this is the case, then there is a corollary fruitfulness to Balthasar's emphasis on existence for the question of the Church's mission to the world. Not only do we shed a false sense of engagement with the world by shedding an attitude of detachment; we also shed a false sense of what it means to love and to be gift for the world. To be in mission to the world, which Balthasar through Bernanos has claimed can only mean to *love* the world, we must be ready to exist transparently to God in the world. That is, we cannot pretend that our "gift" resides in our identity as a perfect society, because, to quote Balthasar, quoting Bernanos, "Nothing is better organized, hierarchized than the exterior life of the Church, but her *interior life* flows with wondrous freedoms of the Spirit."[35] The Church exists, then, as a holy Church where she lives out her mission; her holiness is a *living* holiness that grows through the deepening of her love for the Father and the Son that then infuses and shapes her love of the world. Such holiness happens through time, and it is always imperfectly realized.

The concrete following is what gives us our identity. The Church's structures are indispensable for the life of concrete following, though

---

33. Ibid., 253.
34. Harrison, "Personal Identity and Integration," 427.
35. Balthasar, *Bernanos*, 257.

the Church is not the sum of her structures alone, nor are the structures themselves sufficient for following. For this, Christians need to follow *the Spirit of the triune God*: the one who, with the Father, sends the Son (Balthasar's concept of Trinitarian inversion) and who is sent by the Father and the Son to the Church to continue Christ's mission to the world. Without a sense that our relationship of unrestricted receptivity to the divinity of Christ *through his Spirit* is the touchstone of our identity, we only "give" ourselves falsely to the world. For it is in Christ that the Church receives her identity. Balthasar refracts the meaning of the Church through an examination of the existence of Bernanos, which highlights the human, living, struggling, "ever dying" and "ever rising" of Christian life. He draws attention to ecclesial *existence* through reflection on the life of a writer in recent times, who continued, with his life, to express the gospel (a "prolongation of revelation").

In Bernanos, Balthasar notices a firm rooting in the Church that nonetheless does not remain blind to its failures and poverty. Bernanos' existence is ecclesial not because he is a "yes-man" for the Church but because he has allowed himself to live her life in Christ, to be a participant in the ever-evolving, ever-moving drama of Christ's life in the world. His existence is ecclesial insofar as he understands his own life to be a mission, a way of living ec-statically in the world, that, in his uniqueness as a writer, in the stirrings of his spirit with love for language, love for the poor, and love for the world, he recognizes and accepts a call to empty himself of this love, to "spill it" into the world, to reveal, thereby, the glory of God whose mystery is the heartbeat of the Church he calls home.

It is notable, thus, that ecclesial existence is not to be confused with any *abstract* notion of participation in the Body of Christ, with certain connotations of perfection and, frequently, of sinlessness. Bernanos' existence is not "ecclesial" because he harbors an uncritical love for the Church. It is ecclesial because his sense of the Church and his critique of the Church is a critique that is *formed* and *in*formed by the Church. The challenges he raises emerge from within his ecclesial sensibility: a thinking of the Church rather than a thinking with the Church. What is the Church's "thinking"? "Reason remains intact only when it transcends itself in the direction of God."[36] The intimacy is so deep that Bernanos' thought is that of person who *is*, by virtue of living in the Church. He has allowed the marrow of the Church's life, namely, the life of Christ, to be

---

36. Balthasar, *Bernanos*, 227–29.

the truth of his own existence. "Existential truth becomes realized within the Church when people who make up that Church know that Christ is divine life and divine Person."[37]

Mission, then, is response to the call to holiness. Balthasar's sense of genuine ecclesial existence is nothing less than sanctity. Thus, if it is our mission to transform our culture, which is to say to make Christ manifest in the world, we do so by living out our call to be holy men and women. With Bernanos, Balthasar attests that "the New Covenant finds its ultimate truth in discipleship; all official functions of the ecclesial institution remain at the service of the concrete following of Christ."[38] Ultimately, the objective holiness of the structural and sacramental order of the Church exists for the creation of saints, for the generation of lives of *persons*, lives illuminated by the "wondrous freedoms of the Spirit."

The Church as Mystery—the Church in Her Saints

"Precisely because Bernanos would have liked to show unbelievers the very essence of Christian existence, he took the way, not of 'ethics,' but of 'mysticism,' which means the mystery of God's Incarnation: the Church in her saints."[39] For Bernanos, the saints "have a genius for love."[40] In unearthing the essence of "ecclesial existence" through a rigorous excavation of Bernanos' literary corpus, Balthasar begins to work out a concept of the Church in mission through hiddenness, through her "inner life," rather than overt apologetics and structures.

> What we have said of today's church—that it is growing closer to the earth and that its former outer structures are becoming a feature of its interior life—lets it appear wherever it does concretely and genuinely make an appearance. It lives in small centers of influence which are scattered over the world like tiny lights in the night. It is in these centers that one experiences the love of God in Christ, sacramentally and existentially, in prayer and in the selfless exchange of love; and the kind of life experienced by this small community can thence be carried by its

---

37. Ibid., 113.
38. Ibid., 263.
39. Ibid., 284.
40. Ibid., 226.

members as individuals and by the community as a whole into the world of non-Christians.[41]

Balthasar stands resolutely with Bernanos, who laments that there is a blindness and wrong-headedness in all attempts to "convert" the world to Christ and Church through a translation approach, through a dialogue on the world's terms. Describing the need of the Church to be youthful and to convert the world through her spirituality of childhood, her simple faith, which Balthasar believes the world understands, he alludes to Bernanos' situating of the unbeliever in the pulpit demanding that the spirit of Therese be translated for contemporary man to understand:

> To be sure, the saints are marvelous human beings, at once heroes, geniuses, and children. But what can the world do with them? "What can our politicians and moralists do with a Therese of Lisieux? In their mouth, her message would lose all meaning, or at least every chance of being effective.... It is clear that you [the Church] alone can and must communicate the saints' message; but, alas, you are very far from having always discharged this duty to the best advantage for us [unbelievers]...." The unbeliever then shows Christians the ways to accomplish such a "translation." He shows them what, at bottom, Bernanos was attempting to do throughout his whole work. There is a childlikeness, an impulse of youthfulness, which the world understands because the world naturally loves what is young and knows from experience what it was to be young; and this same childlike and youthful impulse can also be the expression of a most profound, supernatural childhood—the expression of sanctity itself. But this reality needs to be lived by Christians convincingly before the world. Instead of a senile, abstract faith, the world should be shown a vibrantly youthful and really *believing* faith: "Hurry up and become children again that we in turn might do the same!"[42]

Official Ministry and Personal Sanctity

It is through Bernanos that Balthasar outlines the mutually necessary relationship between the official Church and the Church of the saints. Bernanos, according to Balthasar, unlike other writers on the saints, refuses to separate the visible or hierarchical Church from the less visible

---

41. Balthasar, *Razing the Bastions*.
42. Balthasar, *Bernanos*, 330.

Church of sanctity. On the contrary, for Bernanos, the saint cannot come into being without the priestly order and the sacraments, and the end of the official Church is in fact, sanctity. While the Church of the saints is indeed the Church in its most exemplary form, the ecclesial order is not incidental or irrelevant to the formation of the saint. Balthasar points out that faithfulness to Christ will always lead to ecclesial obedience, as holiness is ultimately a received grace and is an act of obedience in light of such grace. He notes that those who have the most reason to be appalled and critical of the awkward movements of the visible Church, namely, the saints, are the same ones who never criticize her. For they have a clearer sense of the true Church than those who raise protest and critique.[43]

The Importance of the Ecclesial Horizon for the Formation of Persons

The point of unity that gives us certainty about the meaning of our existence is God, not the cosmos and not man. This emphasis on God does not come at the expense of the modern emphasis on the human person; rather, Balthasar re-narrates what it means to be a person by reference to Christ. Christ is the foundation of personhood; this foundation transforms our understanding of human freedom as that which entails divine freedom. God's action and human action are transfigured in a way that has profound ramifications for Christian ethics.

One way in which this theodramatic vision of existence recasts a Christian conception of living well is that it involves, necessarily, the ecclesial dimension. Genuine ecclesial existence is nothing but the concrete following of Christ in one's own life. It is the grace of attentiveness in prayer that is accompanied by openness to the call so as to receive one's name, one's mission from God. The communion of the Church mediates such contemplation and openness, as well as acceptance of the mission, which allows one to be "sent" to the world as a holy presence that reveals the "face" of God to others and invites them to participate in the same life of freedom. Christian freedom, however, almost in opposition to contemporary secular understandings of the same, involves an expropriation of self by God for the appropriation of self by God. In allowing ourselves to be appropriated by God, we participate in the "yes" of Mary to God's action in our lives. The result is fecundity, fruitfulness that is only possible because of the activity of the Spirit, to whom we have given our assent.

43. Ibid., 250–70.

The Church as Expressive of Childlike Christianity

John Saward has commented that the spirituality of childhood is key to Balthasar's whole understanding of what it means to live the Christian faith. He shows how the Child of God, Jesus, is the template of what it means to be Christian, and our vocation is to become like a child, to become like this Child. He notes Balthasar's profound analytical studies of persons who exemplified the spirituality of childhood—Therese of Lisieux, Charles Peguy, and Bernanos. The whole essence of this task, of embodying the spirituality of childhood, is "the unaffectedness of letting themselves be given, and owing themselves."[44] There is, of course, a notable similarity between the self-surrender of Mary to the will of her Father, which finds its source in the child Jesus, and the way we are called to walk in and as the Church.

"To be a childlike Christian is to live gladly and gratefully in the real, visible, hierarchical Church, Christ's beloved Bride and our Mother and Teacher. Spiritual childhood is the very soul of Catholic life."

> Here is a new dimension of Christian childlikeness: the reception, in the Church, of the sacraments authorized by Christ, of the proclamation of his Word, and of the leadership decreed by him. It is clearest in the case of the sacraments. In the Church God alone holds the great Eucharistic banquet, to which we are invited as children; he alone in the sacrament of penance bestows the forgiveness of sins and the Holy Spirit; he alone takes the promises of fidelity pledged in marriage into the indissolubility of the marriage bond between Christ and his Church; he alone consecrates men to sacramental powers or to a lifelong dedication in definitive vows. Every person who approaches a sacrament is, like a child, a pure receiver; even if he has to make a contribution of his own, that is nothing other than the perfect readiness of the child.[45]

That self-understanding of oneself as a receiver, of Being as good, true, beautiful, and thus trustworthy, allows one to walk in the world with a peace, a confidence. Saward says that Balthasar's claim is that the sense of being a child is the deepest sense of Being, calling children the

---

44. Saward, "Youthful Unto Death," 156, quoting from *Homo Creatus Est*, 172f.
45. Saward, "Youthful Unto Death," 157.

"consummate metaphysicians," even.[46] That sense of being is first experienced in the love of the mother for the child and the child's love of the mother.

One final note of importance is that the Child Jesus should not be confused with one who is weak or immature in mind. On the contrary, Jesus is shrewd: "No man has been more mature than Jesus, none more manly. He is serenely self-controlled. He teaches with authority." This maturity of mind is directly linked and is due to the childlikeness of his heart. The maturity of taking up one's mission is through sharing the childlike obedience and trust that Jesus has to and in the Father.[47]

Anima Ecclesiastica

To give a cursory illustration of how Balthasar's sense of *anima ecclesiastica* is distinct from blind consent to the teachings of "the official Church" we consider his affirmation of the lives of Georges Bernanos and Madeleine Delbrel: both of them were, according to Balthasar, exemplars of Christian authority. An ecclesiasticized consciousness for Balthasar may exist in the person who holds office; it may also exist in the layperson who disagrees with the official Church, provided it meets the criterion set above that the path chosen by the ecclesiastical conscience is more truly in keeping with the evangelical norm of the counsels. Balthasar clarifies that service in office is "an approximation toward a never-attainable ideal"[48] and that "the official Church (as represented by Peter) and the Church of love (as represented by John) have converged only once, in their Founder, who—on account of his transcendence as God-man—could be at one and the same time officiating priest and the sacrifice of love, the sacrificed Lamb."[49] Ecclesial love is nonetheless basic to the meaning of ecclesiasticized consciousness.

Balthasar also notes the challenge of "preserving the fragile balance that exists between obedience to a norm deemed judicious by the believing conscience (*an obedience that also allows an open and fraternal correction of the office holder*), the Christian's appeal to the *sensus fidelium* of the universal Church, and concrete authority instituted by

46. Ibid.
47. Ibid., 153.
48. *ET* IV, 159.
49. Ibid.

Christ." Balthasar asserts, "This balance can be soundly maintained only by a person with living faith; and in today's Church, it absolutely must be maintained."[50] He considers the *sensus fidelium* "the collective conscience within a vital ecclesial tradition,"[51] to bear the possibility of being a "kind of safe middle ground between overbearing self-allocation of the absolute evangelical norm and a defeatist blind obedience; but the opinion that one really possesses this *sensus fidelium* can likewise be subject to all sorts of illusions, traditional or progressive."[52]

Refiguring Authority: The Authority of the Holy Church

Victoria Harrison notes that holiness in Balthasar serves an important communicative function for the Church seeking to communicate the joy of Christ to those who doubt the existence of God. Simply put, the beauty of Christ is revealed in and by his Church through holiness.

This insight is in keeping with the central task of Balthasar's important though short text, *Love Alone: The Way of Revelation*, which is Balthasar's constructive response to the way to reveal Christ to the world today:

> The methodological point this essay seeks to develop represents, at the same time, the proper theological *kairos* of our time: if this approach ["theological aesthetic"—reception, perceived with the eyes of faith, of the self-interpreting glory of the sovereignly free love of God] does not manage to move our age, it has scarcely any chance left of encountering the heart of Christianity in its unadulterated purity. In this respect, this little book stands as the positive, constructive complement to my earlier book *Razing the Bastions*, which cleared the way for this approach.[53]

Balthasar's approach to witness and the mission of the Church can be understood as guided by two clear *a prioris*: (1) witness involves revealing the divine glory of the triune God; (2) witness is a communal expression of the Church who is the bride of Christ. The second can be seen in this statement of Balthasar: "The Church is the pure outpouring of the Lord,

---

50. Balthasar, *New Elucidations*, 244.
51. Ibid.
52. Ibid.
53. Balthasar, *Love Alone Is Credible*, 13.

the Christian the pure outpouring of Christ and Church. The Christian proceeds from community with Christ, from community with Church."⁵⁴

Holiness is for Balthasar the highest form of authority in the Church. Balthasar notes, additionally, that the saints were never ones to dissent from the official Church, although they had the most ground to criticize her official structure.⁵⁵ Balthasar attributes this forbearance to the profound sense of the Church that every saint has; ecclesiality, a sense of being a member of the body, is, for Balthasar, indispensable for sanctity. Charism is for service, and not for the saint in himself or herself. Balthasar differs from the sociological view of ecclesial authority which models the priesthood of all believers on political democracy in that he understands holiness as unique, and the uniqueness for the sake of the common mission; it may take the form of a Dorothy Day, it may be embodied in a Therese of Lisieux.

The common face of holiness is the service of love, and this holiness, while subjective, rests on the objective holiness of the Church in her official structure, namely, the sacraments and the hierarchical office. This does not emerge out of a belief in the perfection of the Church, but rather from a sense of the Church's "role" in salvation history as intimately tied to the mission of Christ, the mission of love. Love cannot express itself in disunity and agonism. Thus, instead of an invisible Church of saints that distinguishes itself from a visible Church of sinners, often identified with the hierarchy, one could crystallize Balthasar's ecclesiology of authority into the following rubrics: Whose Church? Which obedience? *Christ's* Church. The obedience of *the saints*, formed by the Church. Personal authority in the Church arises from the enactment of one's vocation, and this authority is indeed possible for everyone.

Balthasar recognizes that those who hold official authority in the Church are human, fallible, and prone to sin. He writes, "For Ignatius, then, obedience as the central attitude of the Church as bride of Christ is the true core, the most sublime concept of discipleship: *ecce ancilla*. But obedience, once detached from this inner disposition (perhaps more through the one who gives than the one who receives commands) and seen simply as a tool for the use of the hierarchy as such can and must lead to abuses."⁵⁶

---

54. *ET* II, 28.
55. Balthasar, *Bernanos*.
56. "Office in the Church," in *ET* II, 134.

The Official Church and the Formation of Ecclesial Persons

Importantly, however, Balthasar does not dispense with or downplay the importance of the hierarchy. The Petrine profile is as much a part of the reality of the Church as the Johannine. Moreover, Bernanos shows how the two missions are mutually implicated. The complexity involved in Christian "following" is a reason, according to Balthasar, that office in the Church exists. Balthasar's conception of the Church comprises a crucial aspect of the reality that textures Christian life because it enables personal, communal, and social vocation to become *actual*. Office mediates personhood and participation in divine life as personhood develops through consenting to one's mission; yet mission is the result of a personal call, on the one hand, and the fruit of a communal judgment on the other. Balthasar states, "In order to identify with his mission, the individual cannot look only at an individual ideal of himself in God. Rather, together with others, he has to view the communal ideal of an *ecclesia immaculata* and thus *infallibilis*."[57] Each individual is not to look to his ideal of himself in God by himself and for himself, but must consider the way in which he is forming, with others, the Church of pure receptivity to Christ. A mediating authority thus becomes necessary to guard individuals against individualism in the use of their gifts. Balthasar clarifies that ecclesial authority is fundamentally "rooted in every baptized Christian's 'yes' to the Word of God," and that Christ has instituted ecclesial office for the sake of concretely enacting love.[58]

The office holder has, then, for Balthasar two chief tasks: "to point with authority to the ideal and to the rule that is above everyone, namely to the concrete and pneumatic Christ as he shows himself in Scripture to be authentic and accessible for all the faithful,"[59] and "authoritatively to actualize, re-present, what it points to, for this reason Christ has conferred on it the authority to teach, to make present sacramentally, to govern legitimately."[60] Notably, the absolute sovereignty of Christ is underlined in Balthasar's portrayal of office; all stand under Christ's authority, including the one who holds office.

The importance Balthasar places on ecclesial authority does not overlook, however, the tension in which authority exists. While

---

57. Ibid., 240.
58. Ibid.
59. Ibid., 241.
60. Ibid., 242.

acknowledging that ecclesial authority is divinely instituted, Balthasar makes two claims that signal the *qualified* and *unqualified* aspects of ecclesial authority and ecclesial obedience: (1) "Ecclesial authority and obedience is *qualified* in the case where one may compare ecclesial authority's allusion to the evangelical norm with the norm itself and discern such a divergence from this norm that one's ecclesial conscience compels him to prefer the gospel norm to the directive of the authorities."[61] (2) Yet ecclesial office is unqualified[62] in the sense that the validity of the office stands apart from the authentic witness of the office holder because "the synthesis of authority and witness cannot be institutionalized."[63]

This distinction is another way of clarifying that the source of ecclesial authority is the authority of the Holy Spirit. That Spirit allows one who has an ecclesial conscience to pursue the truth of the evangelical norm if the directive of his religious superior is discerned to diverge from that norm. However, because the authority of ecclesial office is rooted in the Holy Spirit, the lack of holiness of the office holder does not give one grounds for disobedience and can never be used to justify a decision to disobey.

Indeed, Balthasar observes the profound failure of Peter *in* office, and how Christ foresees this failure, noting that Christ predicts that *Peter* will deny him three times and does. Balthasar asks, "Who will ever want or be able to recognize as supreme ecclesial authority him who denied his Lord three times? In Peter it becomes fundamentally evident that mission and person are timelessly identical only in Christ; thus in him alone are the priest who offers and the lamb being offered identical."[64] So, failure in office does not negate the authority of the office. The important reality that Balthasar highlights in his excursus on Petrine office is that the community cannot be dependent on the identity between official authority and personal authority; this perfection does not exist in Peter, nor does such perfection need to exist. To demand such perfection is to fall into the error that the Donatists did in the time of Augustine.[65] Authority comes from "above," from the graced insertion into the life of Christ, by Christ's love and Christ's choosing.

61. Ibid., 243.
62. "Christology and Ecclesial Obedience," in *ET* IV.
63. Ibid.
64. Ibid.
65. Ibid., 246–47.

The Authority of Holiness in the Laity

Attending the shift in emphasis from Church as institution to Church as personal and Trinitarian is Balthasar's passionate interest in the life of the laity. Balthasar's deepest commitment in life was, according to his biographers, less to formulating a theological vision than it was to elevating the laity to what he believed was the highest place of authority: that of the holy life of a people set apart. All of his writings are, he has been quoted as saying, only for the sake of enabling the life of secular institutes to flourish,[66] "to prepare the way for communities of lay Christians that would abide in the world in the spirit of the beloved disciple. His works sought to convey a Johannine spirit 'deeply rooted in the mysteries of the Catholic faith' that would allow laypersons consecrated to the Lord to bear witness through their lives to the organic unity and interconnectedness of the divine mysteries."[67] For Balthasar, the highest, most profound "insertion" or participation in the life of Christ comes through participation in the life of the evangelical counsels. While this has traditionally tended to be reserved for those who have received a call to religious life, Balthasar believed that laypersons can also receive such a high calling to live lives consecrated to a close following of God, which entails "leaving everything" and observing poverty, chastity, and obedience in their lives "in the world." This indicates again that Balthasar's primary sense of the Church is not that of the Church as office, but as the mystery that penetrates the world and responds to the pathos of the world through holy lives infused with the Holy Spirit of Christ and his Father.

Secular Institutes

Balthasar's commitment to a Church that understands itself in terms of representation and substitution emerges in his belief that the life of the evangelical counsels must be retrieved with new seriousness in this age and culture. Believing that the presence of Christ must be lived compellingly in the world, and championing the role of laypersons embodying the living Christ in the world, Balthasar saw the life of the secular institutes as the form that truly transformative, effective witness must take to reach "post-Christian man." Balthasar believed that this way of "entering

---

66. Scola, *Hans Urs von Balthasar: A Theological Style*.
67. Servais, "Balthasar as Interpreter," 192.

into the form of Christ in order to share the fruitfulness of his work,"[68] while coming generally from faith, baptism, and sharing in the Eucharist, comes in a more specific way through the life of the evangelical counsels, which are marked, above all, by openness to a call. The life of the counsels is that life

> through which the act of self-expropriation in faith and of handing oneself over to God contains a completeness that cannot be surpassed by man himself. The first essential condition for this is that one can or may posit this act, not at his own disposal, but only on the basis of a particular *condition of being disposed of, being called, and receiving grace*; otherwise this act would contradict itself as soon as it was posited. For it is not seriously possible to have control over the state in which one is totally subject to control by God; all one can do—though consciously, in love, giving one's consent—is to *allow* oneself to be brought into this state. This insight forms the basis of the entire design of the Ignatian Exercises. It is demonstrated through Mary's existence, with which the life of the New Covenant begins.[69]

Balthasar comes to his conviction in the secular institutes by way of a close look at history, and, in particular, in the proposal and limitations of Catholic Action. He believed that the movement, and others like it, rightly urged laypeople to further involvement but "left the forces of the counsels unused" even as they required total commitment, formation, and involved contemplative practices.[70] Balthasar believes, however, that the present hour is indeed that of the lay apostolate, the fullness of which requires nothing less than the life of the counsels;[71] thus, the synthesis called for is "the synthesis between lay existence[72] and the state of the counsels."[73]

68. *LLC*, 22.
69. Ibid., 25.
70. Ibid., 58.
71. Ibid.
72. A reasonable question to pose to Balthasar is whether only laity who profess the counsels are capable of evangelizing this age. It would seem that Balthasar would acknowledge the virtue and grace that flow from committed and faithful married persons, for example, laity who don't profess the counsels, but that he would consider there to be something more, and that which is urgently needed today that can only be provided by the radicality of the secular institutes. Here is where the author would ask whether Balthasar gives sufficient scope to the possibilities arising from the witness of faithful families.
73. Ibid.

Balthasar realizes, of course, that the counsels have fallen into disrepute for their tendency to be forms bent toward individualistic self-perfection, ideals of personality. He notes that "this situation will not improve until the decision has been made to abandon the ideal of spiritual self-development and perfecting, the religious 'ideal of personality,' in favor of an ideal of being free for Christian mission, which never coincides with the personality of the one sent, or derives from it, but lays claim to everything in the person—possessions, body, and soul—in order to be able to make him in all respects God's messenger in the world."[74] What is needed is a theology of the institutes infused by the concept of *mission*.

Balthasar notes the role of the Holy Spirit in the founding of religious orders, and that the secular institutes emerge in like fashion, that is, somewhat unpredictably for the Church; he uses the analogy of "a meteor" to describe the experience of holiness by the Church in general.

The point of the secular institutes is that they seek to meet the call for the Church to be present to the world through her laypeople, and laypeople who live in the world a radical existence for Christ, where their lives are an expression of love, which is perfected through the form of poverty, chastity, and obedience. The secular institutes, then, hope to bring about an equality between clergy and laity, through shared participation in the life of the counsels, and to leave persons in the world, in their realms of professional expertise, there to meet the everyday person and to reveal something of that intimacy with Love which saves the world.

Balthasar deems the "leveling out" of the ecclesial states of life to be

> the most important of these theological decisions, which, since the Middle Ages, have often shut each other out in a virtually caste-like way. Strictly speaking, since the members of secular institutes belong neither to the "religious" nor to the "laity" as they are defined in canon law, they participate in both forms of life, or rather, in their return to the basic New Testament rock, they have opened up a place wherein the distinction between the religious and those in the world has not yet been made.[75]
>
> Certainly, they have to be sowers and planters of a new Christian community, not to dwell there in comfort but to continue their journeying from there as apostles in a new solitude. It is obvious that this spirituality as a form of life is not for everyone, but it belongs, in however attenuated a degree, to

---

74. Ibid., 66.
75. Ibid., 230.

the ecclesial maturity and responsibility of those who have been confirmed. One cannot be simply—today less than ever—the Church as a product; one must always be the Church producing. The Church community can never definitively be rounded off and self-contained; once it has reached this stage it must open out in the "*Ite, missa est*" to the world and to solitude.[76]

The Pauline Profile

Looked at ecclesiologically, the interrelationship of the two instituted poles of unity (Peter and Mary) is the true place of living coming-to-be in contrast to a distorting absolutizing of the one pole and to a one-sided orientation to it of being-Catholic. That is where the veneration of Mary gets distorted into Mariolatry which gets disruptively mixed in with christocentrism and theocentrism; or where one finds the distortion of the official function of unity into ultra-Montanism and "popolatry." Then one forgets that both principles point beyond themselves to a higher, founding centre: Mary is only the handmaid, Peter only the servant of the servants. The unity of the *Catholica* then lies ultimately in the vitally lived interrelationship of two poles which as such guarantee the real indwelling of the unity-founding head in his body: the "in" of the "over."[77]

"The dynamic of the becoming-Catholic within a being-Catholic can be illustrated with the dynamic of the life of Paul: 'Not that I am already perfect; but I press on to make it my own, because Jesus has made me his own': In the being-made-his-own lies the surrendering; in the pressing-on lies the demand to be met in it. Paul insists, 'Brethren, I do not consider that I have made it my own; but one thing I do, forgetting what lies behind and straining forward to what lies ahead'; but after this emphasis on the purely being-moved, he can once again dwell on being-taken-over from above: 'Let all those of us who are mature be thus-minded . . .' In the final substantive, it becomes clear that *Catholics can claim for themselves the title of being Catholic only under the condition that they are minded like Paul and do not kid themselves and others that they have comprehended it.*

---

76. Balthasar, *Bernanos*.
77. Balthasar, *Office of Peter*.

This could be the starting point of *a whole Catholic ethics and aesthetics,* but we cannot go into that now."[78]

Is Balthasar successful at combining his recognition of how God's glory brings about conversion and the subject-centered reality of modern social imaginaries? We have gleaned from our study of Charles Taylor that secularity is a development over five hundred years that has entrenched a certain immanence in the collective consciousness or social imaginary of modern Western culture and that

(1) within this situation, faith is still possible;

(2) there exist unmet spiritual yearnings or malaise, and the search for fullness may indicate that faith alone can yield authentic or whole selves (cf. spiritual lobotomy); and

(3) there exist lives open to transcendence, and something in the Latin Christian tradition seems to meet this quest for "fullness."

Does Balthasar have an answer, with the "opening" Taylor has provided into the modern Western psyche, to how the Church can meet the needs of this age?

In the first sections of chapter 3 I argued that Balthasar understands much of what Taylor seems concerned to elucidate in *A Secular Age, Modern Social Imaginaries, A Catholic Modernity?, Malaise of Modernity,* and *Sources of the Self.* The burden of chapter 3 was to depict the convergence of diagnosis between Taylor and Balthasar on modernity. The second part of the chapter showed how Balthasar connects up the issues of fragmented and incomplete personhood with a theology of time and personhood in Christ within a theodramatic horizon. The aim was to demonstrate that Balthasar's theologically robust understanding of personhood in Christ is necessary for the Church to express her transformative message in a secular age of persons yearning for authenticity, true beauty, and goodness.

In the present chapter, I complete the argument for Balthasar's contribution to clarifying Catholic witness in a secular age by expounding Balthasar's understanding of how the Church forms persons in Christ, and how the Church's commitment to being a receptive Church that understands mission in terms of the formation of holy persons may succeed at creating a radically different sense of mission for a secular age. I draw out the implications of the importance of Balthasar's emphasis

78. Balthasar, "The Absoluteness of Christianity and the Catholicity of the Church" in *Explorations in Theology*, volume 5.

on eschatology and ecclesiology for effective mission in a modern age. Balthasar engages modernity precisely at the point where he expounds the meaning of holiness in this age: his account of the diversity of missions in the Church, all of which are underlined by a profound sense of ecclesiality; a nuanced understanding of authority that privileges the receptive face of the Church according to the example of Mary; and a notion of the official Church as being called, above all, to form persons, or to foster the subjective holiness of individual Christians. The latter, the advancement of transformed Christian persons, becomes the new priority for the Church's mission in a secular age.

In the end, however, mission becomes immensely simple as Balthasar sees it: it comes down to a true faith that sets one free for loving service without need for self-defense, and for joy in that service. Balthasar underlines the problem with "programs" as a way to think about mission, and an overdetermination in advance of how mission should appear in any one individual's case. Mission is, rather, the thing that comes when one gives oneself completely in trust and loving obedience to the Lord. The witness comes in the form that divine love then takes within us, and Balthasar clarifies how deeply intangible that reality is.

Quoting St. Paul, the deepest reality the Christian can offer the world is the "garden of love, which here bursts forth into new life, with many different names" (Balthasar's eloquent description):

> "Compassion, kindness, lowliness, meekness, patience, forbearing one another ... the peace of Christ ... and above all these put on love" (Col 3:12–15). And again: "Love, joy, peace, patience, kindness, goodness, faithfulness, gentleness, self-control" (Gal 5:22), in connection with which it is important to observe that joy is mentioned immediately after love, and that from this joy should emanate, like the fragrance from flowers, all the various kinds of love and forgiveness that are a reflection of that love vouchsafed to Christians (Col 3:13) by Christ himself and therefore by God (Eph 4:32)—"a fragrant offering and sacrifice to God" (Eph 5:2).

So, Balthasar offers only the "formula" of a true response of self-giving love to God, a relationship of complete trust and confidence in God's love and goodness that leaves one free to make a total gift of self for the redemption of the world.[79]

---

79. "Cordula," in *MCW*, 133–41.

What arises from the total and complete following of Christ in and through his Church is the happiness of the neighbor, a sense of who she or he truly is:

> Because, however, the most significant thing in life that can happen to our neighbor is his being laid claim to and taken seriously as a person, an event that leaves on him the most lasting impression, a state that constitutes for him the source of the greatest happiness he can know on earth, in this above all lies the credibility of the Church, and the success of the mission of Christianity.[80]

As we have become persons in and through Christ, so, too, are we to invite others to the gift of such personalization. Through the love that is offered in the person of Christ through his Church, through the Church that forms persons, can faith, love, and hope transform the world.

---

80. *EG*, 55.

CHAPTER 5

Conclusion

TAYLOR AND BALTHASAR EACH offer rich resources out of which to develop a proposal for how to express Catholic witness and mission in a secular age. Their stances, social and ecclesial, can appear to come down reductively to two options: (1) dialogue with a pluralistic culture with an aim of greater mutual understanding of others' spiritual orientations and, ultimately, some reconciliation, or (2) proclamation of Christ through the radiance of holy lives. Taylor's fundamental answer regarding Catholic mission and witness could be described as affirming the plurality of spiritual paths toward God and embracing the diversity of religious experience in various local cultures so as to deepen catholicity. He would thereby advocate dialogue, openness, and much more freedom and respect in the relationship between the hierarchy and the rest of the Roman Catholic Church. Within this analysis, Taylor would also call for attention to the "seekers" and openness to how faith may look in a secular age. He reassures that faith will not simply disappear.

Balthasar would have a different perspective. Balthasar would hold that the necessary form of mission today is not dialogue, primarily, as much as a radiant existential, personal revelation of God's love. To that end, he would advocate openness to an age of secular institutes, a life of love expressed by laypersons arising from a total gift of self to God through a life according to the evangelical counsels of poverty, chastity, and obedience. Balthasar is keenly aware of the situation of secularity and does not advocate retrenchment in any way but, instead, a going out into the world, with a difference. The vows, for Balthasar, are a way of crystallizing the radical self-surrender at the heart of true sanctity. Holiness is not simply a matter of exemplary "good works." The saints participate in the radical obedience of the Son. Revealing Christ in the world means having the relationship of utter disposability to the divine will that characterized Mary's life.

This work has sought, however, to bring out the complexity in their projects and to locate a point of convergence between their visions. It has found the latter in Taylor's account of lives that give witness to an experience of real conversion and the formation of ever-greater "networks of agape." Despite Taylor's great affirmation of modernity and even secularity, he ends his account of the conditions of belief with a confession of his personal conviction that Christian faith may be the best way to live amidst the dilemmas and "unquiet frontiers" of modernity insofar as he sees life most truly in the lives of "saints." When comparing the work of Taylor on modernity with that of Balthasar on Christian existence, an unexpected complementarity and richness emerge for the question of Catholic witness in "a secular age." One configuration of this complementarity is to describe Taylor's work as raising the question of religious faith in a new way, which expresses the questions, attitudes, and frameworks of religious seekers today and proposes, ultimately, Christian existence as a possible answer to such seeking; and Balthasar's work as providing a substantive vision of Catholic existence through a retrieval of the Church's relevance to modern persons in terms of sanctity, and the Church's spirituality of communion. My claim in this work is that the modern search and striving for authenticity and community show the relevance of Taylor and Balthasar to the question of contemporary Catholic witness in the West. I go further to clarify that both approaches are required for Catholic mission today to move from a first reception of Vatican II's call to engage modernity to a second reception; and that Taylor's approach must be deepened through an appropriation of Balthasar's theology of personhood and my interpretation of Balthasar's ecclesiology. Both indicate the power of the communion of saints to offer something truly exemplary and meaningful for this age.

However, it is precisely this agreement that leads to a deeper affirmation of Balthasar and acknowledgment of the limits of Taylor's contribution for understanding the necessary shape of Catholic mission in a secular age. For Taylor's own earlier work reveals the importance of social horizons to personal formation. If his account of the immanent frame is accurate, then keeping the possibility of openness to transcendence as an option through lives that reveal true conversion will require a community that operates out of an alternative social imaginary to form such persons, a community inscribed with an awareness of the transcendence that is largely denied by the secular social imaginary of Western modernity. Saints, too, emerge from a "social matrix," one that is transformed, however, by the presence of Christ and his Spirit, who welcome and accompany receptive persons on the way to the Father. It is true that saints themselves transcend, according to Balthasar, the bounds of ecclesial imagination, nonetheless, they do not arise *ex nihilo* either, on his account.

Taylor's work, read in a certain manner, can highlight the way in which an exploration of the making of the moral self of modernity reveals spiritual roots to problems that are ultimately linked to theological configurations (or lack thereof) of time and space. Taylor also illustrates with his work on secularity and social imaginaries that secularity is a development that has occurred over a period of five hundred years and, therefore, is not easily dismissed or upended (the last of which is impossible to do, actually, without grace). The development of secularity means that a new horizon of "functional" consciousness exists in contemporary modern Western cultures—a default "tilt" toward immanence frames all discussions of religious belief. This frame of immanence means that contemporary persons have different fundamental referents, ones that are seemingly indifferent to transcendence but highly attuned to freedom in terms of "options," economic productivity, and benevolence (restricted to what humanity can do on its own). Secular or exclusive humanism is the dominant life "option" in Western societies today. In short, Taylor articulates the substantive normative developments in contemporary Western cultures and societies in a new way, which leaves cultures with an awareness of their fundamental social horizon, as well as the option to live for and out of the awareness of something more. Taylor also presents the Church with a picture of the culture she seeks to transform in a manner that moves beyond description of the age as that of "crisis."

It is indeed true that in many contemporary Western societies today the experience of genuine Christian faith is in crisis. Taylor's work shows, in some measure, just how profound the crisis is. *Modern Social Imaginaries* and *A Secular Age* demonstrate that modern Western cultures have an immanentist normativity inscribed in their social imaginary. The secular social imaginary of liberal Western societies is not neutral. Religion is only one option and it is not the one most frequently taken. Selves are much more inclined to pursue and reveal authentic individuality rather than personhood formed by God with and through a community of faith. Modern selves, one might derive from Taylor's works taken cumulatively, suffer from atomism, instrumentalism in thinking, and a lack of fullness because of this loss of openness to transcendence.

Taylor thus gestures to authentic lives of conversion that nonetheless remain possible amid the ever disappearing horizon of Christian faith. But Taylor can only gesture to the possibility of a truly self-transcending life; Balthasar, as a theologian, fleshes out the spiritual conditions for a truly self-transcending life. Balthasar's articulation of human freedom as a gift, fundamentally underwritten by the gratuitous love and freedom of God, and fulfilled human existence as one that allows oneself to participate in the "drama" of life in, with, and through God (and authenticity as that which is only possible through an engagement with God), is both Balthasar's answer to a secular age and what the Church is called to reveal to this age in her contemporary saints. Appealing to the desire for wholeness in all human persons and rearticulating the desire for self-transcendence through a theodramatic narrative of human freedom and redemption of the world through life in Christ and his Church, Balthasar proposes a way in which mission today must be conducted inductively. That is, rather than an approach of inculturation, Balthasar argues for living catholicity in our age by bringing people to an encounter with Christ through becoming persons in Christ. This approach follows the logic of revelation: revealing the presence of God in the world through the Church's cultivation of love and holiness in herself, and a recognition that this love and holiness do not exist apart from the slow and bumbling institution of the Church but precisely must pass through it, because of its reality as a gift of Christ to the world.

Thus, Balthasar leads us to recognize, I believe, that contemplation, spiritual formation, and deepening a sense of ecclesiality are the most important actions for evangelizing mission that the Church can take in and for the contemporary world. Action arising from contemplation receives its life from the Passion of Christ. It is, inevitably, a different kind of action and becomes, cumulatively, a different kind of life. The life that stems from a profound sense of unity as a body rooted in the One who precedes us provides new dimension to Christian ethics also. Ethics that might manifest itself as moralism is then replaced by an ethic that aspires to holiness both in its sense of love as unity and, above all, in its childlike dependence and trust in the ever-living God for sustenance, and above all, as Pope Francis has emphasized, in its mercy. Contrary to a form of rejecting *aggiornamento* or endorsing insularism,[1] Balthasar, in light of Taylor, upends the belief that prayer and the formation of holy persons are world-denying and shows that holy intimacy with God is, ultimately, the most profound way in which the Catholic Church may engage the world, especially in a secular age.[2]

Reconciliation takes the form of a "yes" and a "no" to culture, in the manner that Balthasar so convincingly shows in "The Fathers, Scholastics and Ourselves." Balthasar helps us retrieve the "no" implicit in *aggiornamento*, for we are to bring the Church up to date while remaining the Church; Taylor shows us how to do so without moralism.[3] Both recall us to the centrality and the glory of the human person made in the image of God, and Balthasar, in particular, to the equally defacing dimension of sin in human lives. Together, they help shape a vision of mission that places a centrality on the Church's understanding and valorization of the human person at the heart of modernity and the faith of the Church, and underscore the increasingly lived form that apologetics must take. Together, they show that mission in a secular age requires communion between persons and the triune God and a love of modern man, who seeks and discovers the truth of his identity, above all, in God.

Most simply put, our engagement of Taylor and Balthasar on the question of Catholic mission and witness yields the following: mission's form in a secular age is to reveal that the true expression of authenticity in person and existence and the height of creative self-expression lies in

---

1. One can point to texts in the church fathers where they rejoice in the fact that there exists no other holy land than the world in its totality, for Jesus, the Risen One, is everywhere present. This openness of the Church, her mystery notwithstanding, stands in contradiction to the erection of earthly "bastions" and makes the apostolic movement less believable to people who perceive this contradiction. Balthasar, *Test Everything*, 10.

2. Especially with the poverty of the visible Church, does the Church of the saints show its strength . . . does Church need to be seen in terms of *anima ecclesiastica* and a spirituality of communion rather than as an institution opposed to the world. This is not to minimize, however, the great importance of the Church's commitment to social justice, which is also a crucial form of Catholic witness and mission in this age.

3. To clarify, Taylor's vision of reality can exhibit signs of moralism, but his approach is not rooted in a fundamental suspicion or negative judgment of modern cultures, the latter of which is a great stumbling block to the world's recognition of God in the Church.

personal and communal relationship with God. Witness must be to the reconciliation that fundamentally exists between God, humanity, and the cosmos.

What, then, are the implications of thinking with both Taylor and Balthasar for the Church and specifically for mission? In the introduction, I shared three tropes for mission for a postmodern age, as outlined by David Bosch: "the Church with others," "inculturation," and "common witness." These have guided the analyses and study here of the resources available in the works of Taylor and Balthasar for understanding and conceiving of mission for contemporary Western cultures. In light of this research, some new ways of articulating the shape of Catholic mission proposed by this work include the following: (1) To be *the Church with others* means that the Church is called today to assist modern secular persons in their quest for authenticity and the challenges that attend this quest, such as instrumentalism, subjectivism, and atomism. (2) To be the *Church inculturating* means that the Church must learn the *lingua franca* of modernity—"expression," "authenticity," "benevolence," "rights"—and speak to the genuine desires implicit in it. It also means that the Church must know the person of Christ in order to share him with the world. (3) To be the *Church as common witness* means affirming that ecclesial unity is a necessary dimension of effective mission, and that an ecclesial hermeneutic must be retrieved in Catholic self-understanding such that worship, prayer, catechesis, and formation foreground the discourse and understanding of Catholic moral teaching and practices.

The complementarity I have striven to underscore should not occlude the ways in which Taylor and Balthasar diverge in their understanding of effective Catholic witness in this age. The Church's first priority, for Balthasar, is to love the Lord and one another; this leads to a genuine love of one's enemy. The Church cannot concentrate, however, on "looking" or being interested in understanding culture without a sense of the true end of her mission to be to give glory to God. Such an end requires listening. Tradition and dialogue are mutually involving. When the Church has dissipated herself in "affirming the difference of the other, all others,"[4] thinking then that she has found the formula to imitating the triune God, she needs to go back to the Lord, repent, and renew her relationship with the Father, Son, and their Spirit. In such a vision of Catholic witness,

---

4. For example, the difference of the other who affirms violence and terror as a rule of life is not to be affirmed.

prayer, worship, formation, and an ecclesial spirituality become the necessary priorities of mission.

Thinking in the vein of *aggiornamento* today with Taylor *and* Balthasar means that the Church must again receive her responsibility for transforming the culture around her. George Marsden, commenting on *A Catholic Modernity?*, helpfully indicates how Taylor's approach to modernity does not alienate the culture, but also how modernity even as Taylor has described it is inimical to Christianity. Thus, he suggests "the metaphor of the prodigal" over Taylor's approach to modernity, with Matteo Ricci's mission to China as example. Appreciating Marsden's critique, I, too, wish to invite a deeper openness to culture that first sees culture with the compassion of the Father and stands with open arms ready to receive a culture, recognizing all the while the manner in which it has strayed.[5] Marsden is clearer than Taylor is on what needs to be recognized in the culture as anti-Christian:

> The image of the prodigal helps clarify another dimension that I think is faithful to what Taylor intends to say. It highlights the deep ambivalence that Christians should have toward modernity. It is not just non-Christian. It is, in part, an anti-Christian rebellion with all the bitterness that a broken family relationship can engender. Ultimately, it is a rebellion not only against Christianity but also against God's love (even if institutional Christianity often must share the blame for keeping people from seeing God's love). It is, moreover, a rebellion that takes God's gifts that are potentially good and turns them to evil by absolutizing them. In Augustinian terms, it is a rebellion of directing one's most impassioned love toward some limited aspect of creation rather than to the Creator. Such misplaced love is ultimately destructive both of self and of the ability to love others.[6]

Although Taylor gestures to the problems and costs associated with the transition to a secular understanding of the world—a "flattened" horizon, a disquieting sense of a lack of fullness, spiritual lobotomy—Taylor de-emphasizes the need for the culture itself to be transformed. Rather than

---

5. To clarify, we should love culture as the Father loves the world, but we should be clear that the task of the Church is to accompany the world on the way to the Father, to be a handmaid to the Lord in this task. My adoption of Marsden's metaphor should be taken with the assumption of an entirely analogical understanding of the Church as Father. But this should be clear from Balthasarian emphases on Church as Marian, Church as handmaid and spouse of the Word.

6. Marsden, "Matteo Ricci and the Prodigal Culture," 86.

name its rebellion against God's love in a direct way, Taylor discusses the problems of radical immanence rhetorically, taking into account the kind of strong evaluations at play for most people living within the immanent frame. While this move may be effective in opening up skeptics to faith, it ultimately requires a more truthful judgment about what happens when one mistakes the horizon of immanence for the sphere of ultimate ends. This latter vision can only be clear for one who has experienced the good beyond immanence, the givenness of God in revelation. Only then does the rejection of the same show its brutality and cost.

Dialogue and an ever-deepening understanding of what it means to engage in transforming dialogue must continue,[7] but it is ever important that the Church remind herself that her only answers to the world's needs (for example, "social justice" or "a universal life ethic") are those that express an ongoing relationship with the eternally self-divesting Lord and to model self-emptying in turn. In this time, amidst the chaos of the world, the task of the Church must be to reveal God's love for the world to the world by allowing herself to live out of God's own deep love for his Church. Rooted in such love, the Church can then go forward into the world, affirming it with a discerning spirit, loving it into change.

Taken together, Taylor and Balthasar generate an alternative understanding of church and culture that may prevent the understandings that cause division in the Church, that is, love of laity at the expense of respect for ecclesial authority or church as a truly inclusive body, or vice versa. Culture has changed dramatically since the time of the Second Vatican Council. We have come to realize, for example, that "the secular" does not simply connote a sphere—social, institutional, or otherwise—that is characterized by the absence of religion. Rather, the secular is also "a presence,"[8] and is represented or becomes coded in a social imaginary that takes certain beliefs to be ultimately true: human beings are fundamentally economic agents, identity is public, and self-rule is the will of all peoples.

What Taylor offers with his close analysis of the situation of modernity and secularity is some clues as to how to "speak" to a culture of faith in the Christian God. Rather than use the traditional language of the Church, which argues against secularism because of its detrimental

---

7. Too often we have asked, "Is the way forward going to be dialogue or retrenchment?" This work suggests that dialogue, in itself, cannot be "the answer." In many ways, it has become an ideology or "code" rather than a fruitful act of mutual self-gift.

8. Calhoun et al., *Rethinking Secularism*.

effects on the relationship of people to truth and goodness, Taylor speaks to the strong-evaluating subject, who looks at life in terms of experiences of "fullness." One's life in a pervasively secular world will not be as full, Taylor avers. Taylor locates his critique of the secularity, however, within a more general affirmation of the goods of secularity and the goods of the desires of modern selves. This is Taylor's long-standing approach to the culture of Western modernity and how he sees the possibility of Catholic modernity being realized. One must discern the goods of modernity and become humbled by the historical failures of the Church. He celebrates the worldwide movements of solidarity and sympathy and works to bring about equality and rights to all persons. He affirms the ethos of authenticity that arose from Romanticism and expressivism. He thinks that the ordinary life of production and reproduction is where we can indeed live out our true callings. This willingness to acknowledge the goods in modernity is at the least an expression of acceptance and hospitality that expresses a truth beyond words.

Taylor's account of modernity is important for the Church, however, not only because it clarifies a direction in which charity may be expressed but also because it diagnoses the kinds of unmet desires and needs from which the world is suffering and proposes that a life open to transcendence may help the project of human freedom. His early work on humans as strong evaluators who make moral judgments on the basis of hypergoods sought to open up the way for a retrieval of the theistic sources. As consistently as Taylor has argued for a need to recognize the gains made in and through modernity, and through the devolution of Christendom, Taylor has also shown that modern selves have incurred losses: they have become buffered, atomistic, instrumentalist in their thinking, and subjectivistic. In Taylor's narrative of secularity, the twists and turns of intellectual history and the history of peoples on the ground lead to the development of a moral order that actually closes off openness to transcendence ("the immanent frame"), the very thing that Taylor argues can free selves from the malaises that ail them in modernity. Taylor provides a picture of how the world has developed a secular imaginary and shows how this imaginary has to some degree seemingly closed out the option for faith. He notes that lives that reveal true conversion may nonetheless emerge and seems to imply that this opens up the possibility of transcendence to those living within the immanent frame.

With this discernment of what is good in the culture of modernity, it may be the ideal of authenticity in contemporary culture that is one of the key resources for evangelical and missiological efforts today. Perhaps speaking to the religious seeker and all who strive to live authentically will invite people to consider living an ecclesial existence again. The Church needs to speak to those desires of modern selves who are, in many cases, living an arbitrary life of self-expression that is more akin to subjectivism than to truly generative, admirable creativity. The cult of being original, of making something one's own, is the culture in which we live; breaking with tradition is valorized as the mark of true creativity. Taylor's awareness of the importance of self in determining its freedom is evident in the way he proposes faith as *an option*, and possibly a better option because it helps people transcend some of the limitations and tyranny of life within the immanent frame.

There thus exist real possibilities in and limits to Taylor's use for understanding Catholic mission in a secular age. While Taylor makes great strides with his philosophical work toward conceiving of how to witness to the triune God of Christianity in a secular age—on the genesis of modern moral identity, the malaises that attend modern selves, the shape and constraints of the modern social imaginary, the approach of charitable discernment as a model of truly Catholic modernity, and the development of modern secularity—he is also reluctant to speak definitively on the uniqueness of the message that Christianity offers to humanity. Indeed, Taylor seems to underscore from time to time that he does not say Christian faith is the only way. He leaves faith as an option, true to the culture of our time, and alludes explicitly to the non-necessity of a life of conversion or holiness coinciding with membership in the Catholic Church.

Taylor's vision can thus only take the Church so far, for while he can rightly say that individual lives that are living signs of a network of *agape* are what will enable culture to live out its best ideals, he also seems to want to suggest that the Church move into some ways of being modern that are actually in tension with the gift that the Church offers to help modern selves out of their moral predicaments. For example, Taylor is openly critical of the structure of authority in the Church. However, part of the need for the Church to live in the mode of institution is that institution supports unity through history. Without tradition, there is no sharing of the gospel. Without contact with Christ, mediated by a verticality that emphasizes the majesty and otherness of God, there is nothing to share. Taylor's analysis of modernity can only serve the Church's question of mission to a point because its point of departure is the modern world and it to some degree capitulates overly to the ethos of modernity such that it cannot fully mount the immanent critique it would like.

Otherwise stated, Taylor can only bring the Church so far in his approach to incarnating the catholic principle today. He needs to say more about the person of Christ and the Church. As a modern liberal philosopher, Taylor will not say, "The Church brings to humankind the truth about human existence and the human condition." He can only clear the ground for this to be addressed by someone else. Taylor in his account of the Church can also be overly sociological; that is, the Church or Christians are simply another group whose interests must be negotiated and reconciled with the rest. The Church can only go so far with Taylor because he himself is internally inconsistent and prevents the Church from attaining the orientation toward herself that she needs to have in order to serve the world. That is, let us suppose that the following three premises of Taylor are true:

1. Secularity has developed to the point that it forms the horizon of most modern selves in the West and has occluded the horizon of a reality brought about and sustained by a loving Creator God who is invested at every moment in the lives of his creatures.

2. What keeps plurality and richness in play is a retrieval of the possibility of being open to transcendence—those whose lives reveal conversion are the ones who can keep the possibility of transcendence open as an option for persons living in a secular age.

3. Persons are formed by their horizons, by their traditions.

It would seem that Taylor would want to support those who sustain and keep the Catholic tradition alive. However, Taylor is, in places, very critical of the hierarchy. This shows the tension or weakness in his account of Catholic Christianity. Even as Taylor celebrates "conversions," changed lives as the realities that may transform social and personal life for the better, in the end, his account of the Church undercuts the potential of those "saints" to emerge. Despite his own profound contributions to understanding the role of larger horizons in identity formation, the link between tradition and transformation is not sufficiently strong in his analysis of Christianity. Precisely because of the power of the secular social imaginary, what seems to be needed today is a heightened awareness of the alternative imagination of Christianity, but the tradition that passes on such an alternative vision and social imaginary is undermined by Taylor's critique of ecclesial hierarchy (symbol of unity). Taylor is right to decry the codified dimension of Christianity, which he names as its corruption. The moral profile of the Church will need to reorient itself around formation for virtue and holiness in everyday life rather than judgment of special cases of life and death (such as abortion and euthanasia) alone. However, as Long indicates,[9] it is not the case that dogma need always be reduced to code, and Balthasar shows us how it is precisely the possibility of freedom, rather than its opposite:

> Down through the centuries the Church's longing may seem to have embraced many a secular element, enlivening it, kindling it and ultimately leaving it behind as a charred relic. But this is true of peripheral forms and formulae. Where she sees forms and formulae that express the very essence of her mission, however, she never lets go of them. She keeps them safe in her supra-historical, eschatological core, however much, from the merely historical standpoint, they may seem to be the inert ballast of tradition. This is true of decisive conciliar definitions (Nicaea, Chalcedon, etc.); their continued vitality cannot be explained in purely historical terms. They are not merely baggage carried on the journey: they actively journey along with us.[10]

To recapitulate, Taylor's contribution to understanding contemporary Catholic mission is the following: Taylor helps the Church understand how deep secularity is in our culture; he enables the Church to see it for what it is: the background that shapes how most people generally think and view the world, and, too, how the Church is mixed in with the development of secularity. He assists the Church in understanding the modern world in terms of individuals' desires for authenticity and justice, and the Church's need to respond to the many spiritual seekers in this age. Taylor's approach highlights what is good in the culture and brings faith into consideration as a proposal, an option that helps the culture achieve the ends they most deeply seek. He also challenges the Church to see where she has contributed to the development of secularity in the West, how she might grow from her mistake in rendering Christianity "a code morality" rather than something more true to her organic nature as a communion of love.

What Taylor does not do is this: he is not able to name, as a philosopher, Jesus Christ as the answer to every human person's seeking. He does

9. Long, "How to Read Charles Taylor."
10. Balthasar, *In the Fullness of Faith*, 56–57.

not provide certain answers given the priority of his concern from a social and political perspective, namely, mutual respect and harmony amidst diversity; thus, his emphasis on dialogue and reconciliation through knowing one another. The latter are of course important concerns, but his focus on them leads, it seems, to an underestimation of the special need for unity at this time in the life of the Church. In short, Taylor seems at times too programmatic in his thought of how Catholicism should look, even as he talks about the unfolding of many different possibilities, and he underestimates the importance of unity and sympathy when he talks about the institution.

However, Taylor does show the powerful overlay of the modern social imaginary such that certain forms of reality, such as religious reality, already find themselves interpreted by an overarching framework that is inimical to receiving the otherness of faith. This is deeply valuable. If the Church can recognize this and thus disarm it, which means to some extent accepting that she will not be "understood," and if she can also realize that she can only see beyond the limits of the present with the Lord's help, then the Church will be on the way to retrieving her identity as a missionary Church.

Balthasar provides an ecclesiology rooted in Christology, and an anthropology grounded in ecclesiology. Balthasar thus moves beyond the immanent frame to give an account of the infinite love that grounds human freedom and enables it to become complete. His drama of love between God and humanity, revealed through the life and person of Jesus Christ, articulates with the conviction of a kneeling theology the difference God makes. The question of how to live authentically and with a sense of real ends is answered in Balthasar's account of the person who receives her identity in, through, and with Christ.

Balthasar, while recognizing the modern situation, does not treat it as normative for mission. For Balthasar, Christ is the norm, and Christ is the norm with true objectivity. Balthasar's response to the malaises and the quest of modern persons, which Taylor properly diagnoses—the losses of meaning, of a sense of ends, noninstrumental thinking, moving beyond atomism is that objectivity and one's true identity can be found only in Christ and only in a response that participates in what Christ and his Spirit make possible, namely, a relationship with the Father who sends, who gives one one's name. Balthasar's account of personhood and mission is something the Church needs to appropriate if it is to speak to and to serve the spiritual needs of the present age, particularly the loss of a sense of teleology.

Part of the problem of mission and witness is that the Church has moved away from her center, from the One who sends her, and this is evident in the division that exists within her between "the left" and "the right." The unity she needs to be a credible witness to Christ is the unity of holiness, which can only be achieved through prayer, worship, and right doctrine. Extending the analogy of the individual person who finds her or his identity in Christ, the Church as a body needs crucially to develop her relationship with Christ. She needs to deepen and rediscover her relationship to Christ if she is to have anything to offer the world. In addition to recognizing the secularity of the age and the need of the Church to be aware of the historical situation of the world, Balthasar elucidates how Jesus meets our quest for authenticity (person as mission), and he also shows us how to be authentic persons through community rather than "conscious subjects," individuals. While both Balthasar and Taylor claim that the communion of saints is the most credible face of Christianity today, Balthasar offers also a vision of how a saint is "generated."

Balthasar articulates the relationship between hierarchy and the rest of the Church in a way that shows its necessity, but also its modernity. Once we root ourselves in God as Balthasar suggests, then we are called to live our creativity through obedience to the Father, which the Church as institution can help us to embody. We are challenged and invited by the Church to become who we truly are in God, which means that we offer all that we are and have to the Lord and invite him into our processes of discernment and daily life. We pray for a discovery of where our gifts meet the world's greatest needs; we pray for a sense of how our lives can serve the kingdom; and, on a moment-by-moment basis, we cultivate our relationship of intimacy and trust in the Lord. The deeper the interior life in God, the more we are set free to love others with generosity, charity, and hope. This was, of course, Augustine's deep insight.

Balthasar shows us too that the Church needs to change in some ways, to see herself as called to form persons to become saints and members of the communion of saints. This requires the hierarchy to understand their task differently and to see themselves in a different light. It is the case that the Church must find her true center in her orientation of service to the world, and the hierarchy must be the first to emulate this, and first within the body of the Church. The hierarchy must reorient itself to the formation of saints, the development of subjective holiness that can then "launch the Church" into the world, in the words of Balthasar.

Balthasar challenges the Church to cultivate Marian receptivity in all her members, to foster holiness and christological obedience, that is, a constant listening for God in the present rather than an obedience that lives from a past experience of God. Balthasar strongly criticizes a Church that already has the answer" for the way in which the Spirit is calling her to move. Christian existence, mission, and witness are, on the contrary, an exercise in ongoing discernment, self-surrender and trust in imitation and participation in the kenosis of Christ. It is also needful to retrieve an ecclesial spirituality in each one's attempt to be holy and to glorify God so as to truly live the experience of being one body. While it is not a claim of Balthasar's, a natural extension of the ethos of ecclesiality would seem to be that diverse charisms, as long as they are not understood in ultimate or categorical terms and are properly discerned personal missions, ought to be received by and given to the body. Indeed, true personal mission always coincides with building up the mission of the Church.[11]

Balthasar reminds us, "The living model presents the best access to the Gospel message." He recalls us to what testimony comprises: "whatever things are true, honorable, just, holy, lovable, worthy of praise" (Phil 4:8).[12] We need to participate in the world as people desiring to be living works of art for God. In a similar vein, we ought to work harder to transform the moral profile of the Church from one of judgment to one of service and a path to ever-greater goodness and holiness. Thus, we need to retrieve the virtue tradition and allow it to orient our moral theology and our practices of moral formation. As Melanie Barrett has helpfully shown, our ethic needs to be one through which love's beauty shines clearly.[13]

We need to continue to reach out and do works of justice, and we need to keep working on liturgy and deepening devotion and formation. These are not in tension, and those in the Church who work on the one

---

11. I might suppose that, as an interim measure, those whose mission lies in living in solidarity with the unborn or working to purify the liturgy ought not, for example, to trivialize those whose mission is to engage in the work of social justice. Nor should those who are working for women's ordination insist that everyone hold this view. Rather, dialogue among ourselves and communal prayer so as to better understand and coordinate our mutual missions seems important so that each personal mission builds unity and is not a diversity leading to dissipation and disagreement.

12. Balthasar, *Test Everything*, 49, 51.

13. Barrett, *Love's Beauty at the Heart of the Christian Moral Life*.

should not be denigrating the call of the other. What is essential today is that the work is done with an ecclesial spirituality because of the profound strength of the secular imaginary and the diminishing credibility of the institutional church. We have to be one if we are going to witness at all.

The institutional church is in service of subjective and objective holiness. The institutional church is also entrusted with transmission. Laity that openly fight and rail against the hierarchy is destructive; so also is a lack of openness and humility in the hierarchy's approach to the laity. "Silencing" from on high and a fear-based approach to power profoundly undermine the process toward true unity.

In some sense, others have said many of the things that I am saying here about the vision and direction that the Catholic Church should take going forward. My motivations for writing this work, though, were quite different. I wanted to performatively underline the need to overcome the division in the Church between "the left" and "the right": Taylor tends to be more popular with "liberal" theologians and Balthasar with "conservatives."[14] I also sought to underscore the richness that is possible with the complementarity of labor between contemporary philosophers and theologians and to envision what some version of that engagement might look like today for understanding the Church's encounter with the secular world.

Taylor's historical, philosophical approach together with Balthasar's systematic theological approach speaks to the concerns of both sides and illuminates our current situation more clearly: we need to see that reading the signs of the times with Taylor shows that secularity is the reality of the world in the West that the Church is called to meet; Balthasar reminds us of how abiding in Christ through the Church enables one to be the Church in mission to this culture. It is important to situate the present time historically because it leads to a correction of the description of the Church focused on holiness as being in a time of retrenchment. Looking to Christ in prayer and forming disciples may seem to be inwardly focused activities, but this work tries to show that this "turning to Christ" is necessary in light of the secularity of the culture, for the Church to maintain and propose the alternative "imagination" of God to and for the world. Moreover, contemplation cannot be done at the expense of action

---

14. Or, perhaps I should say with the orthodox: it is not possible to be the Church without Christ!

on behalf of the oppressed. In this way, the Ignatian roots of Balthasar's spiritual vision are deeply salient for mission today.

This change or naming of the world in terms of its "positivity," which is also a negative charge toward religion, and especially Christianity, means that the affirmation of the world that is often the characterization of Vatican II sensibility must be renegotiated. While Vatican II documents themselves have always affirmed the goodness of the world and the need of the Church to open herself to it *in and through Jesus Christ*, there is also now an opportunity to retrieve that sense of the Church's need to transform the world into a praising, reverencing, serving reality of the Lord.[15] This is a recognition that the change needs to take place, not "out there" but "in us."[16] Recognition of the cultural shift is at the same time an opportunity to shift ecclesiological priority into the vertical relationship—and this new emphasis should not be considered a form of retrenchment.

In terms of a second reception of the Vatican II documents, then, it means that we may come to see these not as a second set of sacred scripture but as a collection of works that describes and postulates an alternative social imaginary. Embracing the Council means that we work toward the development of a social imaginary that helps redeem and transform persons who live within the existing imaginary of their lives as completely horizontal, determined by their identity as economic, public agents whose deepest right is to collective self-rule. We do this through living from the heart of the relationship between the Father and the Son—that is, through living in and into the most profound depths of the Spirit.

The narratival horizon of Western morality has been wiped almost entirely clean, as Nietzsche had hoped; in the midst of this vacuum, people are still searching for meaning and a sense of purpose. Charles Taylor shows us that there is an opportunity in this "secular age," in which the unquiet frontiers of modernity are still rumbling with ennui: Is this all

---

15. Balthasar: *The Fathers, the Scholastics and Ourselves: Dying to the World*.

16. In 2000, as a graduate student in philosophy of religion and ethics, I had the privilege of participating in a graduate student meeting with Stanley Hauerwas, arranged by Travis Kroeker for students in his course "Ethics, Politics, and the Apocalypse." Getting into a lively debate with Hauerwas about the virtues of dialogue and the biblical injunction to "love your enemies," Hauerwas laughed and said, "But where's the enemy? The enemy's within!" This comment continued to resonate and forms, in part, a sense of where the challenges truly lie in the relationship between church and culture, which this work has sought to make clearer.

that there is? Regardless of the theoretical structures (ironically) that postmodern and critical theory supply us, there is still this more basic hope in the eternal, the ultimate, the transcendent.

What we receive from the postmodern is an affirmation of subjectivity that can be perverse if not tempered by the One who relativizes everything to His Goodness and His Truth. In the triune God, Christians find that their freedom entails a peace and a joy that stays, and a solidity of personhood that persists, pervades, and transforms the world. This is what the Church can offer, if it retrieves once again its sense of forming disciples as its chief task and mission.

Bibliography

Abbey, Ruth, ed. *Contemporary Philosophy in Focus: Charles Taylor.* Cambridge: Cambridge University Press, 2004.

———. "Turning or Spinning? Charles Taylor's Catholicism." *Contemporary Political Theory* 5 (2006) 163–75.

Ackermann, Stephan. "The Church as Person in the Theology of Hans Urs von Balthasar." *Communio: International Catholic Review* 29 (2002) 238–49.

Aikin, W. Carter. "Narrative Icon and Linguistic Idol: Reexamining the Narrative Turn in Theological Ethics." *Journal of the Society of Christian Ethics* 28 (2008) 87–108.

Alberigo, Giuseppe. *A Brief History of Vatican II.* Translated by Matthew Sherry. Maryknoll, NY: Orbis, 2006.

Alberigo Giuseppe, and Joseph A. Komonchak, eds. *History of Vatican II.* 5 vols. Maryknoll, NY: Orbis, 1995–2005.

Alison, James. *Raising Abel: The Recovery of the Eschatological Imagination.* New York: Crossroad, 1996.

Anderson, Benedict. *Imagined Communities: Reflections on the Origin and Spread of Nationalism.* Rev. ed. London: Verso, 2006.

Augustine, St. *The Trinity.* Translated by Edmund Hill. Edited by John Rotelle. Works of Saint Augustine 5. Brooklyn: New City, 1991.

Babini, Ellero. "Jesus Christ, the Form and Norm of Man According to Hans Urs von Balthasar." Translated by Therese Bonini. *Communio: International Catholic Review* 16 (1989) 446–57.

Balthasar, Hans Urs von. *Bernanos: An Ecclesial Existence.* San Francisco: Ignatius, 1996.

———. "Catholicism and the Communion of Saints." *Communio: International Catholic Review* 15 (1988) 163–68.

———. *The Christian State of Life.* Translated by Mary Frances McCarthy. San Francisco: Ignatius, 1983.

———. "*Communio*—a Program." *Communio: International Catholic Review* 33 (2006) 153–69.

———. "The Council of the Holy Spirit." In *Explorations in Theology III: Creator Spirit,* 245–67. San Francisco: Ignatius, 1993.

———. *Engagement with God: The Drama of Christian Discipleship.* Translated by R. John Halliburton. San Francisco: Ignatius, 2008.

———. *Explorations in Theology*. Vol. 1, *The Word Made Flesh*. Translated by A. V. Littledale and Alexander Dru. San Francisco: Ignatius, 1989.

———. *Explorations in Theology*. Vol. 2, *Spouse of the Word*. Translated by A. V. Littledale et al. San Francisco: Ignatius, 1991.

———. *Explorations in Theology*. Vol. 3, *Creator Spirit*. Translated by Brian McNeil. San Francisco: Ignatius, 1991.

———. *Explorations in Theology*. Vol. 4, *Spirit and Institution*. Translated by Edward T. Oakes. San Francisco: Ignatius, 1995.

———. *Explorations in Theology*. Vol. 5, *Man Is Created*. Translated by Adrian Walker. San Francisco: Ignatius, 2014.

———. "The Fathers, Scholastics, and Ourselves." Translated by Edward T. Oakes. *Communio: International Catholic Review* 24 (1997) 347–96.

———. *The Glory of the Lord*. Vol. 1, *Seeing the Form*. Translated by Erasmo Leiva-Merikakis. San Francisco: Ignatius, 1982.

———. *The Glory of the Lord*. Vol. 3, *Studies in Theological Style: Lay Styles*. Translated by Andrew Louth et al. San Francisco: Ignatius, 1986.

———. *The Glory of the Lord*. Vol. 5, *The Realm of Metaphysics in the Modern Age*. Translated by Andrew Louth et al. San Francisco: Ignatius, 1991.

———. *Heart of the World*. Translated by Erasmo S. Leiva. San Francisco: Ignatius, 1979.

———. *In the Fullness of Faith: On the Centrality of the Distinctively Catholic*. Translated by Graham Harrison. San Francisco: Ignatius, 1988.

———. *The Laity and the Life of the Counsels: The Church's Mission in the World*. Translated by Brian McNeil with D. C. Schindler. San Francisco: Ignatius, 2003.

———. *Love Alone Is Credible*. Translated by D. C. Schindler. San Francisco: Ignatius, 2004.

———. *Love Alone: The Way of Revelation*. Edited by Alexander Dru. London: Sheed & Ward, 1968.

———. *Mary for Today*. Translated by Robert Nowell. San Francisco: Ignatius, 1988.

———. "The Meaning of the Communion of Saints." *Communio: International Catholic Review* 15 (1988) 160–62.

———. *The Moment of Christian Witness*. Translated by Richard Beckley. San Francisco: Ignatius, 1994.

———. *Mysterium Paschale: The Mystery of Easter*. Translated by Aidan Nichols. San Francisco: Ignatius, 2005.

———. *My Work: In Retrospect*. Translator not named. San Francisco: Ignatius, 1992.

———. *New Elucidations*. Translated by Mary Theresilde Skerry. San Francisco: Ignatius, 1986.

———. "Nine Propositions on Christian Ethics." In *Principles of Christian Morality*, translated by Graham Harrison, 77–104. San Francisco: Ignatius, 1986.

———. *The Office of Peter and the Structure of the Church*. Translated by Andrée Emery. San Francisco: Ignatius, 1986.

———. "On the Concept of Person." Translated by Peter Verhalen. *Communio: International Catholic Review* 13 (1986) 18–26.

———. "On the Tasks of Catholic Philosophy in Our Time." Translated by Brian McNeil. *Communio: International Catholic Review* 20 (1993) 147–87.

———. *Our Task: A Report and a Plan*. Translated by John Saward. San Francisco: Ignatius, 1984.

———. *Prayer*. Translated by Graham Harrison. San Francisco: Ignatius, 1986.
———. *Razing the Bastions: On the Church in This Age*. Translated by Brian McNeil. San Francisco: Ignatius, 1993.
———. *Sponsa Verbi*. Einsiedeln: Johannes, 1961.
———. *Test Everything: Hold Fast to What Is Good; An Interview with Hans Urs von Balthasar*. Translated by Maria Shrady. San Francisco: Ignatius, 1989.
———. *Theo-Drama: Theological Dramatic Theory*. Vol. 1, *Prolegomena*. Translated by Graham Harrison. San Francisco: Ignatius, 1988.
———. *Theo-Drama: Theological Dramatic Theory*. Vol. 2, *Dramatis Personae: Man in God*. Translated by Graham Harrison. San Francisco: Ignatius, 1990.
———. *Theo-Drama: Theological Dramatic Theory*. Vol. 3, *Dramatis Personae: The Person in Christ*. Translated by Graham Harrison. San Francisco: Ignatius, 1992.
———. *Theo-Drama: Theological Dramatic Theory*. Vol. 4, *The Action*. Translated by Graham Harrison. San Francisco: Ignatius, 1994.
———. *Theo-Drama: Theological Dramatic Theory*. Vol. 5, *The Final Act*. Translated by Graham Harrison. San Francisco: Ignatius, 1998.
———. *A Theological Anthropology*. 1967. Reprint, Eugene, OR: Wipf and Stock, 2010.
———. *Theo-Logic: Theological Logical Theory*. Vol. 1, *Truth of the World*. Translated by Adrian Walker. San Francisco: Ignatius, 2000.
———. *The Theology of Henri de Lubac: An Overview*. San Francisco: Ignatius, 1991.
———. *A Theology of History*. San Francisco: Ignatius, 1994.
———. *The Theology of Karl Barth: Exposition and Interpretation*. Translated by Edward T. Oakes. San Francisco: Ignatius, 1992.
———. *Tragedy Under Grace: Reinhold Schneider on the Experience of the West*. Translated by Brian McNeil. San Francisco: Ignatius, 1997.
———. *Truth Is Symphonic: Aspects of Christian Pluralism*. Translated by Graham Harrison. San Francisco: Ignatius, 1987.
———. *Unless You Become Like This Child*. Translated by Erasmo Leiva-Merikakis. San Francisco: Ignatius, 1991.
———. *Who Is a Christian?* Translated by John Cumming. London: Burns and Oates, 1968.
Barrett, Melanie. *Love's Beauty at the Heart of the Christian Moral Life: The Ethics of Catholic Theologian Hans Urs von Balthasar*. Lewiston, NY: E. Mellen, 2009.
Baum, Gregory. "The Response of a Theologian to Charles Taylor's *A Secular Age*." *Modern Theology* 26 (2010) 363–81.
Beabout, Gregory. "Personhood as Gift and Task: The Place of the Person in Catholic Social Thought." *Catholic Social Science Review* 9 (2004). http://catholicsocialscientists.org/cssr/Archival/Volume%20IX/Kraynak%20symposium--Beabout.pdf.
Benson, Bruce Ellis. "Love Is a Given: Jean-Luc Marion Tests the Limits of Logic." *Christian Century* 120.3 (2003) 22–25.
Block, Ed. "Hans Urs von Balthasar and Some Contemporary Catholic Writers." *Logos: A Journal of Catholic Thought and Culture* 10 (2007) 151–78.
Bonnici, John S. *Person to Person: Friendship and Love in the Life and Theology of Hans Urs von Balthasar*. New York: Alba House, 1999.
Bosch, David J. *Transforming Mission: Paradigm Shifts in Theology of Mission*. Maryknoll, NY: Oribs, 1991.
Bracken, Joseph A. "Toward a New Philosophical Theology Based on Intersubjectivity." *Theological Studies* 59 (1998) 703–19.

Braman, Brian. *Meaning and Authenticity: Bernard Lonergan and Charles Taylor on the Drama of Authentic Human Existence*. Toronto: University of Toronto Press, 2008.

Bramwell, Bevil. "The New Tension between Individual and Community in Christ: 'Community' in the Work of Hans Urs von Balthasar." *Catholic Social Science Review* 9 (2004). http://catholicsocialscientists.org/cssr/Archival/Volume%20IX/Article--Bramwell.pdf.

Bretzke, James T. Review of *Natural and Divine Law: Reclaiming the Tradition for Christian Ethics*, by Jean Porter. *Zygon* 38 (2003) 197–99.

Brueggemann, Walter. *The Prophetic Imagination*. Minneapolis: Fortress, 2001.

Burrell, David B. "Reflections on 'Negative Theology' in the Light of a Recent Venture to Speak of 'God without Being.'" In *Postmodernism and Christian Philosophy*, edited by Roman Ciapalo, 58–67. Mishawaka, IN: American Maritain Association, 1997.

Calhoun, Craig, et al., eds. *Rethinking Secularism*. New York: Oxford University Press, 2011.

Carpenter, Anne. *Theo-Poetics: Hans Urs von Balthasar on the Risk of Art and Being*. Notre Dame: University of Notre Dame Press, 2015.

Casarella, Peter. "Experience as a Theological Category: Hans Urs von Balthasar on the Encounter with God's Image." *Communio: International Catholic Review* 20 (1993) 118–28.

———. "On Frederick Bauerschmidt's 'Theo-Drama and Political Theology.'" *Communio: International Catholic Review* 25 (1998) 553–58.

———. "Waiting for a Cosmic Christ in an Uncreated World." *Communio: International Catholic Review* 28 (2001) 1–35.

Casarella, Peter J., and George P. Schner, eds. *Christian Spirituality and the Culture of Modernity: The Thought of Louis Dupré*. Grand Rapids: Eerdmans, 1998.

Cavanaugh, William. "The Body of Christ: The Eucharist and Politics." *Word and World* 22 (2002) 170–77.

———. *The Myth of Religious Violence: Secular Ideology and the Roots of Modern Conflict*. Oxford: Oxford University Press, 2009.

———. *Theopolitical Imagination*. London: T. & T. Clark, 2002.

———. *Torture and Eucharist: Theology, Politics, and the Body of Christ*. Oxford: Blackwell, 1998.

Cernera, Anthony, ed. *Vatican II: The Continuing Agenda*. Fairfield, CT: Sacred Heart University Press, 1997.

Chapp, Larry. "The Retrieval of *Gaudium et Spes*: A Comparison of Rowland and Hans Urs von Balthasar." *Nova et Vetera* 3 (2005) 119–45.

Chau, Carolyn A. "'What Could Possibly Be Given?': Towards an Exploration of Kenosis as Forgiveness—Continuing the Conversation between Coakley, Hampson, and Papanikolaou." *Modern Theology* 28 (2012) 1–24.

Chenu, Marie-Dominique. "A Council for All Peoples." In *Vatican II Revisited*. Minneapolis: Winston Press, 1986.

Coakley, Sarah. "*Kenosis* and Subversion: On the Repression of 'Vulnerability' in Christian Feminist Writing." In *Swallowing a Fishbone? Feminist Theologians Debate Christianity*, edited by Daphne Hampson, 82–111. London: SPCK, 1996.

Coles, Romand. "'Gentled into Being': Vanier and the Border at the Core." In Stanley Hauerwas and Romand Coles, *Christianity, Democracy, and the Radical Ordinary: Conversations between a Radical Democrat and a Christian*, 209–28. Eugene, OR: Cascade, 2008.

Colorado, Carlos. "Transcendence, Kenosis, Enfleshment: Charles Taylor's Religious Thought." PhD diss., McMaster University, 2009.
Dadosky, John. "The Church and the Other: Mediation and Friendship in Post-Vatican II Roman Catholic Ecclesiology." *Pacifica: Australian Journal of Theology* 18 (2005) 302–22.
———. "The Dialectic of Religious Identity: Lonergan and Balthasar." *Theological Studies* 60 (1999) 31–52.
———. "Philosophy for a Theology of Beauty." *Philosophy and Theology* 19 (2007) 7–34.
———. "Towards a Fundamental Re-interpretation of Vatican II." *Heythrop Journal* 49 (2008) 742–63.
Dalzell, Thomas. *The Dramatic Encounter of Divine and Human Freedom in the Theology of Hans Urs von Balthasar.* Berne: European Academic Publishers, 2000.
Delbrêl, Madeleine. *We, the Ordinary People of the Streets.* Translated by David L. Schindler and Charles F. Mann. Grand Rapids: Eerdmans, 2000.
DeVries, Hent. "The Deep Conditions of Secularity." *Modern Theology* 26 (2010) 382–403.
Dillard, Annie. *Holy the Firm.* New York: Harper and Row, 1977.
Doak, Mary. "The Politics of Radical Orthodoxy: A Catholic Critique." *Theological Studies* 68 (2007) 368–93.
Donnelly, Veronica. *Saving Beauty: Form as the Key to Balthasar's Christology.* Oxford: Peter Lang, 2007.
Dool, John. "Authenticity and Ecclesiology: Charles Taylor and the Post-Conciliar Challenge." Paper presented at the Lonergan Research Institute Seminar, Regis College, Toronto, January 2008.
Doran, Robert. "Lonergan and Balthasar: Methodological Considerations." *Theological Studies* 58 (1997) 61–84.
Downey, Michael. "Disfigurement and Reconfiguration: The Contribution of Jean Vanier and L'Arche to a Renewed Social Order." *Theoforum* 38 (2007) 309–20.
———. "The Heart in Jean Vanier and L'Arche." In *Spiritualities of the Heart: Approaches to Personal Wholeness in Christian Tradition,* edited by Annice Callahan. New York: Paulist, 1990.
Doyle, Dominic. "Retrieving the Hope of Christian Humanism. A Thomistic Reflection on Charles Taylor and Nicholas Boyle." *Gregorianum* 90 (2009) 699–722.
Duffy, Stephen, et al. *Vatican II: Open Questions and New Horizons.* Edited by Gerald Fagin. Wilmington: M. Glazier, 1984.
Dupré, Louis. *Passage to Modernity: An Essay in the Hermeneutics of Nature and Culture.* New Haven: Yale University Press, 1993.
———. *Religion and the Rise of Modern Culture.* Notre Dame: University of Notre Dame Press, 2008.
Elshtain, Jean Bethke. Review of *Tayloring Reformed Epistemology: Charles Taylor, Alvin Plantinga and the de jure Challenge to Christian Belief,* by Deane-Peter Baker. *Philosophical Papers* 38 (2009) 129–31.
———. "The Risks and Responsibilities of Affirming Ordinary Life." In *Philosophy in an Age of Pluralism: The Philosophy of Charles Taylor in Question,* edited by James Tully, 67–80. Cambridge: Cambridge University Press, 1994.
———. "Toleration, Proselytizing, and the Politics of Recognition: The Self Contested." In *Contemporary Philosophy in Focus: Charles Taylor,* edited by Ruth Abbey, 127–39. New York: Cambridge University Press, 2004.

Espezel, Alberto. "La cristología dramática de Balthasar." *Teologia y vida* 50 (2009) 305–18.

Flanagan, Kieran. "*A Secular Age*: An Exercise in Breach-Mending." *New Blackfriars* 91 (2010) 699–721.

Fraser, Ian. "Charles Taylor's Catholicism." *Political Theory* 4 (2005) 231-52.

———. *The Dialectics of the Self: Transcending Charles Taylor.* Exeter, UK: Imprint Academic, 2007.

Gaillardetz, Richard R. *Teaching With Authority: A Theology of the Magisterium of the Church.* Collegeville, MN: Liturgical Press, 1997.

Gallagher, Michael Paul. "Charles Taylor's Critique of 'Secularization.'" *Studies: An Irish Quarterly Review* 97 (2008) 433–44.

Gardner, Lucy, et al. *Balthasar at the End of Modernity.* Edinburgh: T. & T. Clark, 1999.

Gawronski, Raymond. *Word and Silence: Hans Urs von Balthasar and the Spiritual Encounter between East and West.* Grand Rapids: Eerdmans, 1995.

Godzieba, Anthony J. "Ontotheology to Excess: Imagining God without Being." *Theological Studies* 56 (1995) 3–20.

Goulding, Gill. *Creative Perseverance: Sustaining Life-Giving Ministry in Today's Church.* Ottawa: Novalis, 2003.

Gratton, Peter, ed. *Traversing the Imaginary: Richard Kearney and the Postmodern Challenge.* Evanston: Northwestern University Press, 2006.

Greenway, William. "Charles Taylor on Affirmation, Mutilation, and Theism: A Retrospective Reading of *Sources of the Self.*" *Journal of Religion* 80 (2000) 23–40.

Griffiths, Bede. *The Universal Christ: Daily Readings with Bede Griffiths.* Edited by Peter Spink. London: Darton, Longman and Todd, 1990.

Gschwandtner, Christina M. *Reading Jean-Luc Marion: Exceeding Metaphysics.* Bloomington: Indiana University Press, 2007.

Gula, Richard. *Reason Informed by Faith: Foundations of Catholic Morality.* New York: Paulist, 1989.

Gutting, Gary. *Pragmatic Liberalism and the Critique of Modernity.* Cambridge: Cambridge University Press, 1999.

Habermas, Jürgen, and Joseph Cardinal Ratzinger. *The Dialectics of Secularization: On Reason and Religion.* San Francisco: Ignatius, 2006.

Hankey, W. J. "Theoria versus Poesis: Neoplatonism and Trinitarian Difference in Aquinas, John Milbank, Jean-Luc Marion and John Zizioulas." *Modern Theology* 15 (1999) 387–415.

Harak, G. S. "Commenting on 'Recent Studies in Aquinas's Virtue Ethic: A Review Essay,' by Jean Porter." *Journal of Religious Ethics* 27 (1999) 181–83.

Harmon, Thomas. "Reconsidering Charles Taylor's Augustine." *Pro Ecclesia* 20 (2011) 185–209.

Harrison, Victoria S. *The Apologetic Value of Human Holiness.* Dordrecht: Kluwer Academic, 2000.

———. "Homo Orans: von Balthasar's Christocentric Philosophical Anthropology." *Heythrop Journal* 40 (1999) 280–300.

———. "Personal Identity and Integration: von Balthasar's Phenomenology of Human Holiness." *Heythrop Journal* 40 (1999) 424–37.

Hauerwas, Stanley. "The Politics of Gentleness: Random Thoughts for a Conversation with Jean Vanier." In Stanley Hauerwas and Romand Coles, *Christianity,*

Democracy, and the Radical Ordinary: Conversations between a Radical Democrat and a Christian, 195–207. Eugene, OR: Cascade, 2008.

Hauerwas, Stanley, and Romand Coles. "'Long live the weeds and the wilderness yet': Reflections on *A Secular Age*." *Modern Theology* 26 (2010) 349–62.

Hauerwas, Stanley, and David Matzko. "The Sources of Charles Taylor." Review of *Sources of the Self*. *Religious Studies Review* 18 (1992) 286–89.

Healy, Nicholas J. *The Eschatology of Hans Urs von Balthasar: Being as Communion*. Oxford: Oxford University Press, 2005.

Healy, Nicholas J., and D. C. Schindler, eds. *Being Holy in the World: Theology and Culture in the Thought of David L. Schindler*. Grand Rapids: Eerdmans, 2011.

Healy, Nicholas M. *Church, World, and the Christian Life: Practical-Prophetic Ecclesiology*. Cambridge: Cambridge University Press, 2000.

Heft, James L. "Introduction." In *A Catholic Modernity? Charles Taylor's Marianist Award Lecture*, edited by James L. Heft, 3–11. New York: Oxford University Press, 1999.

Heidegger, Martin. *The Question Concerning Technology and Other Essays*. Translated by William Lovitt. New York: Harper and Row, 1977.

Henrici, Peter. "Hans Urs von Balthasar: A Sketch of His Life." In *Hans Urs von Balthasar: His Life and Work*, edited by David L. Schindler, 7–43. San Francisco: Ignatius, 1991.

Himes, Kenneth, ed. *Modern Catholic Social Teaching: Commentaries and Interpretations*. Washington, DC: Georgetown University Press, 2004.

Horner, Robyn. "The Weight of Love." In *Counter-Experiences: Reading Jean-Luc Marion*, edited by Kevin Hart. Notre Dame: University of Notre Dame Press, 2007.

Howsare, Rodney. *Balthasar and Protestantism: The Ecumenical Implications of His Theological Style*. London: T. & T. Clark, 2005.

Howsare, Rodney, and Larry Chapp, eds. *How Balthasar Changed My Mind: 15 Scholars Reflect on the Meaning of Balthasar for Their Own Work*. New York: Crossroad, 2008.

Illich, Ivan. *The Rivers North of the Future: The Testament of Ivan Illich*. As told to David Cayley. Foreword by Charles Taylor. Toronto: House of Anansi, 2005.

Janicaud, Dominique, et al. *Phenomenology and the "Theological Turn": The French Debate*. New York: Fordham University Press, 2000.

Jenson, Robert. *Essays on Theology and Culture*. Grand Rapids: Eerdmans, 1995.

John Paul II, Pope. "Apostolic Letter *Tertio Millenio Adveniente*." November 10, 1994. http://w2.vatican.va/content/john-paul-ii/en/apost_letters/1994/documents/hf_jp-ii_apl_10111994_tertio-millennio-adveniente.html.

———. "Letter of His Holiness John Paul II to Artists." April 4, 1999. http://w2.vatican.va/content/john-paul-ii/en/letters/1999/documents/hf_jp-ii_let_23041999_artists.html.

Jones, Tamsin. "Dionysius in Hans Urs von Balthasar and Jean-Luc Marion." *Modern Theology* 24 (2008) 743–54.

Keenan, James F. "Commenting on 'Recent Studies in Aquinas's Virtue Ethic: A Review Essay,' by Jean Porter." *Journal of Religious Ethics* 27 (1999) 184–87.

———. Review of *Natural and Divine Law: Reclaiming the Tradition for Christian Ethics*, by Jean Porter. *Theological Studies* 61 (2000) 777–79.

Kehl, Medard, and Werner Löser, eds. *The Von Balthasar Reader*. New York: Crossroad, 1982.

Kerr, Fergus. "Charles Taylor's Moral Ontology of the Self." In *Immortal Longings: Versions of Transcending Humanity*, 136–58. Notre Dame: University of Notre Dame Press, 1997.

———. "Comment: Christians in a Secular Age." *New Blackfriars* 91 (2010) 625–26.

———. "How Much Can a Philosopher Do?" *Modern Theology* 26 (2010) 321–36.

———. "The Self and the Good: Charles Taylor's Moral Ontology." In *Contemporary Philosophy in Focus: Charles Taylor*, edited by Ruth Abbey, 84–104. New York: Cambridge University Press: 2004.

Kilby, Karen. *Balthasar: A (Very) Critical Introduction*. Grand Rapids: Eerdmans, 2012.

Klaushofer, Alexandra. "Faith Beyond Nihilism: The Retrieval of Theism in Milbank and Taylor." *Heythrop Journal* 40 (1999) 135–49

Komonchak, Joseph A. "The Significance of Vatican II for Ecclesiology." in *The Gift of the Church: A Textbook on Ecclesiology in Honor of Patrick Granfield, O.S.B.*, edited by Peter Phan, 69-91. Collegeville: Liturgical Press, 2000.

Kraftson-Hogue, Mike. "Predication Turning to Praise: Marion and Augustine on God and Hermeneutics—(Giver, Giving, Gift, Giving)." *Literature and Theology* 14 (2000) 399–411.

Kuipers, Ronald. "Accommodation, Islamophobia, and the Politics of Mobilization: An Interview with Charles Taylor (Part Three of Three)." *The Other Journal.com*, October 9, 2008. http://theotherjournal.com/2008/10/09/accommodation-islamophobia-and-the-politics-of-mobilization-an-interview-with-charles-taylor-part-three-of-three/.

———. "The New Atheism and the Spiritual Landscape of the West: A Conversation with Charles Taylor (Part One of Three)." *The Other Journal.com*, June 12, 2008.

———. "Religious Belonging in an Age of Authenticity: A Conversation with Charles Taylor (Part Two of Three)." *The Other Journal.com*, June 23, 2008. http://theotherjournal.com/2008/06/23/religious-belonging-in-an-age-of-authenticity-a-conversation-with-charles-taylor-part-two-of-three/.

———. "Stout's Democracy without Secularism: But Is It a Tradition?" *Contemporary Pragmatism* 3 (2006) 85–104.

Laborde, Cécile. "Protecting Freedom of Religion in the Secular Age." *The Immanent Frame: Secularism, Religion, and the Public Sphere* (blog). April 23, 2012. http://blogs.ssrc.org/tif/2012/04/23/protecting-freedom-of-religion-in-the-secular-age/.

Lafont, Ghislain. *Imagining the Catholic Church: Structured Communion in the Spirit*. Collegeville, MN: Liturgical Press, 2000.

Laitinen, Arto. *Strong Evaluation without Moral Sources: On Charles Taylor's Philosophical Anthropology and Ethics*. Berlin: de Gruyter, 2008.

Laitinen, Arto, and Nicholas H. Smith, eds. *Perspectives on the Philosophy of Charles Taylor*. Helsinki: Philosophical Society of Finland, 2002.

Lamb, Matthew L., and Matthew Levering, eds. *Vatican II: Renewal Within Tradition*. New York: Oxford University Press, 2008.

Langan, Janine. "The Culture of Hope and Glory." *Touchstone* 11 (1998) 25–30.

Langan, Thomas. *Human Being: A Philosophical Anthropology*. Edited by Antonio Calcagno. Columbia: University of Missouri Press, 2009.

Levering, Matthew. "Nature as Reason: A Thomistic Theory of the Natural Law." *Pro Ecclesia* 17 (2008) 469–73.

Lindbeck, George. *The Church in a Postliberal Age*. Edited by James J. Buckley. Grand Rapids: Eerdmans, 2003.

Long, D. Stephen. "A Balthasarian Theological Economics: Making Sense of David L. Schindler's Happy Baker." In *Being Holy in the World: Theology and Culture in the Thought of David L. Schindler*, edited by Nicholas J. Healy Jr. and D. C. Schindler. Grand Rapids: Eerdmans, 2011.

———. "How to Read Charles Taylor: The Theological Significance of *A Secular Age*." *Pro Ecclesia* 18 (2009) 93–107.

MacIntyre, Alasdair. *After Virtue: A Study in Moral Theory*. Notre Dame: University of Notre Dame Press, 1981.

———. "Critical Remarks on *Sources of the Self*, by Charles Taylor." *Philosophy and Phenomenological Research* 54 (1994) 187–90.

———. Review of *Philosophical Arguments*, by Charles Taylor. *Philosophical Quarterly* 47 (1997) 94–96.

———. Review of *Philosophy in an Age of Pluralism: The Philosophy of Charles Taylor in Question*, edited by James Tully. *Philosophical Quarterly* 46 (1996) 522–24.

———. *Three Rival Versions of Moral Enquiry: Encyclopaedia, Genealogy, and Tradition*. Notre Dame: University of Notre Dame Press, 1991.

Maclure, Jocelyn, and Charles Taylor. *Secularism and Freedom of Conscience*. Translated by Jane Marie Todd. Cambridge: Harvard University Press, 2011.

Madges, William, ed. *Vatican II: Forty Years Later*. Maryknoll, NY: Orbis, 2006.

Marion, Jean-Luc. "Christian Philosophy and Charity." *Communio* 19 (1992) 465–73.

———. "'Christian Philosophy': Hermeneutic or Heuristic?" In *The Question of Christian Philosophy Today*, edited by Francis J. Ambrosio, 247–64. New York: Fordham University Press, 1999.

———. "God and the Gift." In *God's Advocates: Christian Thinkers in Conversation*, edited by Rupert Shortt. Grand Rapids: Eerdmans, 2005.

———. *God Without Being: Hors-Texte*. Translated by Thomas A. Carlson. Chicago: University of Chicago Press, 1991.

———. *Prolegomena to Charity*. Translated by Stephen E. Lewis. 1st ed. New York: Fordham University Press, 2002.

———. "The Reason of the Gift." In *Givenness and God: Questions of Jean-Luc Marion*, edited by Ian Leask and Eoin Cassidy. New York: Fordham University Press, 2005.

Marion, Jean-Luc, and Janine Langan. "The Blind Man of Siloe." *Image* 29 (2001) 59–69.

Marion, Jean-Luc, et al. "Sketch of a Phenomenological Concept of Gift." In *Postmodern Philosophy and Christian Thought*, edited by Merold Westphal, 122–43. Bloomington: Indiana University Press, 1999.

Markus, Robert. *Christianity and the Secular*. Notre Dame: University of Notre Dame Press, 2006.

Marsden, George. "Matteo Ricci and the Prodigal Culture." In *A Catholic Modernity? Charles Taylor's Marianist Award Lecture*, edited by James L. Heft, 83–93. New York: Oxford University Press, 1999.

Martis, John. "Thomistic *Esse*—Idol or Icon? Jean-Luc Marion's *God Without Being*." *Pacifica* 9 (1996) 55–68.

Mattison, William C., III. "The Changing Face of Natural Law: The Necessity of Belief for Natural Law Norm Specification." *Journal of the Society of Christian Ethics* 27 (2007) 251–77.

McEvoy, James. "Church and World at the Second Vatican Council: The Significance of *Gaudium et Spes.*" *Pacifica* 19 (2006) 37–57.

———. "Living in an Age of Authenticity: Charles Taylor on Identity Today." *The Australasian Catholic Record* 86 (2009) 161–72.

McGregor, Bede, and Thomas Norris, eds. *The Beauty of Christ: An Introduction to the Theology of Hans Urs von Balthasar.* Edinburgh: T. & T. Clark, 1994.

McIntosh, Mark. *Christology from Within: Spirituality and Incarnation in Hans Urs von Balthasar.* Notre Dame: University of Notre Dame Press, 2000.

McKenny, Gerald. "(Re)placing Ethics: Jean-Luc Marion and the Horizon of Modern Morality." In *Counter-Experiences: Reading Jean-Luc Marion*, edited by Kevin Hart. Notre Dame: University of Notre Dame Press, 2007.

Mercier, Ronald. "The Holy Spirit and Ethics: A Personal Gift Making Persons." In *Moral Theology: New Directions and Fundamental Issues*, edited by James Keating, 43–65. New York: Paulist, 2004.

Milbank, John. "Can a Gift Be Given? Prolegomena to a Future Trinitarian Metaphysic." *Modern Theology* 11 (1995) 119–61.

———. "Review Article: A Closer Walk on the Wild Side; Some Comments on Charles Taylor's *A Secular Age.*" *Studies in Christian Ethics* 22 (2009) 89–104.

Mongrain, Kevin. *The Systematic Thought of Hans Urs von Balthasar: An Irenean Retrieval.* New York: Crossroad, 2002.

Newbigin, Lesslie. *The Household of God: Lectures on the Nature of the Church.* New York: Friendship Press, 1954.

Nichols, Aidan. *Christendom Awake: On Re-energizing the Church in Culture.* Grand Rapids: Eerdmans, 1999.

———. *No Bloodless Myth: A Guide through Balthasar's Dramatics.* Washington, DC: Catholic University of America Press, 2000.

———. *Scattering the Seed: A Guide through Balthasar's Early Writings on Philosophy and the Arts.* Washington, DC: Catholic University of America Press, 2006.

Niebuhr. H. Richard. *The Meaning of Revelation.* New York: Macmillan, 1960.

Noble, Tim. "Jean-Luc Marion, Idols and Liberation Theology." *Communio Viatorum* 48 (2006) 131–54.

Norris, Thomas. "The Symphonic Unity of His Theology: An Overview." In *The Beauty of Christ: An Introduction to the Theology of Hans Urs von Balthasar*, edited by Bede McGregor and Thomas Norris, 213–52. Edinburgh: T. & T. Clark, 1994.

Oakes, Edward T. *Pattern of Redemption: The Theology of Hans Urs von Balthasar.* New York: Continuum, 1994.

Oakes, Edward T., and David Moss, eds. *The Cambridge Companion to Hans Urs von Balthasar.* Cambridge: Cambridge University Press, 2004.

O'Hanlon, Gerard. "The Jesuits and Modern Theology: Rahner, Balthasar, and Liberation Theology." *Irish Theological Quarterly* 58 (1992) 25–45.

O'Malley, John W. "Vatican II: Did Anything Happen?" *Theological Studies* 67 (2006) 3–33.

O'Malley, John W., et al. *Vatican II: Did Anything Happen?* Edited by David G. Schultenover. New York: Continuum, 2007.

O'Donovan, Oliver. Review of *Natural and Divine Law: Reclaiming the Tradition for Christian Ethics*, by Jean Porter. *Theology* 104 (2001) 60–61.

O'Regan, Cyril. *The Anatomy of Misremembering: Von Balthasar's Response to Philosophical Modernity.* Volume 1: Hegel. New York: Crossroad Publishing Co., 2014.

———. *Gnostic Return in Modernity.* Albany: State University of New York Press, 2001.

———. *Theology and the Spaces of Apocalyptic.* Milwaukee: Marquette University Press, 2009.

———. "Von Balthasar's Valorization and Critique of Heidegger's Geneaology of Modernity." In *Christian Spirituality and the Culture of Modernity: The Thought of Louis Dupré,* edited by Peter J. Casarella and George P. Schner, 123–58. Grand Rapids: Eerdmans, 1998.

Ormerod, Neil. "Charles Taylor and Bernard Lonergan on Natural Theology." *Irish Theological Quarterly* 74 (2009) 419–33.

Örsy, Ladislas. *The Church: Learning and Teaching; Magisterium, Assent, Dissent, Academic Freedom.* Wilmington: M. Glazier, 1987.

O'Shea, Andrew. *Selfhood and Sacrifice: René Girard and Charles Taylor on the Crisis of Modernity.* New York: Continuum, 2010.

Ouellet, Marc. "L'existence comme mission: l'anthropologie théologique de Hans Urs von Balthasar." PhD diss., Pontificia Universitas Gregoriana, 1983.

Papanikolaou, Aristotle. "Person, *Kenosis* and Abuse: Hans Urs von Balthasar and Feminist Theologies in Conversation." *Modern Theology* 19 (2003) 41–65.

Peperzak, Adriaan. *Philosophy between Faith and Theology: Addresses to Catholic Intellectuals.* Notre Dame: University of Notre Dame Press, 2005.

———. *The Quest for Meaning: Friends of Wisdom from Plato to Levinas.* New York: Fordham University Press, 2003.

———. *Reason in Faith: On the Relevance of Christian Spirituality for Philosophy.* New York: Paulist, 1999.

Pinckaers, Servais. *The Pinckaers Reader: Renewing Thomistic Moral Theology.* Edited by John Berkman and Craig Steven Titus. Translated by Mary Thomas Noble et al. Washington, DC: Catholic University of America Press, 2005.

———. *The Sources of Christian Ethics.* Translated by Mary Thomas Noble. Washington, DC: Catholic University of America Press, 1995.

Pope, Stephen J. Review of *Natural and Divine Law: Reclaiming the Tradition for Christian Ethics,* by Jean Porter. *Journal of Law and Religion* 16 (2001) 679–88.

Porter, Jean. "Christian Ethics and the Concept of Morality: A Historical Inquiry." *Journal of the Society of Christian Ethics* 26 (2006) 3–21.

———. "Natural Equality: Freedom, Authority and Obedience in Two Medieval Thinkers." *Annual of the Society of Christian Ethics* 21 (2001) 275–99.

———. *Nature as Reason: A Thomistic Theory of the Natural Law.* Grand Rapids: Eerdmans, 2005.

———. Review of *Acts Amid Precepts: The Aristotelian Logical Structure of Thomas Aquinas's Moral Theory,* by Kevin L. Flannery. *Theological Studies* 64 (2003) 177–79.

———. Review of *The Call to Personhood: A Christian Theory of the Individual in Social Relationships,* by Alistair I. McFadyen. *Theological Studies* 53 (1992) 365–66.

———. Review of *Religion and the Common Good: Catholic Contributions to Building Community in a Liberal Society,* by Brian Stiltner. *Theology Today* 58 (2002) 636–38.

———. "The Search for a Global Ethic." *Theological Studies* 62 (2001) 105–21.

———. "A Tradition of Civility: The Natural Law as a Tradition of Moral Inquiry." *Scottish Journal of Theology* 56 (2003) 27–48.
Potworowski, Christophe. "Christian Experience in Hans Urs von Balthasar." *Communio: International Catholic Review* 20 (1993) 107–17.
———. "An Exploration of the Notion of Objectivity in Hans Urs von Balthasar." In *Glory, Grace, and Culture: The Work of Hans Urs von Balthasar*, edited by Ed Block, 69–87. Mahwah, NJ: Paulist, 2005.
Quash, Ben. *Theology and the Drama of History*. Cambridge: Cambridge University Press, 2005.
Ratzinger, Joseph. *Called to Communion: Understanding the Church Today*. Translated by Adrian Walker. San Francisco: Ignatius, 1996.
———. *God and the World: Believing and Living in Our Time; a Conversation with Peter Seewald*. Translated by Henry Taylor. San Francisco: Ignatius, 2002.
———. *The Open Circle: The Meaning of Christian Brotherhood*. Translated by W. A. Glen-Doeple. New York: Sheed and Ward, 1966.
———. *Salt of the Earth: Christianity and the Catholic Church at the End of the Millennium; an Interview with Peter Seewald*. Translated by Adrian Walker. San Francisco: Ignatius, 1997.
Redhead, Mark. *Charles Taylor: Thinking and Living Deep Diversity*. Lanham, MD: Rowman and Littlefield, 2002.
Roberts, Raymond. Review of *Natural and Divine Law: Reclaiming the Tradition for Christian Ethics*, by Jean Porter. *Political Theology* 8 (2007) 249–51.
Robinson, Jonathan. *The Mass and Modernity: Walking to Heaven Backward*. San Francisco: Ignatius, 2005.
Rolheiser, Ronald. *Secularity and the Gospel: Being Missionaries to Our Children*. New York: Crossroad, 2006.
Rosemann, Philipp W. "Postmodern Philosophy and Jean-Luc Marion's Eucharistic Realism." In *Transcendence and Phenomenology*, edited by Peter M. Candler Jr. and Conor Cunningham, 84–110. London: SCM, 2007.
Rosenberg, Randall. "The Catholic Imagination and Modernity: William Cavanaugh's Theopolitical Imagination and Charles Taylor's Modern Social Imagination." *Heythrop Journal* 48 (2007) 911–31.
Rossi, Philip J. "Review of *A Secular Age*." *Theological Studies* 69 (2008) 953–54.
Saward, John. "Mary and Peter: The Christological Constellation in Balthasar." In *The Analogy of Beauty: The Theology of Hans Urs von Balthasar*, edited by John Riches, 105–33. Edinburgh: T. & T. Clark, 1986.
———. "Youthful Unto Death: The Spirit of Childhood." In *The Beauty of Christ: An Introduction to the Theology of Hans Urs von Balthasar*, edited by Bede McGregor and Thomas Norris, 140–60. Edinburgh: T. & T. Clark, 1994.
Schindler, D. C. *Hans Urs von Balthasar and the Dramatic Structure of Truth: A Philosophical Investigation*. New York: Fordham University Press, 2004.
Schindler, David L. "Charity, Justice, and the Church's Activity in the World." *Communio* 33 (2006) 346–67.
———. "Hans Urs von Balthasar, Metaphysics, and the Problem of Ontotheology." *Analecta Hermeneutica* 1 (2009) 102–13.
———. *Heart of the World, Center of the Church: Communio Ecclesiology, Liberalism, and Liberation*. Grand Rapids: Eerdmans, 1996.

———, ed. *Love Alone Is Credible: Hans Urs von Balthasar as Interpreter of the Catholic Tradition*. Vol. 1. Grand Rapids: Eerdmans, 2008.

———. *Ordering Love: Liberal Societies and the Memory of God*. Grand Rapids: Eerdmans, 2011.

———. "The Significance of Hans Urs von Balthasar in the Contemporary Cultural Situation." In *Glory, Grace, and Culture*, edited by Ed Block Jr., 16–36. New York: Paulist, 2005.

Schloesser, Stephen. "Against Forgetting: Memory, History, Vatican II." *Theological Studies* 67 (2006) 275–319.

Schmitz, Kenneth. "Selves and Persons: A Difference in Loves?" *Communio: International Catholic Review* 18 (1991) 183–205.

Schreiter, Robert. *The New Catholicity: Theology between the Global and the Local*. Maryknoll, NY: Orbis, 2004.

Scola, Angelo. *Hans Urs von Balthasar: A Theological Style*. Grand Rapids: Eerdmans, 1995.

Servais, Jacques. "Balthasar as Interpreter of the Catholic Tradition." In *Love Alone Is Credible: Hans Urs von Balthasar as Interpreter of the Catholic Tradition*, edited by David L. Schindler, 191–208. Grand Rapids: Eerdmans, 2008.

Sheehan, Jonathan. "Framing the Middle." *The Immanent Frame* (blog), January 14, 2008. http://blogs.ssrc.org/tif/2008/01/14/framing-the-middle/.

Sibley, Robert. *Northern Spirits: John Watson, George Grant, and Charles Taylor—Appropriations of Hegelian Political Thought*. Montreal: McGill-Queen's University Press, 2008.

Smith, James K. A. *Desiring the Kingdom: Worship, Worldview, and Cultural Formation*. Grand Rapids: Baker Academic, 2009.

Smith, Nicholas H. *Charles Taylor: Meaning, Morals, and Modernity*. Cambridge: Polity, 2002.

Speyr, Adrienne von. *They Followed His Call: Vocation and Asceticism*. Translated by Erasmo Leiva-Merikakis. Rev. ed. San Francisco: Ignatius, 1986.

Spink, Kathryn. *Jean Vanier and L'Arche: A Communion of Love*. London: Darton, Longman & Todd, 1990.

Stacpoole, Alberic. *Vatican II: By Those Who Were There*. London: G. Chapman, 1986.

Stanley, Timothy. "Redeeming the Icons." *Journal for Cultural and Religious Theory* 6 (2005) 39–62.

Steck, Christopher W. *The Ethical Thought of Hans Urs von Balthasar*. New York: Crossroad, 2001.

Stout, Jeffrey. *Democracy and Tradition*. Princeton: Princeton University Press, 2004.

Tanner, Kathryn. *Theories of Culture: A New Agenda for Theology*. Minneapolis: Fortress, 1997.

Taylor, Charles. "Benedict XVI." *Public Culture* 18 (2006) 7–10.

———. *A Catholic Modernity? Charles Taylor's Marianist Award Lecture, with Responses by William M. Shea, Rosemary Luling Haughton, George Marsden, and Jean Bethke Elshtain*. Edited by James L. Heft. New York: Oxford University Press, 1999.

———. "The Concept of a Person." In *Human Agency and Language*, 97–114. Philosophical Papers 1. Cambridge: Cambridge University Press, 1985.

———. *Dilemmas and Connections*. Cambridge: Belknap Press of Harvard University Press, 2011.

———. *The Explanation of Behviour*. London: Routledge & Kegan Paul, 1964.

———. "Foreword: What Is Secularism?" In *Secularism, Religion, and Multicultural Citizenship*, edited by Geoffrey Brahm Levey and Tariq Modood, xi–xxi. New York: Cambridge University Press, 2009.
———. *Hegel and Modern Society*. Cambridge: Cambridge University Press, 1979.
———. *Human Agency and Language*. Philosophical Papers 1. Cambridge: Cambridge University Press, 1985.
———. "Magisterial Authority." In *The Crisis of Authority in Catholic Modernity*, edited by Michael J. Lacey and Francis Oakley, 258–69. New York: Oxford University Press, 2011.
———. *The Malaise of Modernity*. Concord, ON: Anansi, 1991.
———. *Modern Social Imaginaries*. Durham: Duke University Press, 2004.
———. *Multiculturalism: Examining the Politics of Recognition*. Edited by Amy Guttman. Princeton: Princeton University Press, 1994.
———. "On Social Imaginaries." In *Traversing the Imaginary: Richard Kearney and the Postmodern Challenge*, edited by Peter Gratton and John Panteleimon Manoussakis, 29–47. Evanston: Northwestern University Press, 2007.
———. "The Person." In *The Category of the Person: Anthropology, Philosophy, History*, edited by Michael Carrithers et al., 257–81. Cambridge: Cambridge University Press, 1985.
———. *Philosophical Arguments*. Cambridge: Harvard University Press, 1997.
———. *Philosophy and the Human Sciences*. Philosophical Papers 2. Cambridge: Cambridge University Press, 1985.
———. "The Politics of Recognition." In *Multiculturalism: Examining the Politics of Recognition*, edited by Amy Gutmann, 25–43. Princeton: Princeton University Press, 1994.
———. *A Secular Age*. Cambridge: Belknap Press of Harvard University Press, 2007.
———. "Self-Interpreting Animals." In *Human Agency and Language*, 45–76. Philosophical Papers 1. Cambridge: Cambridge University Press, 1985.
———. *Sources of the Self: The Making of the Modern Identity*. Cambridge: Cambridge University Press, 1989.
———. "Two Theories of Modernity." In *Alternative Modernities*, edited by Dilip Parameshwar Gaonkar, 172–96. Durham: Duke University Press, 2001.
———. "What Drove Me to Philosophy." The 2008 Kyoto Prize Commemorative Lecture: Arts and Philosophy. October 2008. http://www.inamori-f.or.jp/laureates/k24_c_charles/img/lct_e.pdf.
———. "What Is Human Agency?" In *Human Agency and Language*, 15–44. Philosophical Papers 1. Cambridge: Cambridge University Press, 1985.
———. "What Is Secularity?" In *Transcending Boundaries in Philosophy and Theology: Reason, Meaning, and Experience*, edited by Kevin Vanhoozer and Martin Warner, 97–130. Aldershot, UK: Ashgate, 2007.
———. "What's Wrong with Negative Liberty." In *The Idea of Freedom: Essays in Honour of Isaiah Berlin*, edited by Alan Ryan, 175–93. Oxford: Oxfod University Press, 1979.
———. "Why We Need a Radical Redefinition of Secularism." In *The Power of Religion in the Public Sphere*, edited by Eduardo Mendieta and Jonathan VanAntwerpen, 34–59. New York: Columbia University Press, 2011.
Thames, Bradley J. "Authentically Virtuous: Heidegger, Taylor, and MacIntyre." Paper presented at the annual conference of The Notre Dame Center for Ethics and

Culture at the University of Notre Dame, South Bend, Indiana, November 10–12, 2011.

Tracy, David. "The Hermeneutics of Naming God." *Irish Theological Quarterly* 57 (1991) 53–64.

Tully, James, ed. *Philosophy in an Age of Pluralism: The Philosophy of Charles Taylor in Question*. Cambridge: Cambridge University Press, 1994.

Vacek, Edward Collins. Review of *Nature as Reason: A Thomistic Theory of the Natural Law*, by Jean Porter. *Horizons* 34 (2007) 380–81.

Vahanian, Gabriel. *Praise of the Secular*. Charlottesville: University of Virginia Press, 2008.

Vanier, Jean. *Becoming Human*. Toronto: House of Anansi, 1998.

———. *The Broken Body: Journey to Wholeness*. New York: Paulist, 1988.

———. *Community and Growth: Our Pilgrimage Together*. Toronto: Griffin House, 1979.

———. *Finding Peace*. Toronto: Anansi, 2003.

———. *The Heart of L'Arche: A Spirituality for Every Day*. New York: Crossroad, 1995.

———. *Jean Vanier: Essential Writings*. Edited by Carolyn Whitney-Brown. Maryknoll, NY: Orbis, 2008.

———. *Made for Happiness: Discovering the Meaning of Life with Aristotle*. Edited by Kathryn Spink. Toronto: Anansi, 2001.

———. "The Place of the Mentally Handicapped in the Modern World." In *Social and Religious Concerns of East Africa: A Wajibu Anthology*, edited by Gerald J. Wanjohi and G. Wakuraya Wanjohi, 229–33. Washington, DC: Paulines, 2005.

Van Nieuwenhove, Rik. "Catholic Theology in the Thirteenth Century and the Origins of Secularism." *Irish Theological Quarterly* 75 (2010) 339–54.

Vatican Council II. *The Basic Sixteen Documents of Vatican Council II: Constitutions, Decrees, Declarations*. Edited by Austin Flannery. New York: Costello, 1996.

Vogel, Jeffrey A. "The Unselfing Activity of the Holy Spirit in the Theology of Hans Urs von Balthasar." *Logos: Journal of Catholic Thought and Culture* 10 (2007) 16–34.

Ward, Graham. *Cultural Transformation and Religious Practice*. New York: Cambridge University Press, 2005.

———. "History, Belief and Imagination in Charles Taylor's *A Secular Age*." *Modern Theology* 26 (2010) 337–48.

———. "The Theological Project of Jean-Luc Marion." In *Post-Secular Philosophy: Between Philosophy and Theology*, edited by Phillip Blond, 229–39. New York: Routledge, 1998.

Warner, Michael, et al. *Varieties of Secularism in a Secular Age*. Cambridge: Harvard University Press, 2010.

Watkins, Keith. "The Church as Contrast Society: A Review Essay." *Encounter* 67 (2006) 87–99.

Weigel, George. *A New Worldly Order: John Paul II and Human Freedom*. Washington, DC: Ethics and Public Policy Center, 1992.

Wells, Samuel. *Improvisation: The Drama of Christian Ethics*. Grand Rapids: Brazos, 2006.

Welz, Claudia. "God—a Phenomenon? Theology as Semiotic Phenomenology of the Invisible." *Studia Theologica* 62 (2008) 4–24.

Westphal, Merold. "Vision and Voice: Phenomenology and Theology in the Work of Jean-Luc Marion." *International Journal for Philosophy of Religion* 60 (2006) 117–37.

White, Thomas Joseph, ed. *The Analogy of Being: Invention of the Antichrist or the Wisdom of God?* Grand Rapids: Eerdmans, 2011.

Williams, Rowan. "Balthasar and Rahner." In *The Analogy of Beauty: The Theology of Hans Urs von Balthasar*, edited by John Riches, 11–34. Edinburgh: T. & T. Clark, 1986.

———. "Balthasar and the Trinity." In *The Cambridge Companion to Hans Urs von Balthasar*, edited by Edward T. Oakes and David Moss, 37–50. Cambridge: Cambridge University Press, 2004.

———. *Lost Icons: Reflections on Cultural Bereavement*. Edinburgh: Morehouse, 2000.

Wynands, Sandra. Review of *The Erotic Phenomenon*, by Jean-Luc Marion. *Christianity and Literature* 57 (2007) 142–46.

Yenson, Mark L. *Existence as Prayer: the Consciousness of Christ in the Theology of Hans Urs von Balthasar*. New York: Peter Lang Publishing Inc., 2014.

Yoder, John H. *The Royal Priesthood: Essays Ecclesiological and Ecumenical*. Edited by Michael G. Cartwright. Grand Rapids: Eerdmans, 1994.

Zizioulas, John. *Being as Communion: Studies in Personhood and the Church*. Crestwood, NY: St. Vladimir's Seminary Press, 1985.

Name Index

Ackermann, Stephan, 143, 164
Anderson, Benedict, 67n21, 76
Aquinas, 111, 150
Augustine, 19, 24, 31, 34, 47, 64, 107, 163

Bacon, Francis, 124
Barrett, Melanie, 203
Barth, Karl, 135n63
Benedict XVI (pope), 6, 90–91
Berlin, Isaiah, 98
Bernanos, Georges, 119, 146, 156, 159, 161, 170–73, 176, 177
Bhargava, Rajeev, 20n39
Bosch, David, 3, 194
Braman, Brian, 54
Bruce, Steve, 60n7

Calhoun, Craig, 18–19n38
Cavanaugh, William, 78n44
Celestine (pope), 113
Coakley, Sarah, 15
Congar, Yves, 4, 8, 87
Cox, Harvey, 18

Day, Dorothy, 179
de Lubac, Henri, 19, 150, 162
Delbrel, Madeleine, 177
Descartes, René, 31, 31n18, 34, 36, 54, 124, 143
Diana, Princess (Great Britain), 48
Eliade, Mircea, 66

Elshtain, Jean Bethke, 94–99, 102, 106

Feuerbach, Ludwig Andreas von, 111, 124
Fichte, Johann Gottlieb, 124
Francis (pope), 6–7, 193
Francis of Assisi, 72, 103
Fraser, Ian, 12–13, 28

Gallagher, Michael, 75, 82
Goulding, Gill (sister), 21n41
Greenway, William, 49n79
Griffiths, Bede, 72, 73
Grotius, Hugo, 31, 46, 54

Harmon, Thomas, 64n13
Harrison, Victoria, 59n2, 143, 145, 171, 178
Hauerwas, Stanley, 64n13, 205n16
Havel, Vaclav, 73, 96
Heft, James, 4n8, 13
Hegel, Georg Wilhelm Friedrich, 10, 65, 118, 123, 125, 125n41, 136
Heidegger, Martin, 120, 151, 152
Herder, Johann Gottfried, 12, 36
Hobbes, Thomas, 124
Hölderlin, Friedrich, 120
Hopkins, Gerard Manley, 72, 73, 101, 103
Hutcheson, Francis, 32, 33, 52

Name Index

Ignatius of Loyola, 133–34, 134n58, 140n73, 168, 179
Illich, Ivan, 72

James, Apostle, 167, 168
John Paul II (pope), 6
Juergensmeyer, Mark, 18–19n38

Kant, Immanuel, 117, 124, 136
Keightley, Georgia Masters, 16–17
Kerr, Fergus, 94, 98, 100–101, 102, 103, 106
Kilby, Karen, 156n2, 165
Klaushofer, Alexandra, 65n15
Kroeker, Travis, 205n16
Kuipers, Ron, 64–65n14, 90n68

Lacouture, Jean, 13n26
Lafont, Ghislain, 2n3
Leibniz, Gottfried Wilhelm, 122
Locke, John, 31, 32, 33, 36, 46, 54
Lonergan, Bernard, 29, 110, 117n14
Long, D. Stephen, 8n5, 79, 85–88, 106, 200
Luther, Martin, 68, 135n63

MacIntyre, Alasdair, 70n29, 83, 91, 94, 97–98, 102, 106
Marion, Jean-Luc, 31n18
Marsden, George, 83, 94, 99, 103, 195
Marx, Karl, 116n13, 123, 124, 125, 125n41
Mary, mother of Christ, 135n63, 158, 167–68
McEvoy, James, 76
McIntosh, Mark, 6n10, 140n73, 141
Mercier, Ronald, 4n6, 49, 79
Montaigne, Michel de, 31
Mother Teresa, 50n80, 72, 73, 103

Newbigin, Lesslie, 17
Niebuhr, H. Richard, 94

Nietzsche, Friedrich, 36, 39, 45, 48, 50–51, 65n15, 116n13, 119, 126, 159, 205
Norris, Thomas, 166n16

O'Regan, Cyril, 151–52

Paul, Apostle, 111, 167–68, 185, 187
Peguy, Charles, 72, 73, 103, 176
Peperzak, Adriaan, 77n41
Peter, Apostle, 134, 149, 166–67, 181
Philip II (king of Spain), 113
Pinckaers, Servais, 93
Plato, 35
Potworowski, Christophe, 143, 144
Pufendorf, Samuel von, 31

Rahner, Karl, 110
Ricci, Matteo, 12–13, 27, 28, 84, 195
Rousseau, Jean-Jacques, 35

Saward, John, 176
Schindler, David, 94, 159
Schmitz, Kenneth, 143, 144
Schneider, Reinhold, 112–13
Schreiter, Robert, 14
Shaftesbury, Lord Anthony Ashley Cooper, 32–33

Thérèse of Lisieux, 72–73, 101, 174, 176, 179
Thomas of Aquinas, 111, 150
Tonstad, Linn, 165
Tracy, David, 31n18
Tully, James, 70n29

VanAntwerpen, Jonathan, 18–19n38
Vanier, Jean, 50n80, 71, 72, 73

Weber, Karl Emil Maximilian (Max), 117
Williams, Rowan, 16

Zizioulas, John, 88

Subject Index

active receptivity, 144
aesthetic, theological, 104, 104n108
affirmation of ordinary life, 29, 30, 34–35, 55, 95–96
After Virtue (MacIntyre), 70n29
agency, 44, 48
aggiornamento, 1, 1n1, 4, 38, 125, 128, 193, 195
alienated humanity, 79
angels, 65–66
anima ecclesiastica, 177–78
anthropology, 128, 129n51, 141, 141n76
anti-Christian culture, 195
The Apologetic Value of Human Holiness (Harrison), 171
apologetics, 59, 59n2, 63
appreciation, of ordinary life, 34
art, linking nature with transcendence, 53
artistic languages, 65–66
atheism, 111, 123, 126
atomism
    in politics, 29, 39–40
    selfhood and, 38–41, 192
    social fragmentation and, 40
    in social life, 129
authenticity
    Christ as condition for, 108
    community and, 190
    ethic of, 56
    ethos of, 29
    living life with, 198

moral ideal of, 26, 35–37
personhood and, 116–17
search for, 74, 190
through self-expression, 54–55
authority, 90–91, 91n73, 106, 169, 178–79, 182, 196, 198–99
autonomous rationality, 54–55
autonomy, 130–31, 137, 137n67

Balthasar, Hans Urs von (works of)
    Bernanos, 16, 119, 142, 157
    The Christian State of Life, 137
    "On the Concept of Person," 110
    "The Council of the Holy Spirit," 7n12
    "On Defining the Place of Christian Mysticism," 140n73
    "The Fathers, Scholastics and Ourselves," 193
    Love Alone Is Credible, 135n63, 139n72, 178
    The Moment of Christian Witness, 122
    Prayer, 149
    Razing the Bastions, 7, 178
    Test Everything, 7n12, 87n63, 193n1
    theodrama, 22, 151
    Theo-Drama III, 142
    "Trends in Modern Theology," 139

Subject Index

Balthasar: A (Very) Critical Introduction (Kilby), 156n2
basement level discourse, 60, 60n7
being, primal value of, 126, 126–27n45
belief
    conditions of, 59–61, 105
    fragilization of, 71, 105, 115
    possibility of conversion, 71–73, 190
    term usage, 18
"Benedict XVI" (Taylor), 90
benevolence, 29, 32–34, 89
Bernanos (Balthasar), 16, 119, 142, 157
buffered identity, 63n11, 71
buffered self, 66, 69, 79, 84, 117, 126

Calvinism, 32, 33, 35, 47, 68
Catholic identity
    authenticity of, 29
    critique of Taylor's affirmation of, 99
    in the modern age, 28, 28n8
    See also Roman Catholic Church
A Catholic Modernity? (Taylor), 12, 22, 24, 26–27, 48, 51, 75, 195
charisma, 111
charitable giving, 29
charity, 197
Christian community, 79, 89, 179, 184–85
Christian love, 140n73
Christian memory, 75
Christian order, 158, 159
The Christian State of Life (Balthasar), 137
Christianity
    childlike expression of, 176–77
    disestablishment of, 84
    as lived experience, 108
    means of becoming Christian, 148
    need for secular society, 26
    post-Christian man, 117, 130–31
    relationship to the world, 112–13
    roots of secularity in, 114
    as a way of life, 157
Christology, reduced to anthropology, 128, 129n51
Christology from Within (McIntosh), 6n10
Church, term usage, 19
    See also Roman Catholic Church
code morality, 61, 101, 147
codified ethics, 55
communion and mission, 16–17, 86
communion of saints, 166–67, 202
communitarian, Taylor as, 40
community
    authenticity and, 190
    Christian, 79, 89, 179, 184–85
    of faith, 6, 16, 19, 91n73, 93, 134
    human freedom and, 136, 136n64
    political, 31, 39, 40
conformity, 39
Confucianism, 68
confusion, with respect to morality, 38, 38n41
contemplation, 148–50
Contemporary Sociological Theory (Taylor), 20n30
conversion
    approach to, 174
    ethic of authenticity, 56
    human fulfillment and, 14
    language of, 82
    possibility of, 71–73, 103, 106, 190
cosmos, meaning found in, 40
"The Council of the Holy Spirit" (Balthasar), 7n12
creativity, 39
cultural shift, 85–87
cultural understanding, 29
culture
    church and, 76–78
    dialogue with, 105
    evangelization and, 12–14
    human culture, 50, 50n80
    transformation of, 195–96
culture of rights, 29, 31–32, 39

Das Heilige in der Geschichte
    (*The Sacred in History*,
    Schneider), 112
deconstructionist theories, 39
deism
    Calvinism and, 35, 68
    freedom and, 40
    human freedom and, 122
    impersonal order of, 67
    Lockean deism, 32, 33, 68
    providential, 64, 67, 115
    Shaftesbury on, 32
    Taylor on, 61
democratic model of harmony, 92, 92n74
dialogical character of identity, 44–45
dialogue
    with culture, 105
    as mission, 2n3, 189, 196, 196n7
    with the world, 76, 76n39
direct access society, 47, 67
discernment
    gospel message and, 53–56
    modernity and, 125
disciplined society, 79
disenchantment, 40, 43, 61, 117
disengagement, 36, 41
diversity, 27, 27n4, 27n6
doctrine, 93
doing, process of, 139
Donatists, 181
double-faced goods, 30n14
double-movement, 159
drama, 118–19

earth, heaven and, 135–36n63
ecclesial existence, 88, 170, 172
ecclesial hermeneutic, 16
ecclesial imagination, 4n6
ecclesial persons, 142–43, 180–81
economic activity, 46
emptiness, experience of, 42
enemies, 204n14
Enlightenment era, 34, 35, 51, 54, 55, 64, 77, 126
epistemology, 143
equal rights, 29

equality, 32, 46
ethic of authenticity, 56
ethics, 129–130, 139, 139n72, 147–48, 193–94
The Ethics of Authenticity (Taylor), 37
Eucharist, 78n44, 82
evangelization
    authenticity and, 56
    challenges, 69
    meaning of, 27n4, 27n5, 27n6, 28
    new evangelization, 6–7
    personhood as locus of, 5
    power of expressivism, 51
    Ricci model of, 84
    Taylor's reflection on, 11–12, 11n21
    Vatican II and, 38
    See also mission
excarnation, problem of, 70–71, 101
expressivism, 36, 51, 61, 64, 197

faith
    community of, 6, 16, 19, 91n73, 93, 134
    conditions of, 105
    fragilization of, 71, 105
    as a moral horizon, 42n56
    as an option, 105–6, 191–92, 198
    possibility of conversion, 71–73, 190
    possible in a secular age, 130
    seeking understanding, 121
"Faith Beyond Nihilism"
    (Klaushofer), 65n15
family life, 34
"The Fathers, Scholastics and
    Ourselves" (Balthasar), 193
femininity and receptivity, 163
feminist critiques of Balthasar, 15n31
finite freedom, 135–36, 135n63, 147–48
flourishing, 46
formation of persons, 175
founding moments, 47

Subject Index

fragilization of faith and tradition, 71, 102, 105
fragmentation
    marker of modern identity, 29
    personal, 43
    social, 40
freedom
    deism and, 40
    finite freedom, 135–36, 135n63, 147–48
    as gift, 192
    human attainment of, 121–130
    humanism and, 124
    in the Incarnation, 127–28, 127n46
    infinite freedom, 136
    loss and losses of, 38
    modernity and, 126
    Nietzschean thought on, 48
    personhood and, 108, 110
    self-determination and, 36, 39, 40
    social imaginary and, 46
    theodramatic approach to Christian doctrine, 114
    See also human freedom; theodramatic account of human freedom
friendship, 70
fulfillment
    human, 14, 115–17
    personal, 110
    self-fulfillment, 36, 37, 39
    subjectivism and, 39
fullness
    experience of, 42
    lack of sense of, 29
    of life, 110, 197

Gaudium et Spes
    Church to serve the world, 25
    important legacy of Vatican II, 1, 6
    modern identity in the West, 29
    See also Second Vatican Council
gender identities, 104, 104n109
gift and gift giving, 86–87, 132–33, 145, 148, 192

good, our notions of, 55
goodness, 148
grace
    effect of, 135n63
    need for, 87, 108
    possible substitutes for, 52
gratitude, 135n63
Great Chain of Being, 41, 47
guilt, 113

harm principle, 55n89
harmony, democratic model of, 92, 92n74
heaven and earth, 135–36n63
Hegelianism, 123
heroism, 41–42, 41n55
hierarchy, in Church, 129, 167–69, 199–200, 202–3
"higher times," 66–67
holiness, 15–16, 169, 171, 179, 182, 190
horizons of meaning, 36–37, 40
horizons of significance, 36, 37, 40, 56
horizons of understanding, 43
horizons to identity, 44–45
human agency, 43
human culture, 50, 50n80
human existence in God, 102–3
human freedom, 121–53
    Balthasar's response to, 129–30
    Christ the "acting area," 132–35
    (*See also* theodramatic account of human freedom)
    as gift, 192
    God's honor of, 142
    irreversibility of, 125
    in isolation from God, 121–22, 131
    modernity's problems with, 122–25
    necessity of God, 126–28
    positivism, 126
    theodramatic account of, 131–32
    See also freedom
human fulfillment, 14, 115–17
human person, nature of, 129

humanism, 42, 117, 122, 124, 191
    See also secular humanism
humanity, alienated, 79
hypergoods
    of the individual, 46
    moral goods and, 94
    moral hypergood, 51
    ontological commitments, 25
    of universal benevolence, 33, 33n26

identity, self-transformation, 54
identity formation, 44–45, 61
idolatry, 122
Ignatian Exercises, 183
Imagining the Catholic Church (Lafont), 2n3
immanent frame, 61–63, 63n10, 63n11, 72–73, 75, 102, 118–19, 125, 191, 197
"The Immanent Frame" (Taylor), 80
immeasurable time, 67
impending social dissolution, 38
impersonal universe, 61
Incarnation, 86, 104, 122, 127–28, 127n46, 134
incompleteness, marker of modern identity, 29
inculturation, 3, 12–14, 13n26, 28, 192
individualism
    belonging and, 48
    as a loss of ends, 38
    personhood and, 192
induction, mission through, 99, 192
infinite freedom, 136
instrumentalism
    Balthasar's response to, 120
    challenge of undoing, 69
    loss of meaning and, 40–41
    selfhood and, 38–41, 192
    in thinking, 29, 42–43
intellectual loss, 38
intellectual mission, 74
interpretations of Balthasar
    to instrumentalism, 120
    literary styles, 9–10

of mission, 149–50, 201–2
on modernity, 120
response to human freedom, 129–30
Roman Catholic Church, 4–5, 103–4, 154–161
Second Vatican Council, 3–10
to secularity, secularization and secularism, 112–15
the world, 150–51
interpretations of personhood, 43–49
interpretations of Taylor
    literary styles, 9–10
    missiological significance of *A Secular Age*, 80–81
    narrative, appeal of, 78–80
    overview, 73–76
    theological language, 81–85
    unthought, articulating, 76–78
inwardness, evolution of, 31

Jesus Christ, as central to belief, 93–94, 101, 101n105
    See also Christian, Christianity, and Christology entries
Johannine principle, 166, 169
Judeo-Christian spirituality, 35
judgments, 80n48

"kairotic knots," 66–67
key terms
    Church, 19
    mission, 3, 16–17
    modern, 19–20
    person, 20–21
    secular, 18–19
    self, 21
    witness, 18
kingship, 113
knowing, process of, 139

laity, role of, 160, 182, 183n72, 189, 196
languages, artistic, 65–66
liberty, 62

life, affirmation of the ordinary, 29, 30, 34–35, 55, 95–96
literary styles, Taylor and Balthasar, 9–10
living a life of conversion, 71–73
Lockean deism, 68
Lonerganian approach to mission, 14n29
loss and losses
    of ends, 26, 38, 42–43, 74, 103, 103n107, 120
    of freedom, 38
    heroism, 41–42, 41n55
    of meaning, 40–41
    of relationality, 41–42
    soft despotism, 26, 38, 40
love
    Christian love, 140n73
    expression of, 189–190
    genuine, 194, 194n4
    God's absence leads to absence of, 116, 116n11
    Johannine principle, 166, 169
    moral examples of, 139n72
    names for, 187
    needed for condition of faith, 71
    order of, 143–44
    as part of our nature, 32–33
    preceding understanding, 24
Love Alone Is Credible (Balthasar), 135n63, 139n72, 178

"Magisterial Authority" (Taylor), 90
The Malaise of Modernity (Taylor), 24, 27, 44–45
Marian principle, 166–69
Marian receptivity, 166–67
Mariolatry, 185
market and state power, 40, 40n47
marriage, 34
Marxism, 123
meaning, search for, 36–37, 40, 41, 42–43, 74
mercy, 193
metaphysics, 64, 65n15
Middle Ages, time in, 66–67
mission
    approach to, 114

    authenticity and, 56
    Balthasar's views of, 149–50, 201–2
    to be Church as common witness, 194
    to be Church with others, 194, 194n4
    Catholicism and, 48
    of the Church, 11n21, 17, 48, 56, 160, 189, 194, 202–3, 203n11
    dialogue as, 2n3, 189, 196, 196n7
    holiness and, 171–73, 190
    Lonerganian approach to, 14n29
    meaning of, 26–27, 27n4, 27n5, 27n6, 29, 193–94
    personal identity and, 138, 144
    power of expressivism, 51
    relationship to Christ, 23
    roots of, 137
    Taylor's views on, 11–12, 11n21, 200–201
    term usage, 3, 16–17
    through inculturation, 3, 12, 13n26, 28, 192, 194
    through induction, 99, 192
    Vatican II and, 1–3, 38
    vocation as, 111
    the world and, 150–51
modern, term usage, 19–20
modern identity, Taylor's account of, 29
modern morals, 25
modern selfhood malaise, 37–43
    loss of ends, 26, 38, 42–43, 74, 103, 103n107, 108, 120
    overview, 37–38
    principle of, 29
    relationality, loss of, 41–42
    search for meaning, 42–43
    subjectivism, instrumentalism, and atomism, 38–41, 192
    Taylor's path for mission and, 100
Modern Social Imaginaries (Taylor), 5, 24, 25n2, 45, 55, 75, 191

modern world, Taylor's picture of, 24–56
  ethic of authenticity, 56
  gospel message and, 53–56
  interpreting Taylor, 26–30
  modern selfhood malaise, 37–43
  modernity, alignment with, 50–53
  modernity's achievements and laudable ideals, 30–37
  overview, 10–16, 24–26
  phenomenology of personhood, 43–49, 74
  transcendence in, 26, 42
  Vatican II, alignment with, 49–50
modernity
  Balthasar on, 120
  complementarity of differences, 190
  critique of, 94–99
  discernment of, 125
  freedom and, 126
  irreversibility of, 125
modernity's achievements and laudable ideals, 30–37
  affirmation of ordinary life, 29, 30, 34–35, 55, 95–96
  authenticity, 35–37
  culture of rights, 29, 31–32, 39
  modern selfhood malaise, 37–43
  overview, 30, 30n13, 30n14
  universal benevolence, 29, 32–34
The Moment of Christian Witness (Balthasar), 122
monasticism, 35, 35n30
Montanism, 185
moral certainty, 79
moral code, 61, 101, 147
moral identity, spirituality and, 42n56
moral motivation, 78
moral order, 46–47, 62–63, 86, 102, 115, 197
moral political order, 47
moral self, 39, 50, 65, 191
moral traditions, 91

moralism, 26, 193, 193n3
morality
  challenge to worth of, 51
  as common ground, 26
morals, genealogy of in modern world, 25
multiple modernities, 20, 20n39
mutual benefit, 62
mystery, recovering the Church as, 161–181
  anima ecclesiastica, 177–78
  authority, refiguring, 178–79
  as bride, 164–65
  as communion of saints, 166–67
  ecclesial persons, 180–81
  expressive of childlike Christianity, 176–77
  formation of persons, 175
  hierarchy, reconfigured, 167–69
  laity, 160, 182
  official ministry, 174–75
  Pauline profile, 185–88
  as person, 161–64
  personal sanctity, 174–75
  revealed as, 157
  secular institutes, 182–85
  solidarity with the world, 160, 170–73
  the world, 170–73
mysticism, 140n73, 173

narrative
  appeal of, 78–80
  in making sense of our lives, 55
natural law, 46, 129
naturalism, 41n55, 50n80
nature, of ordinary life, 34
neo-Nietzschean, 25, 26
neo-Platonist philosophers, 32
new evangelization, 6–7
new order, 62–63, 86
Nietzschean thought
  critique of a false Christianity, 51
  critique of Christianity, 26
  freedom and, 48
  moral hypergood, 51

Nietzschean thought (*continued*)
  self-authenticating will to power, 50–51
  subjectivism and, 45
  understanding of values, 36
no harm principle, 55
Nova effect, 8, 16n32

obedience, 140–41, 140n73, 179
official ministry, of the Church, 174–75
"On Defining the Place of Christian Mysticism" (Balthasar), 140n73
"On Social Imaginary" (Taylor), 20n30
"On the Concept of Person" (Balthasar), 110
options in a secular society, 71, 105–6, 191–92, 198
ordinary life, affirmation of, 29, 30, 34–35, 55, 95–96
original sin, 132

Pauline mission, 166
Pauline profile, 185–88
person
  church as, 161–64
  ecclesial persons, 180–81
  formation of, 175
  term usage, 20–21
personal fragmentation, 43
personal fulfillment, 110
personal sanctity and the Church, 174–75
personhood
  agency, 44
  authenticity and, 116–17
  definitions of, 44, 142
  experience of human person, 74
  freedom and, 108
  as gift, 145
  holiness and, 15
  horizons to identity, 44–45
  individualism and, 192
  as locus of evangelization, 5
  moral ontology of human person, 84
  overview, 43–44
  personal identity and mission, 138
  phenomenology of, 43–49, 74
  as relation, 88
  secularity of social imaginary, 45–49
  significance and, 44
  theological understanding of, 110, 111, 143–44
  theological vision of, 155, 155n1
Petrine principle, 166
phenomenology of personhood, 43–49, 74
philosophical discourse, Taylor's view of, 15n30
philosophical hermeneutics, 43
pluralism, 94, 104n112, 105, 108, 189
political atomism, 29, 39–40
political community, 31, 39, 40
political order, 47
political power, 113
porous self. *See* buffered self
positivism, 126, 126–27n45
post-Christian man, 117, 130–31
power
  of expressionism, 51
  as new order benchmark, 62
  political, 113
  self-authenticating will to, 50–51
  state and market, 40, 40n47
prayer, 141–42, 148, 193, 202
Prayer (Balthasar), 149
pre-understandings, 158
primal value of being, 126, 126–27n45
"Proclamation as Dialogue" (McEvoy), 76
prodigal son metaphor, 99, 195
production
  doctrine of person as relation, 88
  as locus of human fulfilment, 29, 34, 42, 197
profane time, 46

Subject Index

Protestant Reformation
    affirmation of ordinary life, 30
    Catholic understanding of the sacred, 34–35
    equality, 32
    heroism and, 42
    secularism and, 68
providential deism, 64, 67, 115
public sphere, as an association, 25n2
punctual self, 70–71
Puritans
    affirmation of ordinary life, 30
    reform movement, 68
    universal calling, 35

rationality, 34
Razing the Bastions (Balthasar), 7, 178
realsymbolic persons, 143, 166
reason, 62
Reason in Faith (Peperzak), 77n41
receptivity
    active receptivity, 144
    Church as unity based on, 164–65
    description of, 163
    femininity and, 163
    Marian receptivity, 166–67
reconciliation, 12, 193
re-conversion, possibility of, 71–73, 106
Reformation and Reformers. *See* Protestant Reformation
relationality, 41–42
relationships
    characteristics of, 41
    self-fulfillment and, 37
relativism, 39, 64
"Religious Belonging in an 'Age of Authenticity'" (Kuipers), 65n14
religious experience and religious seeking, 83
religious imaginary, 62
repentance, 99
reproduction

doctrine of person as relation, 88
    as locus of human fulfilment, 29, 34, 42, 197
responsibility, 96
rights
    culture of, 29, 31–32, 39
    social imaginary and, 46
Roman Catholic Church
    anima ecclesiastica, 177–78
    authority and, 90–91, 91n73, 106, 169, 178–79, 182, 196, 198–99
    Balthasar's perspective, 4–5, 103–4
    Balthasar's vision, 154–161
    Body of Christ metaphor, 162–63
    as bride, 164–65
    Bride of Christ metaphor, 163–64
    Christian order, 158
    clergy sexual abuse scandal, 120n23
    communion of missions, holiness, and receptivity, 166–67, 190
    as communion of saints, 166–67, 202
    complicity with secularism, 119–21
    division that exists within, 202, 204–5, 204n14
    doctrine, 93
    ecclesial persons, 180–81
    encounter with secular society, 105, 105n113, 195, 195n5
    eschatological work outside of, 150
    evangelization and, 27n4, 27n5, 27n6
    expressive of childlike Christianity, 176–77
    formation of persons, 175
    formation of saints, 23, 92, 155
    hierarchy, 129, 167–69, 199–200, 202–3
    laity, 160, 182

Roman Catholic Church (*continued*)
    as mediation point between God and man, 142
    mission of, 11n21, 17, 48, 56, 160, 189, 194, 202–3, 203n11 (*See also* mission)
    moral profile of, 200, 203
    as more than institution, 103–4, 204
    as mystery, 162, 173–74
    need for change, 114, 203
    new vision, 156–161
    objective holiness of, 146–47
    official ministry, 174–75
    Pauline profile, 185–88
    as person, 161–64
    personal sanctity, 174–75
    Protestant Reformation and, 89
    relationship with Christ, 202
    salvation outside of, 128
    secular institutes, 182–85
    solidarity with the world, 160, 170–73, 193, 193n2, 197
    spiritualization of, 161
    Taylor's perspective, 4–5n8, 11–12, 104, 104n111
    Taylor's vision of mission for, 87
    tradition and, 91–92, 91n73
    understanding of the sacred, 34–35
    See also Second Vatican Council
Romantic Expressivism, 64
Romanticism, 29, 36, 51, 77, 197

sacraments, 150, 176
The Sacred in History (Schneider), 112
saints
    communion of, 166–67, 202
    divergence of Church and, 113
    formation of, 23, 92, 155
    heart of the Church in, 129, 129n52
    need for, 81–82n52
    obedience of, 190
    personhood and, 145–46
    real conversion and, 109
    relationship with Church, 179
    unbelievers and, 160
science, as serving the ends of practical life, 34
Second Vatican Council
    Balthasar's alignment with, 3–10
    to be in dialogue with the world, 76, 76n39
    first reception/second reception, 22, 22n42
    Gaudium et Spes, 1, 6, 25, 29
    implementation of, 205
    on mission, 1–3, 17
    overview, 1–3
    purpose, methodology, and context, 3–10
    shift in ethos, 38, 52
    Taylor's affirmation of the world and, 100
    Taylor's alignment with, 3–10, 49–50
    Taylor's defense of, 64–65n14
secular, term usage, 18–19
A Secular Age (Taylor), 4, 9, 11n22, 14, 26n3, 42, 55n89, 57, 59, 60n7, 63n10, 69, 75–76, 80–81, 85–99, 102, 191
The Secular City (Cox), 18
secular humanism, 59
secular institutes, 182–85
secular society, Christianity's need for, 26
secularism for the Church, challenge of
    Christianity's contribution to secularization, 68–71
    conditions of belief, 59–61
    development of secularism, 61–62
    excarnation, problem of, 70–71
    fragilization of faith, 71, 102, 105
    as irreversible, 63–66, 64–65n14
    as the new normal, 62–63
    overview, 57–59
    transformation of time, 66–67
secularity, secularization and secularism

Subject Index   235

Balthasar's attunement to, 112–15
challenge of undoing, 69, 105
Christianity complicit in, 105
Church's complicity with, 119–121
as condition of belief, 100, 105
human fulfillment and, 115–17
as ideology, 105
of social imaginary, 45–49
term usage, 18–19, 18–19n38, 59–61, 196
secularization process, 52
security, 46
self
  buffered self, 66, 69, 79, 84, 117
  critique of Taylor's story of, 97–98
  sense of, 88
  term usage, 21
  understanding of, 55
self-authenticating will to power, 50–51
self-centeredness, 39
self-criticism, 124
self-determination, 36, 39, 40
self-discovery, process of, 36
self-fulfillment, 36, 37, 39
self-gift, 135
selfhood. *See* modern selfhood malaise
self-interpreting animals, 44
self-transcendence, 98, 192
sentiment
  as central moral source for moral agents, 32
  as source within us, 33
service, as Church mission, 17
sexual revolution, 104n109
shared spiritual horizon, 118
significance
  horizons of, 36, 37, 40, 56
  personhood and, 44
  of things, 45
social contract theory, 31
social dissolution, 38
social fragmentation, 40
social imaginary

  alternative to, 4n6
  historical enmeshment of church and culture, 76–78
  immanent frame and (*See* immanent frame)
  lived experience, 77, 77n41
  nature of, 10
  pre-reflective secularity of, 26
  secularity of, 45–49, 75, 191
  Taylor's approach to modernity, 5
  Taylor's path for mission and, 100
"On Social Imaginary" (Taylor), 20n30
social justice, 196
society
  conceptions of, 55
  definition of, 48
  ends of, 61
  as instrument for individual good, 39
soft despotism, 26, 38, 40, 129
Sources of the Self (Taylor), 11n22, 24, 27, 37, 41, 50n80, 55, 75, 81–82n52
spirit/flesh distinction, 35
spiritual lobotomy, 48, 49
spiritual mutilation, 25
spiritual quests, 49, 59, 59–60n5
spirituality, in moral identity, 42n56
state and market power, 40, 40n47
  See also political power
subjectivism
  authentic personhood and, 130–31
  authenticity and, 36
  as disengaged rationality and political individualism, 36
  fulfillment and, 39
  immanent frame and, 118–19
  as individualism, 38, 39
  lack of meaning and, 40
  mode of being, 45
  progression of, 64
  reduction of Christology to anthropology, 128
  selfhood and, 38–41

subjectivism (*continued*)
  value of equality and, 32
subtraction stories, 84
subtraction theory, 60n7

Taylor, Charles (works of)
  "Benedict XVI," 90
  A Catholic Modernity? 12, 22,
    24, 26–27, 48, 51, 75, 195
  *Contemporary Sociological
    Theory*, 20n30
  The Ethics of Authenticity, 37
  "The Immanent Frame," 80
  "Magisterial Authority," 90
  The Malaise of Modernity, 24,
    27, 44–45
  Modern Social Imaginaries, 5, 24,
    25n2, 45, 55, 75, 191
  A Secular Age, 4, 9, 11n22, 14,
    26n3, 42, 55n89, 57, 59,
    60n7, 63n10, 69, 75–76,
    80–81, 85–99, 102, 191
  "On Social Imaginary," 20n30
  Sources of the Self, 11n22, 24, 27,
    37, 41, 41n55, 50n80, 55, 75,
    81–82n52
  "What Drove Me to Philosophy,"
    43
terror, difference of others and,
  194n4
Test Everything (Balthasar), 7n12,
  87n63, 193n1
"The Fathers, Scholastics and
  Ourselves" (Balthasar), 177
theo-drama
  doctrines of Christian faith
    through, 120–21
  life conceived as, 110
  subjectivity alternative, 118–19
theodrama (Balthasar), 22, 151
Theo-Drama III (Balthasar), 142
theodramatic account of human
  freedom, 131–53
  challenging modern
    understanding of God,
    135–37
  Christ, the "acting area," 132–35
  contemplation, 148–50

  ethics, 147–48
  human freedom (*See* human
    freedom)
  overview, 131–32, 151–53
  person and, 140–47
  personal identity and mission,
    138
  the world, 150–51
  See also freedom; human
    freedom
theological aesthetic, 104, 104n108
theological language, 81–85
theology
  defined, 121
  Lonergan's understanding of, 29
Theopolitical Imagination
  (Cavanaugh), 78n44
things, significance of, 45
Thou, God called through worship,
  127, 127n46, 135–36n63
three-cornered battle, 25
three-storey house metaphor, 60
time
  refiguring without God, 76
  social imaginary and, 46, 47
  transformation of, 66–67
tradition, 70n29, 91–92, 91n73, 97,
  102
Tragedy Under Grace (Schneider),
  112
transcendence
  action dimensions, 47
  art and, 53–54
  belief in, 52
  Christian's primary task of
    upholding, 106
  immanent frame and, 63n10,
    197
  in modernity, 26, 26n3, 42
  openness to, 89
  options to, 71, 191–92
  theism, 48
  transformations of knowing and
    doing, 139
"Trends in Modern Theology"
  (Balthasar), 139
Trinitarian doctrine, 108, 111,
  132–33

truth, 121

understanding
horizons of, 43
precedes love, 24
unity-across-difference, 27n6
universal benevolence, 29, 32–34
universal calling, 35
universal life ethic, 196
unthought, articulating, 76–78
utilitarians and utilitarianism, 33, 52

value
    as choice, 39
    source of, 41
Vatican II. *See* Second Vatican Council
violence, difference of others and, 194n4
virtue tradition, 70n29, 97–98

vocation
    mission as, 111
    religious, 35

Western modernity, 20
"What Drove Me to Philosophy" (Taylor), 43
wholeness, search for, 55
wisdom, 161
witness
    challenges, 105–6
    term usage, 18
    See also mission
work, value of, 35
world, the
    for Balthasar, 150–51
    Church in solidarity with, 160, 170–73, 193, 193n2, 197
    holy land and, 193n1

www.ingramcontent.com/pod-product-compliance
Lightning Source LLC
Chambersburg PA
CBHW031732230426
43669CB00007B/333